ULRICH VON HUT
AND THE
GERMAN REFORMATION

HARPER TORCHBOOKS

A reference-list of Harper Torchbooks, classified by subjects, is printed at the end of this volume.

Vlrich von Hutten.

ULRICH VON HUTTEN AND THE GERMAN REFORMATION

BY

HAJO HOLBORN

TRANSLATED BY

ROLAND H. BAINTON

HARPER TORCHBOOKS ♦ The Academy Library
HARPER & ROW, PUBLISHERS, NEW YORK

Nos omnia dura et adversa facere et pati, ut constet libertas, par est.

Hutten to Erasmus, 1523.
p. 194 of this volume.

ULRICH VON HUTTEN AND THE GERMAN REFORMATION

Printed in the United States of America.
This book was originally published in 1937 by Yale University Press in their Yale Historical Publications Studies XI. It is here reprinted by arrangement.
First HARPER TORCHBOOK edition published 1966 by
Harper & Row, Publishers, Incorporated
49 East 33rd Street
New York, N.Y. 10016.

CONTENTS

ILLUSTRATIONS

The woodcut first appeared in the German edition of his dialogues which he dedicated to Franz von Sickingen on December 31, 1520.—Copy in the Library of Congress.

The following illustrations will be found in a group, following page 120.

Erasmus of Rotterdam, 1523

The medallion by Hans Weiditz appeared first in the year 1523 in the new edition of Hutten's *Expostulation* which Otto Brunfels published after the death of Hutten together with a reply to the *Sponge* of Erasmus.—Copy in the Yale University Library.

Title-page of Hutten's *Dialogi*, 1520

The book was printed by John Schöffer in Mainz in April, 1520. —Copy in the Yale University Library.

Martin Luther, 1521

The woodcut by Hans Baldung Grien was between 1520 and 1530 probably the most widely distributed picture of the reformer. The papal legate, Hieronymus Aleander, refers to it in his report to Rome, sent from Worms on February 8, 1521. He wrote: "Lately they sold in Augsburg the picture of Luther surrounded with a Saint's halo, here they offered it without it, and such a large crowd assembled that the pictures were sold out before I could get one. Yesterday I saw on one sheet the picture of Luther with a book in his hand and the picture of Hutten in arms with his hand at the sword and above in beautiful letters *Christianae libertatis propugnatoribus*. Underneath was an elegant tetrastich to each of them, but that referring to Hutten menaced with his sword." The second part of Aleander's statement discusses a woodcut very similar to the one given as the last illustration to this volume. The picture of Luther has been taken from Bruder Michael Styfel Augustiner von Esszlingen *Von der Christförmigen rechtgegründeten leer Doctoris Martini Luthers* [1522?].—Copy in the Yale University Library.

Triumph of Truth, 1521

First published in *Triumphus veritatis; Sick der warheyt. Mitt dem schwert des geysts durch die Wittenbergsche Nachtgall erobert.* For further description see p. 163.

Title-page of Hutten's German Dialogues, 1521

The title-page of the same book from which the frontispiece to this volume has been taken. See also the comment on the portrait of Luther above.

PREFACE

THE present book is a thorough revision and expansion of my biography of Ulrich von Hutten, which appeared in German in 1929. The essential features of my former position have scarcely been altered. On the contrary the friendly reception accorded the book has led me to draw the lines with greater confidence and to relieve the text of critical discussions with my predecessors in the field. At the same time further studies in humanism and the Reformation have enabled me to invest the portrayal alike with more color and accuracy. The enlargements are greatest in the sections dealing with Erasmus, with Hutten's life from 1521 to 1523, and with his literary activity and significance.

The changes have been dictated especially by consideration for the English reader. For his sake the account of Hutten research since Herder and Goethe has given place to an introduction to the general condition of Germany at the beginning of the sixteenth century. All along the line insertions have been made for the benefit of those less at home in German relations.

I am heartily grateful to my friend and colleague, Roland H. Bainton, for the great care expended on the translation, which involved no mere rendering of the printed German text, but rather an attempt on the part of us both in collaboration to achieve a better garment for the ideas. The present English version, therefore, is not always a rendering of the original. All the citations are based directly on the German or Latin of the sixteenth century. The translations of Hutten's poetry into English verse merit especial mention.

A grant from the General Education Board Fund for Research in Language and Literature lightened the mechanical labor involved in preparing the translation. In connection with the publication I am indebted to the Yale Historical Series in which the work appears, and to the Yale Graduate School for financial assistance, as well as to Messrs. Quelle and Meyer of Leipsic, the publishers of the German original, for permission to produce the translation. The editor of the series, Professor Leonard W. Labaree, merits my warm gratitude for his many suggestions and careful supervision of the printing. A more competent guide to the art of English book-making I could not have desired. The Yale University Press spared itself no pains in achieving an artistic product. To the library of Yale University and to the Library of Congress I am indebted for permission to reproduce illustrations.

My wife, Annemarie Holborn, has accompanied this book from the outset with counsel and help. In every stage of the present edition she has had a part.

H. H.

New Haven, Connecticut,
October 19, 1937.

INTRODUCTION

GERMAN history in no period displayed such creative power and prodigality of talent as the opening years of the sixteenth century. The only age which can in any sense be compared with it is the classical epoch of German philosophy and literature around 1800, and even this time, though closer and more comprehensible to us, does not exhibit the native German genius in so untrammeled a fashion as does the age of the Reformation. The generation of 1500 spanned a mightier range of ideas and passions, religious revelations, and human dreams than did its descendants. And if we are assessing the contribution of Germany to the development of Western culture we must assign the first place to the birth of Protestantism. The Renaissance in Italy and the Reformation in Germany constitute the decisive emergence of the modern world. Along with these two a third must be mentioned, which has likewise exercised a crucial rôle, namely the idea of nationalism. Its rise is not so intimately associated with any one land but is a comparatively common development throughout West and Middle Europe. The German Reformation and the Italian Renaissance are themselves in large measure the expressions of a nascent nationalism to which in turn both contributed resilience and power. Early the three elements coalesced and since then in European history they have been now allied and now at war.

Humanism, nationalism, and Protestantism in the Germany of the Reformation constitute the real theme of this book and no life is better able to exemplify their interrelations than that of the German poet and knight, Ulrich von Hutten, who first attempted to bring them into a living synthesis. The great interpreter of German intellectual history, Wilhelm Dilthey, called Ulrich von Hutten the first modern German[1] and Kuno Francke in his valuable study on *Personality in German Literature before Luther*,[2] saw in Hutten the consummation of the development of German individualism after the late Middle Ages. Both judgments mean essentially the same thing. Hutten is the first German to achieve free and open expression not for the stereotyped thoughts of a class or calling, but for the spontaneous feelings and yearnings of a marked individuality. This does not mean, of course, that he was not socially and historically conditioned. On the contrary he was distinctly a man of his time. His peculiarity is that he wrestled with the problems of his day in an effort to achieve a solution of his own.

This conscious effort to realize a personality, this lifelong concern for self-education appears first in German history in Ulrich von Hutten. He is for that reason more alluring to the historian than Martin Luther, partly because we lack the sources for Luther's inner personal struggle in the early decisive years, and partly because God's spokesman must speak less of self-development than of the eternal truth of the Gospel. In spite of the titanic human power in Luther his work overshadows his personality. Even though the course of his inner life was as dramatic as the outer, nevertheless there clings to him still something of the anonymity of the theologian of the Middle Ages.

Hutten's whole life is a struggle for self-realization, not in the sense of a superpersonal religious norm, but in the sense of the formation of his own personality in accord with his native gifts and character. His life was short and turbulent. He was born in the year 1488 and died in 1523. From his student days we can follow this career through a mass of telling deeds and intimate confessions. A master of

1. W. Dilthey, "Weltanschauung und Analyse des Menschen seit Renaissance und Reformation," in his *Gesammelte Schriften* (Leipsic, 1921), II, 49.

2. Cambridge, 1916. Compare his article "Ulrich von Huttens Lebensideale," *Internationale Monatsschrift für Wissenschaft, Kunst und Technik,* VII (1913), 151 ff.

Latin and German speech he has called upon posterity in letters, poems, dialogues, educational and polemical tracts to witness to his struggle.

Before taking up our specific subject, however, we must first survey the German scene at the turn of the century.

Germany in the fifteenth and sixteenth centuries was by all odds the most extensive and densely populated land of Europe. Needless to point out, the country was almost entirely agricultural. Most of the towns were little more than local markets or centers of administration. A few cities, however, had undergone an enormous growth since the second half of the fourteenth century and competed with their older French and Italian sisters in importance for international commerce and exchange. By the end of the fifteenth century Germany had reached the zenith of its economic ascent. The great cities of southern Germany such as Nuremberg and Augsburg had won a place alongside of Italy and the Netherlands, and their merchants had worked out more advanced and daring commercial organizations and business methods than were to be found in any other land.

Economic advance was accompanied by cultural revival. Proud buildings arose, ecclesiastical and secular, and artists vied with each other to give an appropriate form to the communal aspirations of the age. How many of these ancient buildings in Nuremberg, Ulm, Schwäbisch Hall, and Dinkelsbühl remain to this day the cherished artistic landmarks of these towns! This is really the flowering of Gothic art in Germany, which became a national style, dominant well into the sixteenth century in spite of the gradual infiltration of Renaissance forms from the end of the fifteenth.

No less may the spiritual culture of the fifteenth century in Germany be described as Gothic. Between 1346 and 1506 eighteen universities were founded, all imbued with the spirit and piety of scholastic theology.[3] They

3. Compare in the first place the illuminating articles by G. Ritter, "Studien zur Spätscholastik I and II," *Sitzungsberichte der Heidelberger*

owed their foundation to the attempt to keep German students away from the French and Italian universities, to train clerics and civil servants in indigenous schools. Political motives are apparent here as well as in the fact that the foundations were made by the territorial princes rather than by the Church. Nevertheless the curricula and educational methods were scholastic and canonical. Even Roman law which had been dominant in the Italian schools for a long time made only a hesitant entry toward the middle of the fifteenth century. Italian humanism played but a subordinate rôle during the whole of the century. French influence was more marked and all the new cultural centers of Germany, Heidelberg, Vienna, Cologne, Erfurt, Tübingen, and Freiburg, sought to imitate the Sorbonne in orthodoxy.

Nevertheless the reform of German education could emanate from these very universities because they performed their tasks seriously. They might be small and provincial compared with the great educational centers of France and Italy, but in spite of all pedantry they were thorough. The universities are to thank for the revival of preaching, secondary education, and the training of a class of civil servants who assisted the princes in the consolidation of the administration of their territories. How deep was the search for truth in the German universities of the late Middle Ages appears from their greatest son Martin Luther. How potent and coveted was the influence of the universities on German life is evident from the passionate struggle for chairs on the part of the German humanists.

Political life apparently stagnated amid this flourishing

Akademie der Wissenschaften, Philosophisch-historische Klasse, 1921–1922, and "Romantische und revolutionäre Elemente in der deutschen Theologie am Vorabend der Reformation," *Deutsche Vierteljahrsschrift für Literaturwissenschaft und Geistesgeschichte,* V (1927), 342 ff. A well rounded history of the University of Heidelberg in the same author's *Die Heidelberger Universität,* Vol. I, *Das Mittelalter 1386–1508* (Heidelberg, 1936). See also J. Haller, *Die Anfänge der Universität Tübingen* (Stuttgart, 1927).

of the cultural and economic. The Holy Roman Empire had never convalesced since the fall of the Hohenstaufen. We are inclined today to regard this development as natural, but we forget, for example, that the French monarchy sank even lower than the German during the Hundred Years' War and only thereafter refashioned itself into a model for the modern state. We forget, too, that the ancient foe of the medieval German emperor, the Papacy, quickly recovered after the humiliation of the Avignonese captivity and the scandal of the schism. The price of recovery was high, for freedom and unity were achieved only through conciliarism which would have reduced the Papacy to a constitutional monarchy had not the popes established themselves as Italian princes, embroiled in all the intricacies and corruptions of European politics. In the meantime the financial system of the Church was developed with an unscrupulousness scarcely befitting the Viceregent of Christ. Both developments contributed ultimately to a loss of prestige and the disruption of the Papacy.

The German emperors of the fifteenth century did not display comparable vigor in regaining their ancient position and lagged behind the Renaissance popes, not to mention the rulers of France and England. The half century after the councils of Constance and Basel is filled with the reign of Frederick III whose unparalleled *vis inertiae*, though attaching the Empire inseparably to the house of Hapsburg, nevertheless from the national point of view permitted the Empire to waste to a shadow. No attempt was made to resist the pretensions of the Papacy by fostering the conciliar movement. Instead of winning for Germany the concessions which England had wrung in fact in the fourteenth and France by law in the fifteenth centuries, Frederick III made a shabby compact with Rome. England and France had snatched benefices and revenues from the grasp of the curia whereas Germany still sent huge sums in the form of taxes, offerings, fees, annates, services, etc., to Rome, and conceded to the curia immense influence in the national life. Frederick III took no notice of the abuses which had already elicited lively protest, but contented himself in the Concordat of Vienna of 1448 with the correction of a few of the most outstanding grievances, and this only in his own princely possessions rather than throughout the Empire. Aeneas Sylvius, once a conciliarist, conducted the negotiations and thereby paved the way for the preferment which made him Pius II.

It was in general characteristic of the Hapsburgs to concentrate attention on their own territories where modernization and centralization were carried through with fair success. No such attempt was made for the Empire as a whole. Frederick was content with the aura of the imperial title and with the feudal dues which he was able to collect. He was a Hapsburg, however, in his matrimonial policies, which made the house ultimately a European power of the first rank, but not a German national state.

The achievement of national consolidation would have been an appalling task even for a sturdier statesman than the flabby Frederick III in view of the political chaos which reigned throughout the Empire. Thousands of independent political powers, ranging from country gentlemen and squires and little spiritual lords to the greater princes and finally the six electors, were fighting with all their might to extend their feudal rights. They were all still feudal lords. Even the greatest among them could not really be called sovereigns. Only a few territories such as those held by the Electors of Brandenburg and Saxony, the Duke of Bavaria, and the Margrave of Ansbach had reformed their administration during the fifteenth century according to the Austrian pattern. Similarly the great cities had developed a more systematic administration, but the great majority of the German governments displayed neither the will nor the capacity for reform in their own houses.

Still less does one discover for a long time any movement in the direction of national reform. An approach had indeed been made in the union of the greater princes, the electors, who had combined and won for themselves the right of choosing the emperor and of stipulating constitutional conditions. When these electors acted in unison they could work their will, but their common interests were limited and most of them were handicapped by the contesting of their authority within their own territories. The electoral college was more effective as a check on the emperor than for the attainment of national objectives.

This is nowhere more apparent than in the Church question. The electors and likewise the princes had achieved gradually certain privileges and supervision in the administration of the territorial churches. These rights formed the nucleus around which the Lutheran state church was formed, but in the negotiations with the universal power of the Roman Church the princes dealt individually on behalf of their own domains.

Along with the princes the most important element was the free cities. Here, too, there was much of the arbitrary. Only a portion of the cities and not all of the really important ones had become free cities of the Empire. Erfurt, for example, one of the greatest centers of the Germany of that day belonged to the electorate of Mainz, the still small but rapidly growing Leipsic to the duchy of Saxony, whereas little towns such as Isny or Lindau in the present Bavaria had won their freedom. At the same time the great cities of southern Germany such as Nuremberg, Augsburg, Regensburg, Ulm, Strassburg, and Frankfort constituted a real power with their huge wealth and well-ordered budgets. One would have expected that, as in other lands, these cities would have been the natural allies of the monarchs in the construction of the national state. Yet this was true only in a very limited measure.

The Empire, hampered in the early period by enterprises in Italy and later through its own enfeeblement, had not been able to help the cities very much in their struggle for freedom from the surrounding feudal powers. In French history the concurrence of the throne and the cities constitutes an important phase in the demolition of medieval feudalism. In Germany, however, the possibility of a direct subject-ruler relationship remained unutilized or at least the emperor was not powerful enough to pursue a consistent and continuous policy in this direction. The cities in their conflict with the princes and knights were dependent very largely on themselves. This was more like the development in Italy, but there the cities were able to subdue the surrounding districts until all the territorial powers disappeared and the boundaries of one city-state touched those of another. The German cities stopped half-way in their progress toward the formation of such states. Territories were developed but of small extent, for the princes successfully blocked wider expansion.

The cities accepted the situation and abstained from any initiative in the larger questions of imperial policy. They respected the imperial authority and paid the duties, grumbling but without resistance. These duties constituted the primary income of the Empire. All the more jealously the cities guarded against any imperial interference in the assessment and collection of these taxes within their own walls. In spite of all their reverence for "His Imperial Majesty" they were more nearly voluntary allies than citizens and subjects. Their position is quite intelligible since no unconditional support of their independence and of their important commercial interests could be expected from him. They had to look rather to constant renewals of alliances, regional security pacts, and similar diplomatic methods. Complete neutrality would unquestionably have suited them best but with conflicts unavoidable the best they could do was to give the least annoyance and keep the doors everywhere open for their commerce.

For a time this was a defensible position, and yet Machiavelli was right when he called the cities "one eyed" since their procedure did not correspond to their future needs. So long as the territorial princes exercised only a limited jurisdiction they were inclined to grant free play to the commercial enterprises of the cities, but the moment the princes consolidated their administration sufficiently to bring industry and commerce under their paternal control the cities suffered restriction in all directions. And what happened in Germany repeated itself on a larger scale throughout Europe. The new national states of England and France and Spain closed their markets to the German cities. Only with the backing of an equally strong German national state could they have made good their pretensions.

We shall pass over a description of the free knights who comprised the third estate along with the cities and the princes in the Empire. Their power was greatly restricted and greatly involved in local conditions. Hutten's youth will afford us occasion to learn more of these relations. On the other hand we must acquaint ourselves with the change of mood in the Empire which came in at the end of the century with the reign of the Emperor Maximilian.

If the period of the inactive Frederick III (1439–1493) was of fatal significance for Germany, that of the imaginative Maximilian was even more determinative for the future. Although the father had already abandoned the Teutonic Knights in Prussia and thereby relinquished control of the Baltic to the Poles, and the son had been compelled to concede independence to the Swiss, yet through the acquisition of the lion's share of the Burgundian inheritance he extended the boundaries of Germany far to the West and through the marriages of 1515 gave to the Hapsburgs the future lordship over Bohemia and Hungary. Thereby the Empire became the defender of Western culture against the Turks, and by placing the frontiers on the Saône, Maas, and the Somme he laid the foundations for the century-long enmity between France and Germany.

For the moment, of greater significance was the resumption of the policies of the Hohenstaufen in Italy, for what Maximilian contemplated was the complete mastery of Italy and the Papacy. For a period he dreamed even of a direct union of papal and imperial power.[4] We must not interpret his Italian policy in terms of political or material interests however. Naturally the desire of the Austrian was great to extend his authority over the neighboring lands. Such expansions of a political, commercial, and geographical nature had already played a large rôle in the Middle Ages, but these attempts were no more decisive for his policy than for that of the French monarch. Maximilian could have increased his income more easily through a stronger concentration of his authority within the Empire whose resources were a long way from full utilization. Yet even France, though well on the road to national centralization, dissipated its powers on Italian conquests, trying to demonstrate its position as a great power by a show of superiority at the most contested point of medieval world politics. A romantic element was a godfather of modern power politics. How much more irresistible must have been the lure of Italy for the highest secular representative of medieval Christendom?

The consequences of Maximilian's whole policy for Germany were contradictory. The accumulation of territories through inheritance and marriage resulted in making the imperial dignity actually hereditary within the house of Hapsburg. No elector or prince of the Empire could seriously aspire to imperial dignity in the face of such a development. This was true even before the marriage of Maximilian's son brought the crown of Spain to the Hapsburgs. The establishment of the hereditary principle might have served for the renewal of the German monarchical power, but here Maximilian was more interested in restoring the imperial than the royal authority. And when he turned for help in the execution of his European plans to the estates of the Empire he encountered the opposition of the princes, who made their support contingent upon the reform of the German constitution.

4. H. Ulmann, *Kaiser Maximilians Absichten auf das Papsttum 1507–1511* (Stuttgart, 1888).

The leader of the movement for the reorganization of the Empire was Berthold von Henneberg, Elector and Archbishop of Mainz (1484–1504). The popular cry, "Peace and Order" was adopted to ingratiate the movement with the masses. Here Berthold von Mainz attacked one of the most pressing problems of the national life, for legal insecurity and turmoil among the feudal members of the Empire destroyed the common weal and crippled every national movement. These attempts had a measure of success in the proclamation of the Eternal Peace and in the establishment of the Cameral Tribunal in 1495. In its organization the political principle was employed which Berthold wished to make the basis of the future constitution, namely the principle of coöperation between the Empire and the estates. Some of the judges should be named by the emperor and some by the princes. In similar fashion Berthold meant to reform the executive. Beside the emperor there should be an executive council of the Empire, composed of princes who should oversee the administration and in the absence of the emperor assume full responsibilities. Only if the emperor granted these demands would the Common Penny and a levy for the Turkish war be accorded him.

These efforts for reform have usually been disparaged in German historical literature.[5] They are generally characterized as an attempt to cripple still further the imperial power. An adequate judgment is difficult to render since the executive council[6] so soon disappeared. Maximilian opposed the idea with all his force and gave in only temporarily when the exigencies of foreign policy drove him to seek the aid of the Empire at any cost. Then with the early death of Archbishop Berthold, whose statesmanship, resourcefulness, and persuasiveness had been the soul of

5. For a bibliography of the subject see F. Hartung, *Deutsche Verfassungsgeschichte vom 15. Jahrhundert bis zur Gegenwart* (3d edition, Leipsic, 1928), pp. 12 ff.

6. The official Latin name *consilium imperiale* is more indicative than the German *Reichsregiment.*

the movement, the whole undertaking collapsed. This, however, is certain that the reform policy of Berthold was a well considered and promising endeavor at a stronger German unity. He only can interpret the reform as a further disintegration of the imperial authority who has forgotten that the supremacy of the emperor over the Empire had become a pure fiction and that the emperor by no means was engaged in consistent efforts to renew a strong central government. But this is precisely what Berthold had in mind, only that he desired to control this monarchical government through a representative body.

This demand that the German estates should exercise a more potent influence in the Empire in proportion to their greater contributions was thoroughly sound. The estates could scarcely be expected to pay new taxes merely on behalf of the non-national interests of the Hapsburg dynasty. The Empire could properly demand that its own interests receive primary consideration. Nor was there any danger that the concurrent rule of the estates would render the emperor nugatory, for the princes, in spite of the advancing consolidation of their territories and in spite of the eminence of the bureaucratic corps, nevertheless were not in a position to make the executive council a political instrument of the first rank. The two chief experiments with such a council, the first just after 1500 under Maximilian and the other in the years 1522–1524 under Charles V, show that this organization was not in a condition to function without or in opposition to the emperor. Only by conjunction could imperial reform succeed. Apart from an understanding either power was strong enough to neutralize the other and paralyze progress.

In the period of the Reformation there were, however, important results of these efforts to reorganize and centralize Germany. The endeavor to erect an executive council failed but at the same time Maximilian's effort to secure heartier coöperation from the German estates for European politics and likewise the attempt of the estates to guarantee legal security in Germany led to the revival of the great imperial diets. In no period of German history did the *Reichstag* play so prominent a part as in the years between 1495 and 1555. Sessions were more frequent and the rules of procedure became more precise. Only tenants-in-chief were permitted to attend, that is electors, princes, counts, and the free cities. The results of the diets for the imperial constitution were, as we pointed out, modest. But Germany found here a public forum for airing her grievances, and this common discussion greatly furthered the feeling of community among the estates and even among the wider levels of the Empire. And, after all, something was achieved towards the solution of practical questions, specifically through the Eternal Peace and the Cameral Tribunal. This judicial body, however, could have been genuinely effective in preserving the peace of the land only if equipped with machinery for the enforcement of its verdicts. Experiments and discussions in this direction dragged on and occupied many diets well into the days of Charles V.

In addition to these questions of internal order there were also the duties of foreign politics to occupy public attention. The Turkish menace was always a black cloud lowering on the horizon. The threat to the German Southeast Mark was, as such, a serious national problem. In these days naturally the question was not regarded merely as an obligation to defend the frontiers, but as a serious philosophical and ethical problem. The immense expansion of the kingdom of the infidels and the inability of the Christian world to grapple with the danger occasioned a sharp examination of the political principles of the Occident. Were not the collapse of the universal medieval system, the *res publica Christiana*, and the emergence of national rivalries responsible? Could anything withstand the conquest of the West by the hordes of the Sultans short of a rebirth of Christian European solidarity and the spirit of the Crusades? Many looked to the Papacy, and the popes indeed repeatedly sounded the trumpets of the Cross.

Others, however, drew different conclusions from the situation. Was the pope the natural protector against the Turk? Was not rather the emperor, the secular head of Christendom, the appropriate leader against the Ottoman war lord? And here the national party revived the old cries against Rome, the grievances of the German nation against the See of Peter.[7] Rome was accused of sucking the life-blood of Germany, the land called to the political leadership of Europe and in need of all its resources for the successful performance of this rôle. Instead the pope was squandering the gold for his own wars and the luxury of his court.

At this point the critique of the pious coincided with the national opposition. Was not the secularization of the Roman Church the real reason for the punishment which God had visited upon Christendom through the Turk? The restitution of Christian faith and the abolition of abuses in the Church were the real object of reformatory attempts. However, some now began to reflect, the secularization and the corruption of public morals were not merely an Italian invention, but were conditioned by the growth of modern commerce and exchange, usury, profits, imports of luxuries, and monopolies. A puritanic life should be the first step in the cure. As a matter of fact, the diets concerned themselves not only with the regulation of usury, but with sumptuary legislation on dress and the table, for German gluttony was notoriously on the increase.

Wide was the range of questions debated in the diets, affecting alike the inner and the outer welfare of the people. It would be mistaken to assume that only the upper classes engaged in these discussions. Again and again the estates declared before the diet that such and such a measure could not be carried out because the common man would not suffer it. Often this was merely a subterfuge. Yet there was genuine concern for the common man. The Emperor Maximilian sent out through his chancellery a

7. B. Gebhardt, *Die Gravamina deutscher Nation* (2d edition, Breslau, 1895).

great mass of popular manifestoes and apologies for his political measures to be placarded or read from the pulpits.[8] Popular songs likewise were utilized and woodcuts, the newspapers of the illiterate.

Thus in the three decades before Luther's appearance in the year 1517 a consciousness of national solidarity was being fashioned. A many-voiced chorus of debaters from diverse quarters of the Empire gave expression to the concern of all classes for the reform of public life. Had it not been for this feeling of solidarity Luther's emergence would probably have remained a provincial event instead of gripping as it did the whole nation in a few months. The creation of a national forum and the rise of national voices speaking through the press constitute one of the most decisive presuppositions if not for the rise, at least for the dissemination and progress, of the Lutheran Reformation. In this regard even the pre-Lutheran years of Ulrich von Hutten, one of the mightiest German publicists and humanists, were intimately bound up with the rise of the Reformation.

8. P. Diederichs, *Kaiser Maximilian I als politischer Publizist* (Jena, s.a. [1932?]).

I

ANCESTRY AND YOUTH

ULRICH VON HUTTEN was born on the 21st of April, 1488, in the Castle of Steckelberg, where the ancient duchy of Franconia looks over into the land of Hesse. He came from a knightly family and this ancestry meant much for his later fortunes. He always considered and described himself as a knight and the sense of belonging to the nobility of the Holy Empire profoundly affected his bearing. Herein lay in large measure the source at once of the greatness and of the weakness of his personality, the fulfilment and the frustration of his life.

The free knights in Germany constituted a definite estate recruited in the first place from the emperor's men-at-arms and heavily represented in the old kernel of the Empire, in Swabia, Franconia, and the Rhine lands. It was no accident that in these portions of the Empire the knights had been able to assert their ancient independence, for precisely here the territorial princes had not yet been able to achieve exclusive dominance. The most important political element in these lands, apart from a few princes, such as the Duke of Württemberg in Swabia, the Margrave of Ansbach in Franconia, and the Elector of the Palatinate on the Rhine and a number of imperial cities, was made up of spiritual lords, the Archbishops and Electors of Mainz, Trier, and Cologne; the Bishops of Würzburg, Bamberg, Eichstätt, and Speyer; the Abbots of Fulda and Hersfeld.

These prince bishops are peculiar to German history and like the knights were the outcome of older phases of German imperial policy. In the Middle Ages the emperors at one time showered the bishops with civil power in order to create an offset to the recalcitrant German princes. With the decline of the imperial authority the spiritual princes, too, had become feudal lords to the prejudice alike of the Empire and the Church, for the military feudal tradition of the bishops was a decided handicap for the cultural development of the German church. Whereas in this period the upper clergy in France and Italy were usually trained in theology, but few of the German bishops were at home in the subject. Studies were not the rule and were limited in the main to canon law. No outstanding German scholar occupied an episcopal see in 1500 in contrast to France and Italy. Among the causes of the survival of the Roman Catholic Church in these lands and of the ecclesiastical revolution in Germany one must not leave this fact out of account.

Not only in the religious area was the contribution of the prince bishops slight, likewise also in the political. One of the most important means of insuring continuity of administration lay in the attempt of the secular princes to secure dynastic inheritance. In the spiritual territories, in the nature of the case, this factor could not enter. The ecclesiastical posts had to be elective. The bishops and abbots were apt to consult the interests of those to whom they owed their posts, who in turn came from the very same class as themselves, primarily that of the counts and knights. Hence it is no wonder that free knighthood flourished in the neighborhood of these spiritual principalities. Only a few hours on horseback from the fortress of the Huttens lay to the north the territory of the Abbot of Fulda, to the east the bishopric of Würzburg, to the south the archbishopric of Mainz, whose elector still bore the title of the Chancellor of the Empire, a testimony to the importance of the rôle once played by the archbishop in the imperial councils. The contemporary occupant, Berthold, undoubtedly had this in mind in his plans for political reform. The Abbot of Fulda was the successor of St. Boniface, who from this foundation with the help of Charlemagne had evangelized the German tribes, while the Bishop of Würzburg carried the title of duke, derived from one of the four ancient Teutonic duchies. Around

1500 this endowment with civil office had come to look like usurpation, but the knights found their scope thereby enlarged and protected.

The surroundings of Hutten's childhood are described for us in fresh and vivid fashion in the long letter to Willibald Pirckheimer in October, 1518.[1] Here we see the world from which Hutten was never fully emancipated, in spite of all his repudiations of knightly manners. He warned his urban patron against a too idyllic picture of the life of the knights in their castles and pointed out the real forces which formed the warp and woof of their existence. "Do not envy me my life as compared to yours," he wrote. "Such is the lot of the knight that even though my patrimony were ample and adequate for my support, nevertheless here are the disturbances which give me no quiet. We live in fields, forests, and fortresses. Those by whose labors we exist are poverty-stricken peasants, to whom we lease our fields, vineyards, pastures, and woods. The return is exceedingly sparse in proportion to the labor expended. Nevertheless the utmost effort is put forth that it may be bountiful and plentiful, for we must be diligent stewards. I must attach myself to some prince in the hope of protection. Otherwise every one will look upon me as fair plunder. But even if I do make such an attachment hope is beclouded by danger and daily anxiety. If I go away from home I am in peril lest I fall in with those who are at war or feud with my overlord, no matter who he is, and for that reason fall upon me and carry me away. If fortune is adverse, the half of my estates will be forfeit as ransom. Where I looked for protection I was ensnared. We cannot go unarmed beyond two yokes of land. On that account we must have a large equipage of horses, arms, and followers, and all at great expense. We cannot visit a neighboring village or go hunting or fishing save in iron.

"Then there are frequently quarrels between our re-

1. Ulrich von Hutten, *Opera,* edited by E. Böcking (Leipsic, 1859), I, 195–217. (Hereafter cited as Hutten, *Opera.*)

tainers and others, and scarcely a day passes but some squabble is referred to us which we must compose as discreetly as possible, for if I push my claim too uncompromisingly war arises, but if I am too yielding I am immediately the subject of extortion. One concession unlooses a clamor of demands. And among whom does all this take place? Not among strangers, my friend, but among neighbors, relatives, and those of the same household, even brothers.

"These are our rural delights, our peace and tranquillity. The castle, whether on plain or mountain, must be not fair but firm, surrounded by moat and wall, narrow within, crowded with stalls for the cattle, and arsenals for guns, pitch, and powder. Then there are dogs and their dung, a sweet savor I assure you. The horsemen come and go, among them robbers, thieves, and bandits. Our doors are open to practically all comers, either because we do not know who they are or do not make too diligent inquiry. One hears the bleating of sheep, the lowing of cattle, the barking of dogs, the shouts of men working in the fields, the squeaks of barrows and wagons, yes, and even the howling of wolves from nearby woods.

"The day is full of thought for the morrow, constant disturbance, continual storms. The fields must be ploughed and spaded, the vines tended, trees planted, meadows irrigated. There is harrowing, sowing, fertilizing, reaping, threshing: harvest and vintage. If the harvest fails in any year, then follow dire poverty, unrest, and turbulence."[2]

Intentionally overdone is the sombre picture which Hutten here paints of the unenviable lot of the knight. Nevertheless there is a touch of genuine realism.

The days were gone when knighthood was in flower, when the man on horseback dominated his epoch and caused a new and more polished society to flourish in the castles. In those golden days the knights were the military arm of the emperors in their pretensions to world domin-

2. Hutten, *Opera*, I, 201 ff.

ion. Military necessity brought forth the knight and gave him his importance. The demands of war justified his endowment with estates, united in his hand as a hereditary possession. Land was the basis of his power, war the norm of his existence. The Church universal consecrated his weapons. But the economic existence of the knightly noble was imperilled by the growth of moneyed economy. Rents fell. At the same time he became no longer indispensable in war. The place of the warrior knight was taken by the mercenary. The heavy man on horseback was displaced by modern infantry.

The cities were the center of the new industry. Within their walls especially late medieval culture was to develop, whereas the knights, impoverished and bereft of the duties which gave them a sense of the ideal, could no longer pretend to their ancient importance. The cities, however, bear by no means the sole responsibility for the decline of the German knights. A still more important factor was the victorious emergence of the territorial princes as a dominant political force. Even in those provinces where the knights retained their ancient status, internal divisions drove them to alliances with neighboring powers by which they were involved in other people's quarrels with no commensurate advantage.

Outward circumstances alone, however, do not explain the fall of knighthood. The disintegration of the cultural ideal of chivalry must also be taken into account. Was not this ideal pitched too high at the outset? Was not the seed of death concealed in it from the beginning? J. Huizinga, who has presented such a penetrating analysis of variations and modulations of life at court in the fourteenth and fifteenth centuries in France and the Netherlands, judges rightly that "chivalry would not have been a motivating ideal for centuries had it not possessed a high worth, social, ethical, and aesthetic, for the development of society. Precisely in its gorgeous exaggeration lies the power of this ideal. The blood and lust of the medieval spirit could be directed only by an ideal pitched too high.

The Church led in this way and so did chivalry."[3] But there was a strong tension between ideal and reality, and the new man in the city, with his sober realism, did not hesitate to unmask the ideal of his hated rival, to expose the dark reverse of knighthood, to point out that chivalry could be a camouflage for the gross and the greedy.

In the judgment passed by Sebastian Franck on this German knighthood one senses an urban feeling. "They have no occupation," he writes in his *Book of the World*,[4] "but hunting with dog and falcon, guzzling, carousing, and gambling. They live in luxury on rent and interest. They will not stoop to civic duty. Shopkeeping and handwork they despise, and they will not deign to marry a city girl. Their dwellings are impregnable fortresses on mountains and in woods, where they live high, with menials, horses, dogs, and other pomp. If offended they seldom avenge themselves according to law, but start a feud with a chip on the shoulder, break off with declarations of war, take the field, and avenge themselves with fire and rapine. The ecclesiastics dissimulate and show them great friendliness, but secretly regard them as a vengeful, swaggering, proud, turbulent class, a menace to the goods of the Church, and often to the ecclesiastics themselves. The German nobility is distinctive in almost everything—dress, residence, gait, speech, pew in church, burial, etc. His gait is overbearing, his speech provocative, his dress wild and worldly, his countenance menacing, his disposition usually insufferably warlike, and vindictive." Such generalizations of course need toning down. The condition of the knightly families varied greatly, according to locality and family. At all events, the majority of the smaller knights, in consequence of divided inheritances and declining rents, seldom had the means to "live high" and the "impregnable fortresses" were open to all the

3. J. Huizinga, *The Waning of the Middle Ages* (London, 1927), p. 94. The above translation, however, has been made from the original Dutch.

4. S. Franck, *Spiegel und Bildnis des ganzen Erdbodens* (Tübingen, 1534), pp. 44 ff.

vexations of the time. The Castle of Steckelberg, like the rest, suffered from the great famine years which plagued Germany in rapid succession at the close of the fifteenth and the beginning of the sixteenth century.[5] Ulrich von Hutten may well have had this memory in mind in his letter to Willibald Pirckheimer.

The knightly class, no longer enjoying social security, naturally tended to exploit all its remaining resources of power and law. This was not merely, as Hutten indicated, to defend personal independence and property, endangered continually on all sides, but also to keep up an appearance with the princes and rich city folk and sometimes to compete with the great territorial rulers in adventurous political enterprises.

Though a gross egoism dominated the knightly fights, feuds, and raids, nevertheless this warrior life developed a certain rugged individualism. The knight was in a better position to transcend the limitations which the culture of the Middle Ages imposed upon the individual than was the city dweller, with his communal life and urban republican consciousness. It is entirely conceivable, therefore, that modern individualism would have arisen with a certain inevitability from German knighthood had its sphere of activity been capable of expansion; but dating from the sixteenth century the independent noble was almost completely excluded from participation in those enterprises which moulded the future life of the nation. Among his decadent successors, the urge for freedom degenerated into nothing better than an absurd petulance.

By the end of the fifteenth century the fall of knighthood was well under way, but the class was not yet obsolete and powerless. What a magical lure chivalry could still exercise in spite of all criticism appears in the enthusiasm with which Emperor Maximilian was received by his contemporaries. What bound the Germans to him and won their hearts was especially the chivalrous in his person-

5. See E. Gothein, "Politische und religiöse Volksbewegungen vor der Reformation," in his *Schriften zur Kulturgeschichte der Renaissance, Reformation und Gegenreformation* (Munich, 1924), II, 59.

ality. And by 1500 knighthood was not yet reduced merely to romantic attraction. In the political and social spheres alike it exercised still an extraordinary influence. Its position was entrenched by widespread control over the goods of the Church. With a few outstanding exceptions the great sees at the end of the fifteenth century were in the hands of the nobles.[6] "Christ himself could not have entered this college without a dispensation," remarked Erasmus when informed that one must have twelve nobles on the father's side and a like number on the mother's side in order to enter the Strassburg chapter. No better illustration could be found of the dangerous domination exercised by the nobility in the German Church. The cathedral chapters especially were claimed by the nobles. Here lay the key to the bishoprics, the possession of which had been sharply contested by the princes since the fourteenth century. But this did not materially alter the almost habitual condition of the Church, which had degenerated into an asylum for the younger sons and the weaklings of the nobility. An interest in the dominance of the Church made the noble conservative, though otherwise his social position often inclined him to revolution.[7]

This was the general situation in Hutten's youth. More

6. A. Schulte, *Der Adel und die deutsche Kirche im Mittelalter* (2d edition, Freiburg, 1923), p. 201.

7. The history of the *Reichsritter,* free imperial knights, has been neglected by modern historical research. The work by K. H. Roth von Schreckenstein, *Geschichte der ehemaligen freien Reichsritterschaft* (Freiburg, 1859–1871), is rather superficial. The legal and constitutional aspects have been treated by various monographs. See: R. Fellner, *Die fränkische Ritterschaft von 1495–1524* (*Historische Studien,* Vol. 50, Berlin, 1905). A. G. Kolb, *Die Kraichgauer Ritterschaft* (Stuttgart, 1909). G. Kuetsch, *Die landständische Verfassung und reichsritterschaftliche Bewegung im Kurstaate Trier, vornehmlich im 16. Jahrhundert* (*Historische Studien,* Vol. 75, Berlin, 1909). O. Eberbach, *Die deutsche Reichsritterschaft in ihrer staatsrechtlich-politischen Entwicklung bis 1495* (*Beiträge zur Kulturgeschichte,* Vol. 11, Leipsic, 1913). Questions of social history have scarcely been touched. See however, P. Schnepp, "Die Reichsritterschaft," *Deutsche Geschichtsblätter,* XIV (1913), 157 ff., 215 ff.; XV (1914), 169 ff. In addition, H. Ulmann, *Franz von Sickingen* (Leipsic, 1872), pp. 229 ff. F. von Bezold, *Geschichte der deutschen Reformation* (Berlin, 1890), p. 28. G. von Below, *Die Ursachen der Reformation* (Munich, 1917), p. 62.

precise information as to his childhood eludes us. The early, and for that matter the later, period of his developing years is enveloped, if not in total, at least in partial, obscurity. At any rate the wind which blew through Ulrich's boyhood forests was no gentle breeze. His family, which can be traced according to a reliable tradition to the tenth century, belonged to the minor ranks of the upper nobility. The quarrels over class and clan, which occupied so much of the daily life of the knight, left little room for spiritual pursuits. One may assume that these were limited to an acceptance of the Church's teachings and obligations, while the political and economic resources of the Roman Catholic system were utilized to the full. This happened without any special reflection. One did not wish to be left behind and therefore grasped whatever means lay to hand. Some members of the family could be taken care of by the Church. At the same time the income could be increased by war and the service of the princes. This was the way in which Hutten's father cared for his children. For a while he fought in the imperial army. Now he lived on his revenues and served occasionally as the agent of a neighboring prince. When we catch a fleeting glimpse of him he appears ruthless and hard.[8] Crotus called him as inscrutable as Ulysses.[9] Nothing would indicate that the father exercised any influence on the son's development. The mother meant more in this regard. What she may have contributed to the inner resources of her son we cannot tell. Yet he felt that he belonged to her and when he started his war on the Romanists, and had in consequence to choose between family and cause, he appealed to her. The verse, "Though my good mother weeps," shows the hold which she still exercised on her eldest son.

When he was eleven his parents placed him in the convent at Fulda. Again we are ignorant of the circumstances. Seldom was it assumed that the eldest son would take or-

8. P. Kalkoff, *Huttens Vagantenzeit und Untergang* (Weimar, 1925), pp. 141 ff.

9. Hutten, *Opera,* I, 18.

ders. Most probable is it that his constitution was too feeble for the life of the knight proper. We do know instances, however, in which the eldest son was destined for an ecclesiastical provision when the continuance of the family was assured through younger children. A cousin of Ulrich's, fifteen years his junior, Moritz von Hutten, was dedicated under these circumstances, and his career shows us what the family expected from such a son. As a boy he was resident in Eichstätt, then studied canon law on chapter funds in the German and Italian universities. At the age of thirty he won a comfortable benefice, and at the age of thirty-six we find him as Bishop of Eichstätt, a prince of the Empire.[10]

Presumably the parents of Hutten entertained similar expectations on his behalf. The father was a beneficiary of the convent at Fulda, whose chapter was filled almost exclusively from the neighboring noble families. The natural assumption is that the father, by putting the son in the convent, wished to assure for him a claim on one of the benefices.[11] For this no promise was necessary, no subsequent profession on the part of the boy. Had he remained, the abbot would not have denied him leave to study at the university. Hutten's opponents while he was still alive sought occasionally to spread the rumor that he was a runaway monk, but this charge, which he strenuously denied,[12] appears so late and in such partisan quarters as to deserve no credence.[13] The assumption that his parents promised him as a boy to the cloister, even though he himself took no vows, admits likewise of no proof. Evidence is lacking, and in the controversy with his opponents Hutten would have been under no temptation to conceal such a dedication because the obligatory character of the parental "oblation" was contested by the dominant theology.

10. K. Ried, *Moritz von Hutten, Fürstbischof von Eichstätt (1539–1552)* (*Reformationsgeschichtliche Studien und Texte,* Vol. 43/44, Münster, 1925).

11. P. Kalkoff, *Huttens Vagantenzeit und Untergang,* p. 76.

12. Hutten, *Opera,* II, 145.

13. P. Kalkoff, *Huttens Vagantenzeit und Untergang,* p. 101.

When Hutten fled from the cloister in 1505 he broke no vow. Rather he wished by timely flight to avoid compulsion to make his profession before departing for the university. The convent, indeed, took his action amiss, but his father was more aggrieved because it defeated his hope that the son would rise rapidly at Fulda and maintain the family stake in this preserve of the nobility, while the other members were advancing the cause of the von Huttens at the neighboring court of the Archbishop of Mainz. To be sure, we do not know the views and motives of the father, but it is clear that by fleeing from the convent the young Hutten desired to escape from the parental plan.

Of the cloister at Fulda and its environment he always spoke with respect.[14] His later utterances may be interpreted as exaggerations designed to get something for his studies, but at least they show that he was not driven out by severe discipline or the enmity of his teachers. In a writing of the later period Hutten declares that as soon as he came to years of discretion he recognized "that he could better serve God and the world in another profession in accord with his nature." Here we have a Lutheran tone. The spontaneous and individual decision of his youth is justified by the religious and ethical feeling of his later years. But one may credit Hutten's assertion that he came early to the recognition of the incompatibility between his innermost desires and the life of the monk. When the seventeen-year-old lad emerged from the cloister he sought not to please God but to enlarge his experience and the sphere of his activity. To be sure, he had not the remotest doubt about the meritoriousness which the Middle Ages ascribed to monasticism, but had not he, who all his life long combatted the monkish-ascetic view of life, had he not already sensed in his early years the gulf which separated him from the world of the monks? The conflict was not merely external and directed against the historical development of Catholic monasticism, but his inner instinct led him to reject every form of monkish asceticism. Even the

14. Hutten, *Opera,* III, 71 ff.

humanist ideal of tranquillity he was to spurn, for it too was ascetic even if not ecclesiastical. This humanist contempt for the world, this flight from the arena into the timeless peace of antiquity, Hutten was to combat with the utmost vigor.

We may assume that he was aware of the cleavage when he left the cloister, although the consciousness of antipathy to asceticism may not have been more explicit than a vague yearning for freer movement, wider experience of the world, and a youthful ambition for fame and importance. The conviction was concrete enough to make him willing to break with his family and trust himself to a future necessarily uncertain, however fair in dreams. No matter how hard the waves dashed against him in later years, he never regretted the step.

The fruits of the six years at Fulda were not lightly esteemed by Hutten himself. We cannot take his tribute altogether literally when in 1510, in the *Elegy of the German Poets*,[15] he enumerates Fulda among the centers of the new learning, for one cannot properly speak of real humanist life at Fulda. The ground was scarcely prepared for an early development along these lines, since the superiors were too much engrossed in maintaining the peace of the abbey against the assaults of the knights without and within the walls. Nevertheless the life of the cloister was not actually disturbed by these feuds during the period when Hutten was there,[16] and we may assume that he received a preparation which was useful for his later poetry. The foundation of his mastery of the Latin language, by which he soon acquired a reputation, must have been laid in the cloister.

The same poem contains a vivid reference to the honorable past of the abbey of Fulda, the oldest foundation in Germany, established by Saint Boniface, the Apostle to the Germans. There was here something of the later humanist exaltation of primitive German history, but one

15. *Ibid.*, pp. 64 ff.
16. See P. Kalkoff, in *Archiv für Reformationsgeschichte*, XXII, 210 ff.

has the feeling that Hutten does not as yet portray Saint Boniface, the first missionary to Germany, and Hrabanus Maurus, the first German theologian, as living figures in their own time, but rather as mythical personages, dazzling to the eye of the cloister student. Such memories he absorbed and later developed.

II

THE WANDERING SCHOLAR

WITH the flight from the cloister Hutten entered upon the career of the goliard, the itinerant, mendicant scholar of the Middle Ages. Definite objectives there were none. Hutten employed his newly won freedom to abandon himself to the life wholeheartedly, though not so much for indulgence as for gleaning, learning, seeing, and discovering.

His course of study cannot have been regulated. The rapid shifting from one university to another, due perhaps to the desire to follow his teacher, Rhagius Aesticampianus,[1] was not conducive to the fulfilment of the academic demands of the well integrated curricula then in vogue. The arts course at the University of Erfurt, for example, leading up to the master's examination, lasted three and a half to four years. The baccalaureate examination had to be preceded by at least a year and a half of study. We find Hutten in the winter of 1505 in Cologne, in the summer of 1506 in Erfurt, while the winter was spent in Frankfort-on-the-Oder. In 1507 he was in Leipsic. Then he traveled north. With regard to this period we know only that he was reduced to extremities. These were the darkest days of his life. The hardy youth had become a humanist parasite, sponging upon friends to avoid begging in the streets. In 1509 he appeared in Greifswald, in Pomerania, and was taken into the family of the burgomaster. He was enrolled also in the university. But soon there was friction with his patrons of Greifswald and he had to go to Rostock, where he was taken in by Ekbert

1. Hutten followed Aesticampianus from Erfurt to Frankfort-on-the-Oder. On this humanist see the articles by G. Bauch, "Joh. Rhagius Aesticampianus in Krakau," *Archiv für Literaturgeschichte*, XII (1884), 322 ff., and "Die Vertreibung des J. Rhagius Aesticampianus aus Leipzig," *ibid.*, XIII (1885), 1 ff.

Harlem; at the end of 1510 he came to stay with the Wittenberg professor, Balthasar Fachus.

This is about all the information we have with regard to his German student days. It scarcely warrants the assumption that he pursued the regular course at the university. He did take the bachelor's degree in September, 1506, at Frankfurt,[2] and apparently intended to complete the arts course, but he seems soon to have lost himself in the "allotria," the term then applied to the humanist studies lying outside the curriculum proper. As time went on, this divergence from the regular medieval course became more and more intentional.

We cannot determine when he first came to have that antipathy for scholastic study characteristic of his later literary work. Camerarius records that Hutten went to Cologne, already desirous of pursuing humanist studies.[3] This is scarcely credible, even though Cologne was not so benighted or Erfurt so emancipated as David Friedrich Strauss contended.[4] Neither "many towered Erfurt" nor "holy Cologne" was dominated by the humanist arts faculty. Not until the end of the next decade did the humanist circle come to have a decisive influence at the University of Erfurt. In 1506, when Hutten was there and Luther was an inmate of the Augustinian cloister, the little humanist group had only a loose affiliation with the university, and even when the relationship became more intimate the humanists were in a position of sufferance rather than of leadership.

2. G. Bauch, *Die Anfänge der Universität Frankfurt an der Oder* (Berlin, 1900), p. 85.

3. Hutten, *Opera,* II, 361.

4. D. F. Strauss based his narrative on the book by F. W. Kampschulte, *Die Universität Erfurt in ihrem Verhältnis zu dem Humanismus und der Reformation* (Trier, 1858 ff.), which has been proved unreliable by more recent research. The best description of the university is to be found in O. Scheel, *Martin Luther* (2d edition, Tübingen, 1917). See also G. Bauch, *Die Universität Erfurt im Zeitalter des Frühhumanismus* (Breslau, 1904); F. Benary, *Zur Geschichte der Stadt und Universität Erfurt* (Gotha, 1919); P. Kalkoff, *Humanismus und Reformation in Erfurt* (Halle, 1926).

We shall have to assume that Hutten's emancipation from scholasticism was gradual, the more so because there was much in the curriculum of the German universities of the Middle Ages which could satisfy for a time the thirst for a knowledge of antiquity. Classical rhetoric, ethics, and political theory were studied, and the classical authors increasingly read throughout the fifteenth century.[5] Even the German theologians were concerned to purify Latin from barbarisms. Antiquity was treasured by late scholastic education as an arsenal of epigrams and proverbs. So much could be incorporated in the dome of the scholastic structure without imperilling the stability and integrity of the architecture.[6]

This development in the German universities has been characterized as "scholastic humanism,"[7] and it is true that only in a very few cases was German humanism anti-scholastic. We must not take too seriously the many complaints of the unchristian demeanor of the young poets, nor the bitter competition for academic posts. The fact remains that humanism did not formulate its position in terms utterly irreconcilable with the dominant theology, or at any rate that it avoided an open breach. Not until the second decade of the century did serious differences develop. Not until then did the aggressive tendencies of humanism come to the fore. Since Hutten contributed to the accentuation of the cleavage, it would be of the highest historical interest to be able to trace more precisely his experiences at the university and his student impressions. But the paucity of the sources enables us to draw only very meagre conclusions.

5. O. Scheel, *Martin Luther,* II, 223 ff. G. Ritter, "Die geschichtliche Bedeutung des deutschen Humanismus," *Historische Zeitschrift,* CXXVII (1923), 393 ff.

6. This process was first adequately described by P. Joachimsen in a study which opened a new period in the treatment of German humanism: *Geschichtsauffassung und Geschichtsschreibung in Deutschland unter dem Einfluss des Humanismus* (*Beiträge zur Kulturgeschichte,* Vol. 6, Leipsic, 1910).

7. *Ibid.,* p. 37.

In the *Elegy of the German Poets*[8] Hutten musters the roll of the German centers of humanistic learning. The list scarcely warrants the assumption that he felt any particular indebtedness to Erfurt for his own humanist preparation and some of the men celebrated can hardly be included in the humanist movement. This confirms our supposition that Hutten emerged only gradually from the classicism of the late scholastics and that during his period as a scholar in the German universities he never so much as dreamed of forging weapons from the culture of antiquity with which to demolish the spiritual presuppositions of medieval theology. Nevertheless humanism did display tendencies toward a philosophy of life essentially alien to scholasticism and it is significant that Hutten met representatives and pioneers of this movement during his student days. Of greatest moment was the friendship with Crotus Rubeanus,[9] whom Hutten met in Cologne and Erfurt. Probably it was Crotus who took Ulrich from Erfurt to Gotha to meet Mutianus Rufus.[10]

We have already pointed out that Hutten's semester at Erfurt was not primarily occupied with relations to the circle of the canon of Gotha, as Strauss assumed. The time spent there was short and the relations with this group were not especially intimate. Yet Hutten kept them up and we may assume that they meant something to him even now, whether or no at this time or only later he was to appropriate and push to their conclusions the stimuli received from the unconventional figure of Conrad Muth, lately returned from Italy and now exerting from his sequestered Gotha a decided influence on the then populous Erfurt. He did so by gathering about him a group of young men whom he indoctrinated with the tenets of the Neoplatonic theism derived from Marsilio Ficino and Pico

8. Hutten, *Opera,* III, 64 ff.

9. On Crotus Rubeanus—his real name was Johannes Jäger—see E. Einert, *Johannes Jäger aus Dornheim* (Jena, 1883); W. Brecht, *Die Verfasser der Epistulae obscurorum virorum* (Strassburg, 1904).

10. On Conrad Muth compare K. Krause, *Der Briefwechsel Mutians* (Kassel, 1885); W. Dilthey, *Gesammelte Schriften,* II, 46 ff.

della Mirandola. The speculative ideas of this spiritualized piety certainly did not affect Hutten. In his later writings there is no trace of it. More important was it that he learned for the first time from Mutianus the possibility of constructing from the writings of classical antiquity a philosophy of life which, if not in direct conflict with that of the Church, none the less rendered the sacramental system and scholasticism superfluous. Mutianus's sceptic quietism and unintegrated nature prevented him from drawing practical conclusions. He was content to rear his unobtrusive temple in the shadow of the Church.

Hutten could observe also in the circle of Mutianus the goodly fellowship of the humanists, who felt themselves bound to exchange ideas and act in concert. Hutten later was fond of referring to the companionability of these new spirits. He had a feeling of the great movement whose cohesion he came to exaggerate. And, further, though Mutianus did not openly break with the Church of which he was a beneficiary, none the less Hutten found in him a disintegrating critic of the institutions of medieval ecclesiasticism, scholastic teaching, and the moral delinquencies of the priests and spiritual potentates.

The vigorous rallying of the Erfurt humanists to the defense of Jakob Wimpfeling attracted Hutten's attention to this Alsatian humanist, whose tract *De Integritate* (1505) had set Erfurt by the ears through an attempt to prove that neither Christ, Paul, nor Augustine was a monk.[11] This criticism from a devout, sincere, and discreet Catholic believer awoke even now the suspicion that scholasticism was not the only Christian theology. Here was the contrast between ancient and medieval Christianity which Hutten was to meet later in his teacher, Rhagius Aesticampianus. In the *Letters of Obscure Men* there are

11. P. Kalkoff, *Reformation und Humanismus in Erfurt,* p. 9. Best treatment of Wimpfeling in Ch. Schmidt, *Histoire litéraire de l'Alsace* (Paris, 1879). See in addition J. Knepper, *J. Wimpfeling* (Freiburg, 1902), and P. Joachimsen, "Der Humanismus und die Entwicklung des deutschen Geistes," *Deutsche Vierteljahrsschrift für Literaturwissenschaft und Geistesgeschichte,* VIII (1930), p. 439.

a number of references to Wimpfeling's controversy with the mendicants. As early as 1510 Hutten spoke of him with respect.[12] Probably he heard of him first at Erfurt, where in the circle of Mutianus the total ecclesiastical criticism was more rationalistic, reckless, satirical, and frivolous than Wimpfeling's.

In Frankfort and Leipsic Hutten attached himself to the circle of the itinerant humanist Rhagius Aesticampianus, whose influence can be traced with more precision because now we have reached the period of Hutten's first poetical compositions. From him Hutten received a better grounding in rhetoric and moral philosophy. Aesticampianus sought to bring the church fathers back to life. In the study of patristics secular and theological learning seemed to him to coalesce. Jerome, Ambrose, and Augustine were for him primarily teachers of morality. The contrast to scholasticism at this point was sharp. A practical interest ran through his work. The scholastics were reproached for hairsplitting and for giving so little counsel on the duties of life, which are more important than logical squabbles. He complains that the fathers are accessible only to the accomplished linguists. Not only was he a poet seeking a place beside the theologians at the university, but also a lay Christian asserting his independence of the sacerdotal. The priest for him was a hypocrite; scholasticism was superstition.

Hutten was close to Aesticampianus, a member of the inner circle for whom the master gave special lectures at home.[13] Through him Hutten first broke into print, in that Aesticampianus incorporated in the Frankfort and Leipsic editions of his works some of Ulrich's poems. This was the usual way in which a young humanist came before the public. He could fill out the free pages in the work of some distinguished author. Here was the almanac or periodical of later times.

The poems which have come down to us from this period

12. Hutten, *Opera,* III, 77.
13. G. Bauch, *Die Anfänge der Universität Frankfurt,* p. 103.

of Hutten's life reflect his studies and do not as yet display the distinctive characteristics of his style.[14] Here we have conventional school exercises. We can see, however, that the pursuit of scholarship was already a serious concern. The ideal was to become good and learned in order to win a name with posterity and gain entry to the fraternity of scholars.[15] His *Art of Versification* of 1511 shows that he could hold his own in the poets' guild. Compared with similar works of the humanists, it rates well.[16]

These verses had been composed in Wittenberg, at the home of Balthasar Fachus. The hardest and for us the obscurest years of Hutten's life in the north were now past. He recounts shipwreck, robbery, and every imaginable calamity in these years. Whether his own instability and levity were in part responsible, we cannot tell. His unusual ability to take care of himself brought him through, even though with diminished health. He was a victim of syphilis which in this period devastated the lands of Europe as the plague had done in earlier centuries. Diseases, too, have a history and our doctors have long been accustomed to trace the graphs of epidemics and the variations in the symptoms of a disease. This is peculiarly apparent in the case of the appearance of syphilis, probably imported on the first boat from the new world to Spain and thence to Italy. At that time men had no notion of the transmission of infection, and no sanitary counter measures. The condition of the inns and public baths defies description in a modern work, so it is no wonder that this new scourge of mankind was disseminated as by the fastest post horses all over Europe. Again the complaint attacked a population obviously unprepared, without immunity and without antidote. The symptoms were mortifying and medical help

14. See O. Clemen in his edition of D. F. Strauss, *Ulrich von Hutten* (Leipsic, 1927), p. 509. O. Flake, *Ulrich von Hutten* (Berlin, 1929), p. 59.

15. Compare F. Gundolf, *Hutten, Klopstock, Arndt* (Heidelberg, 1924), p. 7.

16. C. Bursian, *Geschichte der klassischen Philologie in Deutschland* (Munich, 1883), p. 130. P. Kalkoff, *Huttens Vagantenzeit und Untergang*, p. 118.

negligible at best. Sometimes the patients died of the disease, sometimes of the cures. Particularly in Hutten's case we may wonder whether his early death was due solely to the malady or also to the roughshod treatment to which he frequently submitted, though again we must not forget that he never took care of himself and constantly taxed his strength.

For the critical observer of the time inferences as to Hutten's morality can in no wise be made from his disease. The manifestations and dissemination of the malady permit of no such deductions, and in any case moral concepts were different from our own. In contrast to the ethical demands of the Church the natural morality of the people was often absolutely heathen and unrestrained. A change was first introduced by the tightening of ecclesiastical discipline through the Reformation and Counter-reformation. "Job's sickness," as venereal disease was then called, has contributed not a little to the decline of medieval sexual laxity. Erasmus of Rotterdam, who is often cited as one of the first to reflect on hygiene, was himself, as we have but lately learned,[17] a victim of syphilis, and the list might be almost indefinitely extended from among the celebrities of the time.

This does not mean that Hutten was in any sense fastidious. Yet it is significant that we never find obscene witticisms in his works as so often in the literary productions of his day. The pornographic literature of the Italian Renaissance is notorious. Among the Germans of the time questionable passages if less frequent are more coarse. There is nothing of the sort in Hutten. Only the *Letters of Obscure Men* exhibit ribaldry, but here we have a deliberate attempt to characterize opponents. Hutten's own utterances are entirely free from such suggestiveness. His composition is always disciplined and the reader's attention is never distracted by wanton witticisms. The disease

17. See A. Werthemann, "Schädel und Gebeine des Erasmus von Rotterdam," *Verhandlungen der Naturforschenden Gesellschaft in Basel*, XL (1929), 313 ff.

did not corrode the kernel of his being or his will to live, as we see in the poem composed at the end of this year. The *Lötze Philippics* display already the distinctive Hutten traits which should destine him to a rôle of historical importance.

The poem was occasioned by a very dubious—one might also say, a flimsy—pretext. He wished to avenge himself for the treatment which he had received from his host at Greifswald.[18] Here he had been entertained by the professor of law, Henning Lötz, son of the wealthy burgomaster. Obviously the Lötze family were not sufficiently impressed by Hutten's membership in the group of humanist poets at the university to regard their services on his behalf as a contribution to the Muses. In all probability Hutten had promised later to reimburse them for roof, clothes, and coin. They waited in vain. Hutten held before them the prospect of doing better elsewhere. The Lötze were not satisfied, and when he left Greifswald without their consent and went to Rostock they took his books and clothes in pledge.

This affair scarcely speaks well for Hutten, even though the Lötze may have been too exacting, but he makes out of the episode a momentous question involving humanism as a whole and deserving of wide publicity. He reveals himself as one who could turn the molehills of his life into mountains and charge up and down them with foaming steed. The explanation is not merely that he desired to call attention to himself, but also that he had a real capacity for discerning the larger implications of trivial episodes.

The *Lötze Philippics*[19] show already that Hutten was sensing the power of words, now for personal intrigue, later for politics. In dangerous fashion young Ulrich contemplated the influence of the word which could now be disseminated through all lands by means of the recent invention of printing. He wished to stir not only the humanists but also his knightly relatives and the Duke of Pomera-

18. T. Pyl, in *Allgemeine Deutsche Biographie,* XIX, 290.
19. "In Lossios querelarum libri duo," Hutten, *Opera,* III, 19 ff.

nia. Every means was justifiable to crush the affronter by holding him up to the scorn of the world.

Hutten's activist nature reveals itself, however unworthy the occasion. He was soon to find a greater arena. The deeper motivation of his later efforts appears in the conclusion to this poem, a feeling for the diverse capacities of Germany, for the manifold talents of this great people. As yet he was not able to discern unity. He could merely enumerate a catalogue of humanist elements and centers. Would he be able to combine humanism more deeply with the destiny of the German nation? Would he be at all able to rise above academic performances and envisage the destiny of a people? Already he had a feeling for German antiquity, though as yet no conception of a common history, involving a common responsibility.

III

IN THE CAMP OF MAXIMILIAN. FIRST PERIOD IN ITALY

"FORTUNE hath dashed my resources, leaving me naught but a spirit undaunted."[1] So wrote Hutten in the *Lötze Philippics*. Throughout the work resounds the youthful will to be somebody and to make a name through great deeds. Deliberately Hutten described himself not only as a humanist, but also as a knight. To be sure, the exaggerated picture which he drew of the power and prominence of the Hutten family was intended to intimidate the Lötze; at the same time it served as a gesture to his relatives who might free him from his unhappy condition. The father, however, when approached by Crotus Rubeanus, wished the son to return to Fulda or at least, as a second best, to take up the study of law, which offered the surest prospect of a respectable position.[2] But Ulrich would not be diverted from his humanist studies. Precisely as the flight from the cloister and homeland had been justified as a desire to emerge from obscurity and learn from the world at large, so he explained his renewed decision to continue in these pursuits. When the attempt failed to obtain money from fellow monks at Fulda, Hutten turned to the south and directed his steps to Vienna.

Here he seems to have looked forward to "more comfortable days," as he puts it in his *Salutation to the Austrian Capital.*[3] Perhaps he hoped that his humanist lectures would bring him a position, possibly even thought they might gain for him entrée at Court. He must have heard recently that the Emperor Maximilian fostered the humanist movement and sought to enlist it for political

1. Hutten, *Opera,* III, 45.
2. *Ibid.,* I, 17 ff.
3. *Ibid.,* III, 159.

ends. As late as 1509 Hutten had not included any representatives of the southeast in his roster of the German humanists, but now the *Exhortation to the Emperor Maximilian to Continue the War against Venice*[4] shows a far-reaching acquaintance with the intellectual outlook of the Vienna humanists.[5] One might readily assume that the new tone was occasioned by the extremities to which he was reduced, had one not previously observed similar tendencies and were one not about to discover his ability to effect a deeper fusion of new and old.

The Emperor Maximilian was not in the real sense a humanist.[6] Legend has christened him the "last of the knights," and it is true that the roots of his personality lay in the culture of the Middle Ages.[7] He thought of himself in the first place as the restorer of the ancient imperial dignity and he was easily induced to make great sacrifices to this end. At the same time his policy was thoroughly egoistic and vindictive. Under the cloak of chivalrous generosity and honor he was concerned ruthlessly to further the interests of his family. In breaking political alliances and treaties he was as unscrupulous as the princes of the Italian Renaissance, though in some instances he followed not so much his true interests as his transitory whims. Machiavelli said of him that he dissipated his power by inconsistent designs.[8]

The Germans of his day loved his appearance. His colorful personality reflected the many and contradictory expectations which the people held of a king. He was not a

4. "Ad Caesarem Maximilianum ut bellum in Venetos coeptum prosequatur," Hutten, *Opera,* III, 124 ff.

5. J. Aschbach, *Die Wiener Universität und die Humanisten* (in his *Geschichte der Wiener Universität,* II, Vienna, 1877). G. Bauch, *Die Rezeption des Humanismus in Wien* (Breslau, 1903). P. Joachimsen, *Geschichtsauffassung und Geschichtsschreibung,* pp. 196 ff. F. von Bezold, "Konrad Celtis, 'der deutsche Erzhumanist,'" in his *Aus Mittelalter und Renaissance* (Munich, 1918), pp. 82 ff.

6. H. Ulmann, *Kaiser Maximilian I* (Stuttgart, 1884–1891).

7. P. Joachimsen, *Geschichtsauffassung und Geschichtsschreibung,* p. 218.

8. *Il Principe,* Chapter XXIII.

great general, but brave and experienced in war, a daring mountain climber and hunter. The imagination of the people seized upon such characteristics, and when he appeared among them, unaffected and using their own speech, all hearts were his. A like feeling was to arise once more after his death when the whole nation transferred their picture of him to his unknown grandson Charles, who came, however, from a very different world than his grandfather.

The German humanists, too, paid their homage to Maximilian and were received by him with encouragement. Humanism was useful not only for the genealogical interests so dear to his heart, but also for his dynastic ambitions and imperialistic designs. The humanists could serve him especially in the moulding of public opinion for his plans and purposes. Humanism had much for which to be grateful to Maximilian, though his ulterior interests menaced the cultural aspects of the movement. He it was who drew German humanism out of the schoolroom into the world arena and breathed into it something of the active joy of his own nature. This shift in the mood of the humanists from world-weariness to optimism is to be traced to their relations to the Hapsburg monarch. That Hutten's temper early tended to the active side and could not rest content with the *vita contemplativa*, we have already indicated. Nevertheless, outward circumstances plainly prompted his first political poem. The literary form of the *Exhortation* is cast in the humanist stereotype. As yet there is no inner note, although the peculiar convictions of the knight and his relation to the emperor and the *Reich* begin to come to the fore. Soon, however, the new stimuli occasioned at first only by the outward impressions of the residence in Vienna came to have an inner basis and justification. An indication of Hutten's craving for comprehensiveness and a conscious rounding out of his personality appears in the attempt to combine new and old experiences, as we find him doing in the poem which bears the significant title *Why the Germans Are Not Degenerate in Comparison with Former Times.*[9]

In his earlier period as a strolling scholar he may, indeed, have made some political observations, but he was occupied primarily only with the literary efforts of humanism. Now, however, that he stood on Austrian soil, in the vicinity of the imperial court, his will to political activity awoke. The knightly tradition was revived, with all of its class prejudice. At the same time there glimmered a feeling for the connection between the literary work going on in the Empire and the political might of the Empire itself. He began to wonder whether the greatness of a country consists in its literary culture alone or rather in its attainment of political power. The solution of this problem is the concern of the poem mentioned above.

After an epoch of valiant, warlike unfolding, Germany was now entering upon a period of peaceful development of her resources, among which Hutten counted above all art and scholarship, but also industry. The shift to these pursuits, he held, should not be regarded as a mark of deterioration of the moral health of the German people; they were still sound, even though their warlike energies might fail of full expression. The primitive period, too, was not without its defects in that it neglected to record its deeds and contemporary Germany in consequence was compelled to turn to foreign authors for a recital of the mighty exploits of its forefathers. Did not the modern period mark a comparative advance? Granted that great political enterprises had not been brought to fulfilment, there was nevertheless something more than a flair for *belles lettres.* German soldiers were winning victories all over the world, and could one find a better proof that the Germans were worthy of their fathers than the discovery of gunpowder and printing? Besides, the German state was not contemptible. With good reason the Italians endured the dominance of the German emperors, the Turks were afraid

9. "Quod ab illa antiquitus Germanorum claritudine nondum degeneraverint nostrates," Hutten, *Opera,* III, 331 ff.

to encroach further, and the Frenchman would get a taste of the energies of the Germanic peoples, revivified as they had been by the studies of the last century, should he venture to approach the "ever impregnable Rhine."

The poem, in which for the first time literary and political aspirations are intimately fused, is written in a proud, exalted diction, pulsing with joyous consciousness of the coming generation, at whose end, as a matter of fact, the political status of the nation was to be markedly reduced; for at the conclusion of the Reformation period Germany's political influence on Italy practically vanished, the Turks did advance their boundaries, and with the cession of the Lorraine bishoprics to France the western border lands became autumn leaves. The events and forces which contributed to this outcome could scarcely have been foreseen in 1511. Nevertheless, that the political task of the German people of this period was much more arduous and problematical than Hutten realized might in a measure have been anticipated even then. He came later to have a deeper feeling for the difficulties which a great political destiny would impose upon the German character and soon after leaving Vienna he became more sceptical with regard to Emperor Maximilian, in whose atmosphere the optimistic judgment on the contemporary German situation had been awakened as it came to expression in the *Poem on Germany*.

For all time to come, however, Hutten made a contribution by evolving the conception of a German national history segregated from the universal stream and the constituent conception of a distinct German character, and by popularizing these ideas among his contemporaries with all the drive of his extraordinary energy and through the medium of a newly forged and emotionally expressive language. His complaints over the deficiency of early German historical literature indicate the source of his conception. We find that Conrad Celt was disturbed in the same way and in Vienna Hutten would come to know intimately the historical work of his humanist circle. Whether this was the sole stimulus may well be doubted. The new ideas came to flower contemporaneously in many places, as, for example, through Heinrich Bebel in Tübingen and through Wimpfeling in Alsace, whose works Hutten came to know early, though in another connection. Then, too, there may have been something by way of corroboration in the lectures of Aesticampianus on the *Germania* of Tacitus, which Hutten attended in Leipsic in 1509.[10] In Tacitus' *Germania* were to be found the traits which Hutten ascribed to the character of the German people, namely, purity of morals and manliness. From now on the idealistic picture which Tacitus drew of the primitive German constituted an ever active incentive to Hutten's thinking and wishing. In this penchant for Tacitus old and new spiritual currents and moods of the period are inseparably bound.[11] From the humanist side came a flush of satisfaction that a great classical author should have placed so high a rating on the German people, whom even the German humanist was inclined to regard as barbarian, and in the new mood also was sympathy for a freer type of life. But older motives derived from the Middle Ages likewise contributed to this exaltation of the ideal of Tacitus. He was holding before the eyes of the over-ripe culture of his days the picture of a simple, natural people, and the Middle Ages, also satiated with cultural norms, pined for a less hampered existence, more in accord with the morality of nature.[12] An extensive literature concerned itself with the portrayal of the simple peasant. He was idealized as the man who through his plain toil nourished the whole of society. In this connection one recalls the "wild man game" portrayed in countless pictures of the late Middle Ages. It is symptomatic of a craving for relaxation, beauty, and naturalness in the midst of a reality which

10. P. Joachimsen, "Tacitus im deutschen Humanismus," *Neue Jahrbücher für das klassische Altertum, Geschichte und Literatur,* XXVII (1911), 707.

11. P. Joachimsen, *ibid.,* pp. 697–717, and F. Ramorino, *Cornelio Tacito nella storia della cultura* (2d edition, Milan, 1898).

12. See J. Huizinga, *The Waning of the Middle Ages,* Chapter X.

weighed as a burden. Hutten's Germans bear, if one may say so, something of the essence of the "wild men" of the idyllic game of the waning Middle Ages.

He is affected also in his glorification of primitive German society by the agrarian outlook of the knightly class. Here he discovered simpler economic forms which appeared to him ideal in comparison with the despicable modern commerce and trade. He went so far later as to espouse an agrarian precapitalistic economic system as eminently German. The limitations of his class background are here discernible and also in the *Exhortation* to the Emperor Maximilian, in which Hutten so vigorously expressed his opposition to the Venetian shopkeepers, thereby revealing the resentment of the knights against the bourgeois who threatened their economic status.

The picture of the early Germans derived from Tacitus received at first only a general interpretation at Hutten's hands. It is the contribution of his later period that, in contrast to other humanists, he gave to the German national consciousness, if not a positive content, at least a positive direction, in that he interpreted the conception of German freedom as liberation from Rome. In the poem on Germany there is a soft undertone of enmity to Rome where complaint is made of the influence of the popes and priests on German morals, but this is only a feeble prelude. The consciousness of this enmity was to come to full expression only on Italian soil.

Destiny was to drive him thither, granting him no peace in Vienna. He was, indeed, his own destiny and his own worst enemy, for it was the undisciplined character of his personal deportment, the insolence of his carriage at the university, which rendered a longer residence at Vienna impossible.[13] In April, 1512, he was in Pavia and to satisfy his father must take up the Pandects. From Pavia the disturbances of war drove him in July to Bologna, where again he fell into extremities and, utterly destitute and sick, was reduced to taking military service.

13. D. F. Strauss, *Hutten*, ed. by O. Clemen (Leipsic, 1927), p. 64.

Italy was then the arena in which the great questions of European policy were fought out. Hutten was an eye witness of the variable struggles and battles waged for the control of the Apennine peninsula. But although he was drawn into the midst of great events we need not be surprised to find him as a bystander, unable to penetrate into their motives, for the events themselves, precipitated by unscrupulous policy, were so inconsistent and variable from day to day that even the most experienced statesmen found it difficult to infer from the outward course the inner intent.

In spite of all the reservations which Hutten entertained with regard to the personality and policy of Maximilian,[14] none the less the victory of the German emperor was for him identical with the victory of righteousness. In this one-sided evaluation, which Hutten prosecuted with the utmost vigor of his nature, we perceive once more the renascence of the political polemic of the days of the Hohenstaufen. However much Hutten may have reënforced it with the moral and philosophical conceptions of humanism, the emperor was for him the lord of the world. "As Christ is the Lord of Heaven, so is the German emperor the lord of the earth."[15] The armored figure of Pope Julius II seemed to him in consequence to be trespassing in forbidden territory. The office of the pope consisted solely in the performance of his duties as the Christian shepherd of souls. Such an attitude had been characteristic of Walther von der Vogelweide in the twelfth century, but Hutten went further in that he brought to bear on his treatment of the political drama the reflections stimulated by his humanist studies on the significance of historical events. But how did it come to pass, in the higher scheme of things, that the unquestionably righteous pretensions of the emperor were realized so slowly and with so many setbacks?

14. H. Ulmann, *Kaiser Maximilian I.* E. Fueter, *Geschichte des europäischen Staatensystems 1492–1559* (Munich, 1919). H. Kretzschmayr, *Geschichte Venedigs,* II (Gotha, 1920).

15. Hutten, *Opera,* III, 208.

A religious nature would have been driven to the problem of the justice of God. Hutten left this out of account without thereby abandoning the paths of ecclesiastical thought, for the Church did not deny that the phenomena and occurrences of the natural world follow their own laws.

In this "natural world" the gods of antiquity were still active in the form of demons, and among them stood, above all, the Goddess *Fortuna*,[16] who touched the burning question of humanist thought. One can scarcely say that Hutten broke new ground in his treatment of the Goddess of Chance in the *Epigrams to the Emperor Maximilian* of 1512–1513.[17] Nevertheless it is significant for the relation in his mind of thought and will. Complaints over the freaks of *Fortuna* predominate. They verge even upon scepticism as to whether there is any moral order at all, but this doubt is quickly dispelled by the will to live. He could console himself that the wheel of fortune returns upon itself. To be sure, sometimes there are also intimations of a deeper solution, when he suggests that the variations of *Fortuna* may serve to strengthen the greatness of men or of nations. At any rate, his belief in the world was so great that he remained in general convinced of the ultimate success of stalwart effort and striving.

The progress which we observe from the *Lötze Philippics* to the *Epigrams to the Emperor Maximilian* lies in the extension of the rôle of *Fortuna* from the sphere of individual life to that of the destiny of nations. Here is the especial fruit of this Italian residence, that he had come to have a more intimate appreciation of great events and had come thereby to interpret individual personality in terms of the play of great forces. His national enthusiasm was taking on more concrete political forms and—what

16. See F. von Bezold, *Das Fortleben der antiken Götter im mittelalterlichen Humanismus* (Bonn, 1922). H. R. Patch, *The Goddess Fortune in Medieval Literature* (Cambridge, 1927). A. Doren, "Fortuna im Mittelalter und in der Renaissance," *Vorträge der Bibliothek Warburg 1922–1923* (Leipsic, 1924), Part I, pp. 71 ff.

17. "Ad Caesarem Maximilianum epigrammatum liber unus," Hutten, *Opera*, III, 205 ff.

was of the utmost significance for the future—he began to criticize the position of the Roman curia. Ever since the rise of the *patrimonium Petri* the popes had been torn between their duties as local Italian princes and their universal spiritual tasks. Julius II was really little more than an Italian prince. During his pontificate the papacy in its secular aspects became known to the man who later heavily contributed a sharp anti-papal turn to the German Reformation.

Hitherto Hutten's opposition to the secular pretensions of the papacy had been awakened only by his inborn national feeling. A little later he was to enter the lists as a humanist against the intellectual system of the Church. Herein lies the significance of the Reuchlin feud.

IV

POLEMIC AGAINST SCHOLASTICISM ACQUAINTANCE WITH ERASMUS

BEFORE we follow Hutten's development in the midst of humanist friendships and encounters we must first glance at the outward situation into which he now entered. In 1513 he was back in Germany, and although the immediate family remained cool because he had not distinguished himself, his other relatives were prepared to accept him. Frowin von Hutten and Eitelwolf von Stein secured for their nephew a place in Mainz. The former occupied an important post in the circle of the cathedral chapter there and the latter became in 1514 court prefect to the incoming Archbishop Albert.[1] As their protégé Ulrich seems to have been presented to the young archbishop in whose hands exceptional power was concentrated through an astonishing accumulation of bishoprics. He favored the humanist movement, less out of genuine understanding than through an ambition to parade himself. His interest in the movement awakened hope in Frowin von Hutten and Eitelwolf von Stein, who sought to advise the Hohenzollern in such matters, that their nephew might find favor in the eyes of Albert. On Eitelwolf's motion, Ulrich undertook to compose a panegyric

1. On the history of Mainz during the reign of Albert see J. May, *Der Kurfürst, Kardinal und Erzbischof Albrecht II von Mainz* (Munich, 1865–1875). H. Goldschmidt, *Zentralbehörden und Beamtentum im Kurfürstentum Mainz vom 16. bis zum 18. Jahrhundert* (Berlin, 1908). F. Herrmann, *Die evangelische Bewegung in Mainz im Reformationszeitalter* (Mainz, 1907), and "Evangelische Regungen zu Mainz in den ersten Jahren der Reformation," *Schriften des Vereins für Reformationsgeschichte,* Vol. 100 (Leipsic, 1910). P. Kalkoff, *W. Capito im Dienste Erzbischofs Albrechts von Mainz* (Berlin, 1907), and *Hutten und die Reformation,* in *Quellen und Forschungen zur Reformationsgeschichte,* IV (Leipsic, 1920), 47 ff., and *Huttens Vagantenzeit und Untergang* (Weimar, 1925), pp. 119 ff.

on the accession of the new Archbishop of Mainz.[2] The new prince was celebrated in diverse ways and flattery was not spared. The poem is a real model of court verse and as such enjoyed success: Ulrich received the promise, on the completion of his juristic studies, of a post in the circle of the elector.[3] He obtained in addition, as a regal present for his poetic effusions, a stipend for the completion of his studies in Italy. Hutten was not so pleased, for neither court life nor legal study particularly interested him. He would have preferred to follow his humanist propensities.[4] Still he expected something from Albert. He hoped that the elector, prompted by Eitelwolf, would make Mainz into a center of European culture. The thought that an energetic prince would do something more significant for humanism than all the nobles put together disposed him to a more favorable picture and a higher evaluation of princes than at any other time in his life.

The experience which he had with those of his own class profoundly discouraged him as to the cultural status of the knights who stood in the way of the new learning. He called them "Centaurs," wholly lacking in *eruditio* and *humanitas*.[5] Seldom did one find among them such outstanding men as Eitelwolf von Stein, who did not disdain to belong at once to the knights and to the intellectuals.[6] This was the man whom Hutten held up as a shining example to the knights. The design to make out of the feudal nobility of the Middle Ages a modern cultural aristocracy will engage us again.

Yet, however much Hutten might reproach the knights with the lack of *eruditio* and *humanitas*, he did not cease on the other hand to draw upon his own derivation from the knightly class. Even in his dealings with his humanist friends, like Erasmus, he emphasized his knightly origin.[7]

2. "In laudem reverendissimi Alberthi Archiepiscopi Moguntini panegyricus," Hutten, *Opera,* III, 343 ff.

3. *Ibid.,* I, 43.

4. *Ibid.,* p. 102.

5. *Ibid.,* p. 36.

6. *Ibid.,* pp. 43 ff.

7. See his first letter to Erasmus of October 24, 1515. *Ibid.,* p. 102. P. S. Allen, *Opus epistularum Erasmi* (Oxford, 1906), Ep. 365, II, 155 ff.

Odd it is, indeed, that humanism, with its universal tendencies, succeeded so little in emancipating him from class limitations. We must not forget, however, that knightly blood not only imposed bounds on his spirit but endowed him also with positive strength.

As the sudden death of his patron, Eitelwolf von Stein (1515), dimmed the plans for the transformation of the bishop's court at Mainz into a seat of the Muses, and the hope which Ulrich entertained for his life at Mainz began gradually to crumble, so the murder of his cousin, Hans von Hutten, brought him again into contact with his family and renewed his knightly class consciousness. This is not the place to describe in detail the marital rivalry of Duke Ulrich von Württemberg and his courtier, Hans von Hutten.[8] Suffice it that Duke Ulrich, in order to possess the wife, had murdered Hans von Hutten. To a man the Huttens rose to avenge the insult. At this moment the literary talent of the estranged son was welcome. With fiery passion he now undertook to inflame public opinion against the duke. This agitation against the Württembergs runs through the next years,[9] until Ulrich as a knight at the side of Sickingen was able to expel the duke from his territory. In the controversy with Ulrich von Württemberg Hutten's pen is for the first time sharpened against the territorial princes. For the moment, however, this one vile duke was regarded as a hideous exception. Later Hutten was to turn his venom against the whole class.

In the four *Exposures of Ulrich* we observe the literary progress which Hutten had made since the completion of his student days in Germany. Compared with the *Lötze Philippics*, likewise designed to demolish a personal oppo-

8. See H. Ulmann, *Fünf Jahre württembergischer Geschichte 1515–1519* (Leipsic, 1867).

9. "In Ulrichum Wirtenpergensem orationes quinque," Hutten, *Opera*, V, 1 ff. Copious quotations in D. F. Strauss, *Hutten*, edited by O. Clemen (Leipsic, 1927), pp. 82 ff. The first *Exposure* was written in 1515, the second and third in spring 1517, the fourth in summer 1517, and the last one in summer 1519. That Cicero served as a model has been shown by L. Wellner, "Über die Beeinflussung einiger Reden Ulrich von Huttens," *23. Jahresbericht des Gymnasiums in Mährisch Neustadt*, 1910.

nent, the *Exposures of Ulrich* exhibited a greater maturity not only in the wider scope of the subject but also because the rhetorical style gave freer play to the sweep of his spirit and the power of his feeling.

It would be a mistake to regard the valiant tone of the *Exposures of Ulrich* as an indication of Hutten's mood in these years. All during his German and Italian travels we find a note of deep depression and bitter scepticism, which contrasts markedly with the self-confidence of his personal conduct. He felt himself to be as good as the next man, and better than most, but the riddle of existence still pressed upon him. Humanism filled him with hope for the progress of mankind; yet only gradually could the clouds of barbarism be dissipated. This observation and his own toilsome struggles overwhelmed him with recurring despondency as to destiny. We must not, however, exaggerate the significance of such utterances, deeply conditioned as they were by the fleeting depressions which so readily overtake this period of life. Yet, however transitory, they show us that Hutten was no stranger to the autumn melancholy which in this century ever shadowed the exuberant joy of living. This man, whose figure Strauss employed to tinge the German Reformation with world-approving optimism, was the author of a work which expressed as did scarcely any other the sceptical mood of secular literature. Significantly the *Nobody* was the most frequently read and reprinted of Hutten's poems.[10]

The first draft was already completed at Greifswald.[11] After returning from Italy Hutten took up again the theme of human inadequacy and the narrow limits of life on earth. A letter of 1515 shows that the work was completed at that time, and the characteristic dedication to Crotus Rubeanus must also have been practically finished.[12] One recognizes the outward impressions which accompany the composition of the work: the chilly reception

10. "Nemo," Hutten, *Opera,* III, 106 ff.

11. O. Clemen, in *Theologische Studien und Kritiken,* 1908, has described the first edition which was printed at Erfurt in 1510.

12. Hutten, *Opera,* I, 102.

at home, the indignation of the family that he came back not as a doctor but as a "nobody," the contempt of the father for humanist "humbug." But it is not merely personal circumstances which come to expression, but also deeper concern for the future of the new learning. "O mores, O studia! O ye leaders of this time! Why do we not dispel the clouds and turn to the truth?"

This ejaculation was the fruit of the experiences which he had gathered in Germany. The theologians and the jurists who controlled public life seemed to him to be untouched by the new ideas and movements and to stand in the way of the spiritual emancipation which he championed. This recognition, coupled with a growing dislike of the court at Mainz, almost made him wish for Italy, so that on the death of Eitelwolf von Stein and the murder of Hans von Hutten he could write to Jacob Fuchs: "Germany has nothing now that can stimulate me." One must be rather in Italy, the home of learning.[13]

In the midst of such thoughts and moods disgust over the German ecclesiastical situation found expression in the Reuchlin feud which threatened the whole development of German humanism. John Reuchlin,[14] the first of the German humanists to branch out from classical to Hebrew studies, had foiled the plan of Pfefferkorn, a renegade Jew engaged in a lively propaganda for the collection and destruction of all the Jewish books. Antisemitism was popular in Germany at the beginning of the sixteenth century and the Emperor Maximilian had not the courage to quench the firebrand while yet there was time. Reuchlin expressed his view on the scholarly value of the Jewish literature, first in a memorandum intended for the emperor and then in 1511 in a popular tract, the *Augenspiegel* (eye-glasses). Thereby he evoked the wrath of the German Dominicans and of the theological faculty of

13. *Ibid.*, pp. 40, 42.

14. On Reuchlin see L. Geiger, *Johannes Reuchlin* (Leipsic, 1871). N. Paulus, *Die deutschen Dominikaner im Kampfe gegen Luther* (Freiburg, 1903). Also F. G. Stokes in the introduction to his edition of the *Obscure Men* (London, 1909), and A. Bömer, *Epistolae obscurorum virorum,* I (Heidelberg, 1924).

Cologne, who were backing the apostate. Reuchlin himself was cited before the tribunal of the inquisitor of Cologne, Jacob von Hochstraten.

The humanists were endangered. Basically the question was not simply as to the retention of the Jewish books, but as to something much more fundamental.[15] Should the humanists have a voice in the affairs of faith and the Church? So long as they confined themselves to poetry and rhetoric controversy might arise over academic posts, but the theologians however disgruntled at the incursion of the poets into the universities could not counter with the ban. The case was altered when the humanists turned from diction to dogma. This was precisely what now took place in Germany. Italian humanism was primarily a national revival of the old Roman world and its manner of life. The Latin poet, rhetor, and philosopher should come to life again and engender a new society. Even Valla's criticism of the papacy and of the official Biblical text was an ephemeral political weapon. Fundamentally the temper of the Italian Renaissance was not seriously anti-ecclesiastical. Either humanism entirely neglected the Church and confined its attention exclusively to political and communal interests, which should be infused with the new ideal of *humanitas*, or else the Church and its teachings were so allegorized that every philosopher could find himself at home in them.

For a time it seemed as if such a humanism would transplant itself to Germany. Among the political humanists Aeneas Silvius was the one who brought poetical and rhetorical education from Italy to Germany. Even more this papal diplomat provided the Germans directly with the material for a historical legend.[16] He was the first to

15. Compare P. Joachimsen, "Der Humanismus und die Entwicklung des deutschen Geistes," *Deutsche Vierteljahrsschrift für Literaturwissenschaft und Geistesgeschichte,* VIII (1930), 460 ff.

16. P. Joachimsen, *Geschichtsauffassung und Geschichtsschreibung* (Leipsic, 1910), pp. 27 ff. U. Paul, *Studien zur Geschichte des deutschen Nationalbewusstseins im Zeitalter des Humanismus und der Reformation* (*Historische Studien,* Vol. 298, Berlin, 1936).

describe the land as a great flourishing corporate body in all of its provinces. He it was who praised the progress of German culture, and pointed the Germans to the sources of their oldest cultural history, Caesar, Strabo, and Tacitus.

The patriotic or "romantic" humanism of the Germans, represented by the young Hutten, is based directly and indirectly on the Italian model. Likewise the purely literary ventures of early German humanism arose under Italian influence. The primary work of the young Erasmus, the *Antibarbari*, shows that most clearly.[17] He wanted to become a "poeta." *Humanitas* was originally the program of the new literary education. But then came the transition.[18] The influence of John Colet and his circle with their Biblical studies revived in Erasmus a deeper aspiration, recalling the lessons already learned in his native land from the Brethren of the Common Life with their combination of scholarship and simple mystical piety. The sallies of Lorenzo Valla in Biblical criticism contributed further to make him aware of his own especial task, namely to utilize the new philological tools and ideas for the reform of piety.[19] Here he was met by the deep longing of the world beyond the Alps which was not ready like Italy to regard the Church and religion as incidental, but turned to them for the solution of all the problems of life.

Not by accident did Erasmus introduce his Christian humanism into Germany at the precise moment when the native humanists were drawn into the theological area by

17. P. Mestwerdt, *Die Anfänge des Erasmus* (*Studien zur Kultur und Geschichte der Reformation,* Vol. 2, Leipsic, 1917). A. Hyma, *The Youth of Erasmus* (Ann Arbor, 1930). R. Pfeiffer, *Humanitas Erasmiana* (*Studien der Bibliothek Warburg,* Vol. 22, Leipsic, 1931), and his article "Die Wandlungen der 'Antibarbari' " in *Gedenkschrift zum 400. Todestage des Erasmus von Rotterdam* (Basel, 1936), pp. 50 ff. O. Schottenloher, *Erasmus im Ringen um die humanistische Bildungsform* (*Reformationsgeschichtliche Studien und Texte,* Vol. 61, Münster, 1933).

18. J. Huizinga, *Erasmus* (New York, 1924), pp. 36 ff.

19. A. Hyma, *The Christian Renaissance. A history of the 'Devotio moderna'* (Michigan, 1924). H. Baron, "Zur Frage des Ursprungs des deutschen Humanismus und seiner religiösen Reformbestrebungen," *Historische Zeitschrift,* CXXXII (1925), 413 ff.

the Reuchlin controversy. What embittered the theologians and evoked the condemnation of the universities of Germany one after another and finally of Paris and Louvain was the fact that Reuchlin, the humanist, employed his philological equipment for a new interpretation of Biblical passages. This was for them the mortal sin of the *Augenspiegel.* And at that point the humanists all rallied to the defense of Reuchlin. Not quite all. Mutianus regretted that Reuchlin was bringing humanist knowledge into disrepute among the masses, but this mood did not prevail. In general the German humanists were resolved on a theological reform. No wonder that a few years later they applauded Luther.

Externally, too, Reuchlin's controversy was associated with Luther's. The wrath of the Dominicans in 1516 was thwarted by papal intervention. The stake was all ready to kindle when the messenger of Leo X entered with the announcement that the pope reserved the case. The Medicean pontiff appointed as judge the humanistically inclined Bishop of Speyer, who in 1514 had pronounced the *Augenspiegel* innocuous and Hochstraten a slanderer, who should pay the costs. This was too much for the Dominicans, who appealed to the pope and consecrated all the resources of the order to the prosecution of their case. At first only with half success. The committee of cardinals decided in favor of Reuchlin, with only one dissenting voice, that of Sylvester Prierias, later the author of the first official refutation of Luther. Pope Leo, however, did not dare to go directly in the teeth of the Dominicans and evaded a verdict by a so-called *mandatum de supersedendo,* suspending the legal controversy. There the case would have rested had not Luther's advent inclined the pope toward the Dominicans. The judgment pronounced in 1520 vindicated Hochstraten, declared the *Augenspiegel* dangerous, and saddled Reuchlin with the formidable costs.

This is in outline the course of the famous Reuchlin feud in which, for the first time, the German humanists arrayed themselves with solidarity against the dominant theology. For Hutten, too, this fight constituted a new stage of development. Just as in Italy his German consciousness had been aroused by the observation of papal politics to withstand papal encroachments, so now the heresy hunting of the ecclesiastical court revealed to him the incompatibility of the intellectual worlds of humanism and scholasticism. Not that he broke altogether with the official tradition of the Church. There are unequivocal witnesses from this period that he not only continued to believe in ecclesiastical ceremonies, but also that he had no protest against serious aberrations. Witness his hearty approval of the execution of another Jew named Pfefferkorn for ostensible crimes.[20] Hutten was concerned merely to attack scholasticism as the current version or perversion of ecclesiastical theology. Scholasticism, he felt, is not the old Christian theology, as it pretends to be, but a theology of only three hundred years' standing—a caricature, in fact, of Christian teaching. "When I reflect on this I realize how in the last three hundred years the Christian religion has been undermined. When the old genuine theology collapsed, then religion and learning sank together and the worst of all plagues broke out, namely superstition, which so obscured the purity of the true worship of the Deity that one can scarcely tell now whether the whole thing is meant to serve Christ or a new god who will take for himself this last age of the world."[21]

In this differentiation between the good old theology and the new perverted variety, the influence of Erasmus is discernible, and likewise earlier in Hutten's career, of Rhagius Aesticampianus. The first draft of the *Nobody* already shows acquaintance with some at least of the writings of Erasmus. In the new preface to the *Nobody* Hutten praises him as a godly restorer of early Christian

20. Hutten, *Opera,* III, 345 ff. "In sceleratissimam Pepericorni vitam exclamatio."

21. *Ibid.,* I, 182. The same idea is often expressed in the *Obscure Men.*

teaching and learning.[22] But the picture which Hutten entertained of the "old theology" was very vague and void of content. His conception of the old or of the new theology, if not a mere reproduction of Erasmus, was much more wooden and artificial than Luther's. Such conceptions arise from an essentially rational will rather than from a sense of religious compulsion, and here at the outset lay the limitation of Hutten's polemic against scholasticism. However decisive it might be to point out that scholastic teaching was not an impregnable supernatural deposit, but a product of historical development, however dangerous to scholasticism to be confronted with the Church Fathers, nevertheless it was not to be destroyed by mere historical criticism, but only by the onslaught of the religious consciousness. At this point Hutten was rather weak and that is why his opposition to scholasticism did not lead him beyond the limits of the Church's sacramental system. The intimate connection between the sacramental and the intellectual system of the Church was not adequately clear to him, and his sweeping attack on the medieval Church is inconsistent with his personal relation to its inner life. He was not the one to think anything through systematically. He was a man of action and his thoughts were the servants of his will. His attack on the learning of the Church was a polemic not so much against

22. In the preface to the *Nobody* he talks of *illi nuper Erasmi labores*. Most probably the *Lucubrationes* published in 1515 by M. Schuerer of Strassburg were meant as W. Kaegi has suggested in "Hutten und Erasmus," *Historische Vierteljahrsschrift,* XXII (1924), 204. For a description of this publication see my edition of *Desiderii Erasmi Roterodami Opera Selecta* (Munich, 1933), p. xii. The most important tract contained in the *Lucubrationes* was the *Enchiridion militis Christiani.* Hutten, however, must have known the bulk of Erasmus' writings. In 1517 for example he quoted the *Adages* and the *Praise of Folly* but not in a manner that would indicate only a recent acquaintance (Hutten, *Opera,* I, 146). The *Novum Instrumentum* of 1516 was soon in his possession, for he used after that almost exclusively the new Latin translation of the Bible by Erasmus. See P. Held, *Ulrich von Hutten. Seine religiös-geistige Auseinandersetzung mit Katholizismus, Humanismus, Reformation,* pp. 95 ff. (*Schriften des Vereins für Reformationsgeschichte,* Vol. 144, Leipsic, 1928).

scholasticism as against scholastics. Not so much the system of the Church as its contemporary representatives would he hoist from the saddle. In them he saw what he loathed, a mind closed to the new intellectual movements—and, for that matter, any movement whatever. This sodden inertia—*quies scholastica*[23]—above all provoked his ire and he satirized the academic, formal hairsplitting of the scholastics, who, though knowing better, tied everything up in rules. They were like the Roman jurists, whom from now on he attacked with similar verve. They too, with their new methods, suppressed the German law and corrupted the old German customs.

The fight which he began to wage in the preface of the *Nobody* against the Roman law was hopeless, for it was already too well domesticated in Germany for the development to be reversed, and however much hardship its introduction meant for many, the old legal system, with its diversity and uncertainty, was a severe hindrance to the expansion of the national energies.[24] In the economic sphere more than elsewhere a system of law was needed to give legal unification to the commercial districts already bound together by the trade of early capitalism. Hutten did not know enough about the old practice and its disadvantages. He must have learned something about it during his residence in the north, but his praise of the Saxons and the good old German customs and laws is of a very general nature. Might he not have reconciled himself to the victory of the Roman law by the reflection that it was creating a unified system? For he himself ardently desired a most intimate association of the German states—all branches, as he later said, of one tree.[25] We must bear in mind, however, that the introduction of a unified system of law did not greatly assist the attainment of political unity. In spite of the Cameral Tribunal, the real beneficiaries of

23. Hutten, *Opera,* I, 195.

24. G. von Below, *Die Ursachen der Rezeption des römischen Rechts in Deutschland* (Munich, 1905).

25. Hutten, *Opera,* V, 117.

the introduction of Roman law were the territorial princes. The modern jurists, trained originally in Italy, constituted the staff with which the princes consolidated and centralized their possessions. The more intensive administration and mobilization of the resources of the territories in the following period had been preceded by the development of a technically trained corps of officials.

From this angle Hutten's revulsion from Roman law and modern jurists is comprehensible. Along with the wish to gain parity for the humanists beside the jurists and theologians, Hutten was prompted by the independence of the free noble who saw his domain restricted by the intensive consolidation and concentration of the territories. It would be unfair to regard Hutten's polemic against the jurists as purely reactionary. As a matter of fact, the introduction of modern civil administration helped to perpetuate the particularistic tendencies of Germany; and Hutten, moreover, was something more than a quasi-anarchist, shrinking from the increasing rationalization of civil life. He was also expressly concerned for a state more vitally rooted in the affections of the people by old German forms. Here history vindicates his judgment in so far as the interruption of the living stream of popular common law constitutes a permanent loss for the development of the German people.

But every day polemic against the jurists became less significant than attacks on the scholastic theologians. Lustier even than the preface to the *Nobody* was the *Triumph of Capnio*[26] (Reuchlin), which Hutten showed to Erasmus at their first meeting and withheld from publication for a time on his advice.[27] The supreme example was the *Letters of Obscure Men*, conceived in this period though not fully executed until later.

In the spring of 1514 Reuchlin had published a collection of letters in Latin, Greek, and Hebrew with the title

26. "Triumphus Doctoris Reuchlini sive Johannis Capnionis encomion." Hutten, *Opera,* III, 413 ff.

27. *Ibid.,* II, 318.

Letters of Famous Men. The anthology was intended in part to serve the purposes of philology and style but primarily to exhibit an assemblage of testimonies from distinguished men for Reuchlin's cause and person. The persecuted humanist presented them to the tribunal and to the public as a sort of personal testimonial. Ostensibly a counterblast was the collection which came out in October 1515 with the title *Letters of Obscure Men.* The word "obscure" at that moment had no meaning other than as the opposite of famous. The connotation obscurantist is a result of the work. In the spring and fall of the next year various reprints appeared in Germany, of which the second contained in addition to the original forty-one letters an appendix of seven more. Then followed in the spring of 1517 two editions of a second part containing sixty-two more letters.

The question of the authorship can be regarded as closed in all essential points.[28] Roughly speaking one may say that the first part was the work of Hutten's friend Crotus Rubeanus, the appendix to the first part as well as the second came from Hutten. But friends of the authors contributed to both. Hutten, for example, wrote the first letter of the first part, and Hermann von dem Busche, the Westphalian knight and humanist, did letters nineteen and thirty-six of the first and sixty-one and -two of the second. In the case of four other letters of the second part his hand is likewise traceable. But the essential point is that Crotus and Hutten conceived the plan and gave shape to the whole apart from their preponderant contributions. Hutten's authorship of the priceless epistle with which the first part opens is clear proof that during his residence in Germany Crotus and he hatched the scheme

28. The greatest contribution has been made by W. Brecht, *Die Verfasser der Epistulae obscurorum virorum* (Strassburg, 1904). His results have been modified by A. Bömer in the first volume of his edition *Epistolae obscurorum virorum* (Heidelberg, 1924). Other critical texts of the *Obscure Men* in the supplement of Hutten, *Opera,* edited by E. Böcking, and the Latin and English edition by F. G. Stokes (London, 1909).

of mocking the opponents of Reuchlin by a satire and of exposing the devices and the mind of the conservative theologians through a fictitious correspondence. Thus arose the letters to Ortwin Gratius, the leader of the Cologne theologians. Seldom in history has the maxim been truer that laughter kills.

The *Letters of Obscure Men* win for Crotus primarily the place of originator of a new satirical genre approximating Rabelais and Cervantes. The universities of the Middle Ages were acquainted with the take-offs on the *Quodlibet*, in which every conceivable topic was discussed according to a strict academic ritual.[29] The *Fastnachtspiele* and the books of fools likewise provided material for the comic, but in the *Letters of Obscure Men* one feels already the tone of a new literary age. One may say even that Erasmus' *Praise of Folly* belongs still to the Middle Ages in spite of its humanist philosophy. The *Obscure Men*, however, stand at the beginning of modern literature. These figures require no introduction from their authors, but live for themselves. They do not address themselves to the public but chat among themselves, and the reader listens in as he would follow the conversation of table companions. A new stage of realism in observation and description is here attained. Only once did humanism in this period reach a similar level, in the *Colloquies* of Erasmus, which came out a few years later.

In this great literary venture Crotus' share is to be evaluated higher than Hutten's, for the first part establishes the type and achieves a finer literary level. Hutten was too short of breath for this ambling type of satire. The snappy interchange of the dialogue, adopted a year later, pleased him better. Crotus was less skillful in this medium, but for the genre of his own creation he was well equipped through an intimate acquaintance with the thought and life of the theologians. He was a teacher now in the very cloister school at Fulda from which he had once

29. A. Bömer, *Lateinische Schülergespräche der Humanisten* (Berlin, 1897 ff.).

helped Hutten to escape. Besides he was carrying on theological studies and had no need merely to simulate a superficial theological style. Herein lies the charm and the freshness of his work. His intention was perhaps not so much to brush aside and destroy scholasticism as to rise above it. The artist is stronger in him than the propagandist. His negative criticism of the old outweighs his positive contribution to the new. Finally, the ideal of culture which he opposed to scholasticism was more a matter of taste than of conscience.

The impression of the first part is admirably set forth by Thomas More: "The learned are tickled by their humour, while the unlearned deem their teachings of serious worth. When we laugh, they think we do but deride the style; this they do not defend, but they declare that all faults are compensated by the weight of the matter, and that the rough scabbard contains a brilliant blade! Would that the book had appeared under another title! I verily believe that in a hundred years the dolts would not perceive the nose turned up at them—though longer than the snout of a rhinoceros!"[30]

In the second part no such doubt is possible. There are passages of delicious humor superior if anything to the best letters of the first part, but all in all Hutten's style was a studious imitation of Crotus, lacking in inventiveness and lapsing readily from the comic to the pathetic. Humanist culture was not for Hutten as for Crotus an instrument of detachment by which one could be emancipated through an urbane chuckle. *Humanitas* is worth more and exacts more. That is why the character of the *Obscure Men* changes so markedly from Crotus. Cutting satire becomes bitter invective.

Significant is it also that Hutten gave the work a political cast. The *Epistles* were meant to gain air for the suffocated Reuchlin. In confidential letters the pitiful shabbiness of the complaints of his opponents, the pettiness of

30. *Epistolae Obscurorum Virorum,* edited by F. G. Stokes, p. xlix. Allen, *Opus epistularum Erasmi,* Ep. 481, II, 372.

their ways and minds, should be held up to public laughter. But what Crotus conceived of as a war of two literary movements Hutten envisaged as a cosmic drama. The course of events moved Hutten with more heat and passion and the issue of the Reuchlin controversy was for him not only a matter of his own faith in the world but also the answer to the problem of the future of humanism and the future of Germany. Whether the German nation would overcome barbarism and gain an equal spiritual footing with the Latin countries, whether she would be mindful of her old beliefs, her old political forms, would appear in the Reuchlin affair. Thus had he intensified the significance of the particular event to a tremendous and even a dangerous height: for it was unrealistic and unwise to classify men into two almost equal camps over such issues. The essential position of scholasticism was not grasped and the outward power of humanism was grossly exaggerated. The humanists were not so united among themselves, nor so influential with the princes, as would appear from Hutten's *Obscure Men*. Thomas Murner, for instance, was not by reason of his humanism at one with Hutten's purposes; and could Albert of Mainz be counted on merely because he had thrown a tract of Pfefferkorn into the fireplace? Very few humanists were prepared to be as decisive as Hutten desired. Even the eminent patrons of the movement must be intimidated by a radical polemic, the more so because Hutten, unlike Crotus, attacked not the small fry of the type of Ortwin Gratius, but took by the horns such haughty figures as Jakob von Hochstraten, Inquisitor General of Cologne, and Arnold von Tungern, Dean of the theological faculty.

However much Hutten may have consciously exaggerated humanist influence in order to terrify opponents and make an impression at court, he had not really grasped the situation with precision. The passionateness of the battle blinded him to the realities, the glow of his emotions lifted him all too readily over the hurdles, and he himself had a certain inkling that things were not so simple as he made them out to be: now and then he rattled the sabre, in case persuasion should not suffice. He talked about a conspiracy, unfortunately without giving one any further glimpse into this idea, which plainly occupied him for the moment. In any case he had made up his mind to plunge. Both a humanist and a knight as he desired to be, he considered every means which might lead to the end. Now emerged the characteristic contour of a figure hitherto hazy, due in part to the fluctuations of his early circumstances and impressions, in part to the paucity of our sources—now emerged the humanist in arms, or, as he himself said, an Alcibiades following Socrates.

Thus he described himself in his first letter to Erasmus, who was to be his Socrates and to whom he was to cleave henceforth with a marked inwardness in contrast to his prevailing activism. In August, 1514, at Mainz, in the company of Reuchlin and Hermann von der Busche, he came to know Erasmus.[31] The prince of the humanists was on his way from England to Basel, where he was about to bring out a new edition of the *Adages* at the press of the incomparable Froben and to prepare the great edition of the New Testament and a further edition of the works of Jerome. A second meeting took place in Frankfurt. These two contacts gave rise to the correspondence, unfortunately not fully preserved, and to mutual literary references in the humanist mode.

Thus far every nation had a claim on Erasmus.[32] He was born in the German Netherlands, the son of a Catholic cleric. There and in Paris he received his early education. In Italy and in England he became one of the princes of the European scholarship. At the age of forty-five[33] he was travelling to Switzerland, where he was to reside till

31. See W. Kaegi, "Hutten und Erasmus," *Historische Vierteljahrsschrift,* XXII (1924), 201 ff.

32. J. Huizinga, "Erasmus über Vaterland und Nation," *Gedenkschrift zum 400. Todestage des Erasmus von Rotterdam* (Basel, 1936), pp. 34 ff.

33. Owing to contradictory statements by Erasmus as to the year of his birth the dates of his life are not easy to determine. See P. Smith, *Erasmus* (New York, 1923), pp. 445 ff.

the growth of Protestantism drove him to Freiburg. On the journey he first became acquainted with the world of German scholarship, of which he formed a most favorable impression. He was an important champion of Reuchlin, whose cause he defended in public[34] and in confidential letters, such as those to the Cardinals Raffaello Riario and Domenico Grimani.[35] In particular, from now on he took an interest in Hutten's personality and literary creations. The elegance of the Latin diction and the genius displayed thoroughly charmed him. He entertained hopes for Hutten's literary development and was not unwilling to be called his friend. In a conspicuous place in the annotations to the epoch-making edition of the New Testament in 1516 Erasmus paid Hutten a high tribute of which he might well be proud, rating him on a par with such distinguished German humanists as Sturm and Melanchthon and the brothers Amerbach and Glarean. The wide circle of readers was informed: "How could Attica produce more pith and elegance than this one possesses? Is not his speech divine beauty and sheer charm?"[36]

Erasmus would not agree with everything that Hutten had on foot, nor had he properly appraised him at the two meetings of 1514 and 1515, but he was an excellent judge of human nature and it is significant that he was willing to regard Hutten as a comrade in humanism, even if one take into account the ambition of Erasmus to be able to muster as many pens as possible in case of an encounter such as that with Edward Lee in 1520. Erasmus perhaps hoped that he might curb Hutten and succeeded for a while in keeping the *Triumph of Capnio* out of print, but the urbane irony of Erasmus could scarcely fail to sense the

34. See his letter to Reuchlin, which was published in the collection *Epistulae clarorum virorum.* Allen, *Opus epistularum Erasmi,* Ep. 300, II, 3 ff.

35. Allen, *Opus epistularum Erasmi,* Ep. 333 and 334, II, 68 ff.

36. Hutten, *Opera,* I, 103. The context of the quotation, however, must be examined. Erasmus withheld the passage in those editions that he published after his quarrel with Hutten. It is left out in the Leiden edition of his collected works, too. Accordingly see *Novum Instrumentum* (Basel, 1516), pp. 555 ff.

sharper tone of the younger generation of German humanists. His scepticism and diplomatic variability could not be entirely congenial to the drive and reckless activity of Hutten, nor could Ulrich's militant nationalism conform to the pacific cosmopolitanism of Erasmus. How far Erasmus felt the difference at the outset we cannot tell. We know that he was favorably impressed. We may assume that the differences which separated them personally and historically, and which later occasioned a breach, had not yet come to the fore. We see that in Hutten's youthful temper there were many ruffled and uncertain cross currents. His national feeling was sometimes for the moment almost entirely subordinated to pride in the universal republic of scholars. Prevailingly he envisaged a change in German affairs through peaceful, non-revolutionary means. Here were characteristics which facilitated an understanding with Erasmus better at that time than later. There was perhaps another factor. The unstinted enthusiasm with which Hutten greeted Erasmus warmed his heart and revealed to him what was stirring among the younger Germans. Later on, when he voiced his disapproval of the group, he could not conceal a secret fondness.[37] And was the heart which now warmed to him to be despised? And did not Hutten always display his best side in meeting important and great men?

The first literary utterances of Hutten on Erasmus, the mention in the preface to the *Nobody* and the letter of October 24, 1515, give us all that Hutten found in Erasmus. "Why should I not call you the German Socrates? —for you have helped us as much in scholarship as he in his Greek."

So he wrote from Worms to Erasmus. Thus he took the European scholar into the German fold and in large measure contributed to make Erasmus feel more at home in his fatherland in the larger sense, and to make the Germans proud to have produced one of the great leaders of Euro-

37. Allen, *Opus epistularum Erasmi,* Ep. 967, III, 587 ff. Hutten, *Opera,* I, 269 ff.

pean scholarship. How nicely this fitted in with Hutten's conviction that the Germans were not a degenerate people, one can easily see; and it helped him also to point out to the scholastic obscurantists their backwardness in venturing to oppose a cause which had Erasmus as its patron. The humanist prince was thereby dragged into the antischolastic propaganda more than he relished: the reference in the *Epistles* was most obnoxious. Here we discern plainly a political purpose on the part of Hutten—not that this was the primary motive of his attachment to Erasmus, but without doubt it contributed. Hutten well knew that although Erasmus might have the same end in view he would adopt different tactics than would the young German humanists. He was the *homo pro se,* who would not make common cause with others without more ado. This was what Hutten said of him in the *Obscure Men,*[38] while at the same time seeking to win him entirely for his side.

"I am not perhaps of such a character that I can wholly please you," he wrote to Erasmus, "but it is a stroke of fortune to please you in some regard at least." Hutten was aware of the difference in their characters and in the practical sphere guarded his independence. Here he believed he had something of his own to say and did not hold back out of deference for the person of Erasmus—the more so because he regarded his stand as the practical consequence of the Erasmian position. He sought rather scholarly instruction from Erasmus, while in politics he reserved the right to take the lead. The significance of the contribution of Erasmus in the scholarly realm Hutten would not restrict to languages. His regret for his inability to learn Greek in residence from Erasmus[39] should not lead us to infer an evaluation of the great humanist merely as a philological authority; rather, Hutten looked upon him as

38. Ep. 59 in the second part of the *Obscure Men.* Hutten, *Operum Supplementum,* I, 279.

39. Hutten, *Opera,* I, 102. Allen, *Opus epistularum Erasmi,* Ep. 365, II, 155 ff.

the greatest teacher of the philosophy of life. This is the meaning of the comparison with Socrates, which is explained more fully in the preface of the *Nobody*, where Erasmus is celebrated as the restorer of the old theology.[40]

Hutten was right when he saw in Erasmus something more than a poet, for his humanist poetry was only a part of a much more serious, deep, and comprehensive program. We noted that Erasmus, when he met Hutten, was on the way to bring out a new edition of the Greek New Testament and to publish the works of Jerome. These labors best disclose the ideal pursued by him so unremittingly, namely, the restoration of Western Christianity through the spread of a new or a renewed culture. Linguistic study—or, more precisely, the study of the classical and early Christian authors—constituted the way which should lead men to the height. A better knowledge of the Bible and of the Fathers should awaken an understanding of the primitive and simple Christianity whose teaching was not really in conflict but rather in agreement with classical philosophy: antiquity included Greeks, Romans, and Christians until Augustine, even though one recall that Erasmus demarked the world of the Gospels and the Apostles more sharply from that of the pagans than did Petrarch, the father of European humanism. This syncretism was possible because not only was classical culture prized chiefly for its philosophy of life, but also the content of the Christian message was essentially transformed into an ethical system. It is a "philosophy" of Christ, an optimistic religion favorable to culture and compatible with the humane ethic of classical philosophy. From these sources Erasmus drew the norms with which he hoped to renew Christianity, gradually and from within, without striving and revolution, for these awake the forces of lower egoism and covetous instinct which his moral faith hoped to overcome through education. The Cross meant for him, as he says in the *Dagger of the Christian Soldier*,

40. Hutten, *Opera*, I, 183.

victory over all human passions. He believed in the power of reason, in the harmony of culture and religion, and in the perfectibility of man. He was thus related to the Enlightenment of the eighteenth century, though we must not forget that in many respects he was not emancipated from the abysmal, spiritually tough humanity of the sixteenth century.

From a comparison of the present with primitive Christianity came the critical point of view involving scrutiny of scholasticism and of the medieval ecclesiastical institutions and of the methods of contemporary politics. Scholastic theology, hierarchical church polity, and civil politics pervert the teachings of Christ: they are heathen corruptions. He speaks of the "frivolous, theological hairsplitting" with which the scholastics divert attention from their ignorance of the fundamentals of Christianity. On the contrary, a knowledge of Augustine, Ambrose, Jerome, Origen, but especially of the Gospels and of the Pauline letters, would restore Christianity to the intent of its founders, namely, a popular philosophy, a wisdom free from overrefined speculation, simply to tame the world, despise the bad, and learn to do good. To preach this Christianity is the mission of the Church, which in its secularization and diversion to temporals is not true to the ideal of the Sermon on the Mount. The priests must again take seriously the example of the Apostles, the Church must be not a temporal power, but an educational institution. Then, and then only, will she be in a position to disseminate godly morality and to promote peace in Christendom, now so universally neglected in spite of the precepts of Christ.

We can scarcely tell how exactly Hutten appropriated the point of view of Erasmus. There are traces enough of all of these ideas in his writings. By Aesticampianus he was taught to endorse the attempt of Petrarch to base Christianity on the sources of the New Testament and the Fathers. He wished also that the Church should return to the purely spiritual tasks which alone had been her concern in the beginning, but when Erasmus conceived of the primary task of the Church and the papacy as the establishment of peace, Hutten was a long way off. He could never have said with Erasmus that the grossest abuses of papal dispensations were closer to the simplicity of Christ than was the divinest part of the laws of emperors and the state.[41] The concrete experience of the contemporary papacy had sunk in too deeply. Here precisely was the peace-breaker, the enemy of the German emperors. Pride in the German Empire would not suffer him to concede to the papacy such a dominating position in the *res publica Christiana*, which belonged rather to the emperor. Hutten's contrast to ecclesiasticism arose not merely from the impression of the contemporary priesthood, but went much further. He would have conceded to the true Christian priests only a restricted area. When, however, he put the Empire above the Papacy, he was not combatting the Church in general. He still held to the medieval conception of a political ecclesiastical unity and, only under the influence of Erasmus in the *Epistles of Obscure Men*, began to attack the externals of the sacramental system,[42] in which in the main he believed. He did not attempt, like Mutianus, to read in a new meaning.

These divergences in the appropriation of Erasmian ideas enable us to see that Hutten was not altogether prepared to give up his inner independence. A thoroughly satisfactory solution for the contradictions of his own being and of the turbulent time he could not find in the ideas of Erasmus. Much he could take over, and he was prepared to break a lance for Erasmus while at the same time pursuing other paths. What separated him most markedly at the outset was a deep grounding in German affairs. Particularly when Hutten entered the lists for the Empire against the pope we see how he identified himself with the struggle for independence of the emerging nation. For all this Erasmus had no feeling. Hutten could propagate the

41. D. Erasmus Roterodamus, *Opera Selecta*, edited by H. Holborn together with A. Holborn (Munich, 1933), p. 203.
42. Compare Ep. 16 and 43, Part II of *Obscure Men*.

Erasmian ideal of primitive Christianity without investing it with the same sensitiveness and cultural richness. He retained at the same time the myth of old German freedom and manliness. By identifying the patristic and the ancient German philosophies he tried to bridge the gap, and there are certain points of affinity between Erasmus' early Christians and Hutten's early Germans, for both were constructed with the aid of classical moral philosophy. But we must not forget that the stirring activism of Hutten's Teutonic ideal diverged widely from the rationalist outlook of Erasmus.

V

TERMINATION OF STUDIES IN ITALY 1515–1517

ON the way to Italy in an inn at Worms Hutten wrote his first letter to Erasmus, on October 24, 1515. He complained of his lot, which did not suffer him to complete his studies at the foot of the master but drove him to a course in law, for the completion of the legal studies was the condition on which Albert at Mainz had promised him a position and connections at his court, and probably the father Hutten had made the same condition for his further support. Under these circumstances Ulrich would not have looked forward to Italy were he not consoled by the hope of humanist friendships to be made on the side and for which he desired letters of introduction from Erasmus to humanist friends and patrons.[1] We saw that before Hutten went to Italy the desire to participate in the international republic of letters conflicted with his thought and deed for nation and fatherland and seemed at times to bleach his national ideas. In the following year, too, both tendencies were active. In Italy, on the one hand, acquaintance with the humanists increased his feeling for the significance of pure humanist scholarship, while on the other hand a closer association with the Papacy awakened his national consciousness and spurred him to action. This tendency increasingly prevailed until, when he espoused Luther's cause, the contemplative outlook of humanism was completely overshadowed.

Hutten now travelled to Rome, probably by way of Augsburg, Verona, and Florence. At Innsbruck he found the imperial camp. The emperor's forces were gathering in South Tyrol to attack upper Italy, for the young

1. Hutten, *Opera,* I, 102. Allen, *Opus epistularum Erasmi,* Ep. 365, II, 155 ff. We may assume that Erasmus acceded to this wish.

Francis I had just come into control of Milan through the victory of Marignano. The great arena of the European powers was again seething with war and Hutten eagerly awaited the political outcome. Then in Rome, where he spent the summer of the year 1516, he had an opportunity to observe the Papacy at first hand. He saw all the great machinery of papal temporal administration, the court, and the clerical and legal bureaucrats, with whom at this very moment lay the decision of the Reuchlin case to which Hutten attached so much significance. The news of the progress of the trial which filtered to him through German acquaintances in Rome was embodied in the *Epistles of Obscure Men.* How little did his observations of the reality correspond to the ideal which he entertained for the Papacy! He was in the midst of the gorgeousness of the Roman Renaissance, the inordinate ambition of papal politics, and the corruption of the curial bureaucracy. The Reuchlin trial offered a glaring example of what money could do at the Curia. In Mainz he could already have heard the complaints of the costs of episcopal investiture, which, due to the sudden consecutive deaths of two archbishops, had become especially insufferable. The contrast with primitive Christianity was doubly warranted if German gold was squandered merely to pamper the Roman Curia. Not the successor to Peter but a new Simon ruled the Church. Hutten well voiced his impressions in the verses which he addressed to Crotus Rubeanus:

Nor Roman maids nor Roman men will you find more,
But all is pomp and fleshly lust. The Rome of yore
Had men like Metellus, Curius, Pompey.
O the times! Here manliness hath passed away.
Turn not, Crotus, my friend, your longing eyes from home;
The Roman you will find no more in Holy Rome.[2]

The blame for this state of affairs he sought not merely in the character of the Italian people—of whom he was far

2. Hutten, *Opera,* III, 278 ff. "Ad Crotum Rubianum de statu Romano epigrammata."

from fond due to their contempt of the Germans—nor even in the economic misadventures of Leo X, whom he scourged as "Florentine shopkeeper," but also in the impotence of the German Empire, in which, following the Middle Ages, he saw the heir of the Roman Empire. The retention of this legacy involved the maintenance of a hold on Italy. The absence of the proper lord and protector was for Hutten the cause of Italy's misfortune. This is why she had become the object of the fierce strife of her neighbors. Thus he wrote on learning in 1516 that Maximilian after a brief onslaught had left Italy again and gone back to Germany. In spite of all nationalism Hutten was thoroughly permeated with the conception of a universal Roman Empire,[3] not to be divested of its universal duties and tasks within the *res publica Christiana.* This medieval ideal still exerted its spell over him and he needed it to legitimatize the imperial power, but he saw the Empire also in a new light. The emperor was the embodiment of the virtues of the German people. He was, indeed, the heir of the Roman Empire but also of the imposing German legacy reaching from the victories of the Cimbri and the Teutons, from the wars of Arminius through the times of the Carolingians and Ottos until now. "Thy people is now the greatest. Formerly it was Rome," so Dame Italy is made by Hutten to address the emperor.[4] He envisaged the Empire both in its universal aspects and also in its national significance. To its keeping he would entrust the worth and prestige of the nation. Its might he would derive not only from the idea of the Roman Empire but also from the virility of the great German people which stood behind it and culminated in it.

The contrasts in Hutten's philosophy of the Empire reflect the character of the transitional period in which the ideas of the Middle Ages were still alive, or even were being revived in full splendor on the very threshold of a new

3. "Epistola ad Maximilianum Caesarem Italiae ficticia," Hutten, *Opera,* I, 106 ff.

4. Hutten, *Opera,* I, 109.

era. One can easily characterize Hutten's ideas as politically unrealistic. The road to the universal monarchy of the Middle Ages was closed by the rise of the national states in Western Europe. The power of the Curia was thereby restricted, but at the same time its independence from the Empire was furthered; and besides, the political program of Maximilian was not national in Hutten's sense, but rather based on dynastic conceptions. How could it be otherwise in view of the disintegration of the Empire and the power of the estates? Hutten's ideas would inevitably be shattered by such a lack of realism unless he succeeded better in adjusting them to the actual situation. In one respect he did so. More and more the emphasis shifted to the national basis of the Empire. In 1518 he could write that only the "empty name" of the fallen Roman Empire was transmitted to the Germans.[5] This was after the definitive failure of Maximilian's Italian policy on which he set such high hopes, and after his own return to Germany, when he came to have a better appreciation of the great obstacles to the German imperial organism. To eliminate these became from now on his prime endeavor. Finally, however, not the least of the influences which moved him to advance on the road to nationalism was received in Italy.

Here he came to know the *Annals* of Tacitus, which were printed by Beroaldus in Rome in 1515, with a papal privilege protecting the work against reprint. That Hutten devoured it in order to see the primitive German in the true light from the ancient sources, we could scarcely doubt, even if we lacked the express confirmation of the appearance of the figure of Arminius in his writings.[6] The *Germania* as interpreted by the German humanists had given him the conception of the distinctive entity of the German people and the ideal of a universal German moral purity. Now the *Annals* provided a moral example in the individual figure of Arminius, the first German to receive

5. Hutten, *Opera,* IV, 88.
6. *Ibid.,* I, 109; III, 155; III, 335; V, 45.

a detailed historical delineation, for the notices of Ariovistus are scanty. It is Hutten's contribution to have made Arminius a symbol of the German character. Here he found the ideal of the man of politics after his own heart, possessed of valor, manliness, and will-power which yielded not to obstacles because grounded not on the fluctuation of circumstances but on constancy of purpose. Arminius is invested with the moral content of Roman philosophy and quickened thereby. "This is treachery, to change faith in accord with shifting fortune. The justice of my cause impelled me to withstand even adverse circumstance."[7] Thus Hutten causes his hero to speak in the posthumous dialogue which started the Arminius cult in Germany. Presumably he appeared clothed with these humanist virtues on the first reading of the *Annals*. We must not, however, push the dialogue back into the Italian period, for in all probability it was not composed until 1519 or 1520.[8] The most significant point which Hutten there later expressed and which was to exert a profound influence on the national consciousness, was the transfer of the idea of German freedom from the sphere of local liberty to that of national independence of foreign control. German freedom now became something more than the independence of the estates: it is freedom from Rome. As the champion of such freedom Hutten wished to hold up before the eyes of his people the figure of the German liberator.[9]

7. *Ibid.,* IV, 417.

8. The question as to when the *Arminius* was written is a matter of conjecture. Hutten was, as we saw, already attracted by the subject in 1517 at about the same time when he started to use the dialogue as a literary form. On these grounds it has been concluded that the *Arminius* was written in 1517. See H. Tiedemann, *Tacitus und das Nationalbewusstsein der deutschen Humanisten* (Dissertation, Berlin, 1913). P. Kalkoff has shown, however, that this assumption deserves little credence. He suggests the year 1520. I am inclined to assume an earlier date since this dialogue is comparatively little affected by specific political aims. If we put it in the year 1519 the new "Arminius" for Hutten would be Charles V. This guess would afford an explanation of the suppression of the dialogue by the author.

9. Compare P. Joachimsen's studies, *Geschichtsauffassung und Geschichtsschreibung,* p. 109. "Tacitus im deutschen Humanismus," *Neue*

Hutten had not advanced so far in the years 1516 and 1517. In the third of the *Exposures of Duke Ulrich*, which he composed at that time, he could write that the old Germans would not have suffered the pretensions of Arminius to a crown, even though he had gained for them outward freedom, because such a claim would have imperilled freedom within the group.[10] Hutten's national ideology was not yet clarified. Extraneous elements had not yet been eliminated and the object of his effort was not yet sharply delineated. He retained not only the medieval conception of the *res publica Christiana*—he always did that—but also the idea of the Papacy, however much he might criticize the contemporary form. He inveighed against the warlord Julius II and the shopkeeper Leo X because they did not conform to his ideal of Christian morality and again because they did not bow to the emperor. But he would not have abolished the hierarchy on that account. He hoped rather for a purge through an imperial victory. But the picture already begins to alter when Arminius is placed at the head of the German leaders, and the emperors of the Middle Ages are regarded as his successors. Medieval history is no longer regarded as unified, nor are its conflicts interpreted as an effort to attain order within the framework of the universal Roman imperium, but rather as the clashes of peoples and nations. This feeling was intensified by the Italian residence because Hutten experienced for himself the difference between German and Latin. His criticism of the Papacy, however, was not yet fundamental, because he conceived of the national German task in universal terms as the dominance of the German nation over the Roman Empire, including the Papacy, and also because he had not abandoned the Papacy as a support for the sacramental system of the Church. There are anticipations, but as yet no clear note of the summons which he was

Jahrbücher für das klassische Altertum, Geschichte und deutsche Literatur, XXVII (1911), 697 ff., and the same author's book *Vom deutschen Volk zum deutschen Staat* (2d edition, Leipsic, 1920), p. 26.

10. Hutten, *Opera,* V, 45.

to blow for the renewal of the war of liberation of Arminius against the Romans. If Maximilian was urged to imitate Arminius, it was because the emperor should exemplify the old German valor in fighting for the rights of the medieval Empire. He was the heir of Arminius and of Rome.

Turn not, Crotus, my friend, your longing eyes from home;
The Roman you will find no more in Holy Rome[11]—

"but rather in Germany," we may supply. This experience did much to intensify Hutten's universal imperialistic conceptions.

So much was this the case, in fact, that he had nothing more to say of ancient Rome, whose ruins lay about him.[12] We should not expect him to view Rome as did Winckelmann, or to be captivated by archeology like the Italian humanists. Yet it is characteristic that no saying is recorded of him like that of his friend Crotus in 1519: "I saw the monuments of antiquity. I saw the pulpit of pestilence. The one filled me with joy, the other with antipathy."[13] Crotus Rubeanus saw the abuses of the Roman court perhaps even more sharply than Hutten, but the observations which he made did not cut into his conscience deeply enough to prevent his pictorial talent from enjoying the spectacle. One feels thus early the justice of Hutten's self-characterization of 1522, that the "common sorrow" cut him more to the quick than other people.[14] In more general terms one can say that his horizons had not gone beyond the world of moral energies and efforts. Life for him was worthy of careful scrutiny only where there was a chance for a militant encounter. Both study and external observation were focussed here. His life did not display the same colorful variety as did that of Crotus Rubeanus. Hutten's was a one-track mind, deeply stirred and

11. *Ibid.*, III, 278.
12. The same was true of Erasmus; see P. de Nolhac, *Érasme en Italie* (2. édition, Paris, 1888).
13. Hutten, *Opera,* I, 311.
14. *Ibid.*, II, 137.

indeflectible. Every new insight imposed the duty of reckless effort for outward embodiment. He could no more separate the intellectual and political spheres than he could differentiate word and act. Behind the polemical writings composed in Italy against the Papacy and scholasticism, beyond the *Epigrams to Crotus* and the *Letters of Obscure Men*, was a man who expected by his words to incite deeds, because every intellectual apprehension carried with it a direct practical command. He, too, knew the art of political concession. For a while he could watch and wait whether Fortune would give her wheel a favorable turn, but he could not stay long in ambush. His ideas would start to ferment before he could make correct observations. He was impelled in part by a youthful swagger desirous of dazzling men by his recklessness, but this is not the whole explanation. He had rather a superb and astounding contempt for obstacles and would have arrived somewhere had he first come to grips with reality. His publication gives one the impression of native power of will and conscience, yet contemptuous and even oblivious of the actual state of affairs, as we have already indicated. In the knightly romanticism, with which during his formative period he invested and quickened the humanism of Erasmus and of German patriotism, we see something of the incapacity of medieval culture to face squarely the hard facts of life. Its Utopian aspirations overlooked the devil, who, in spite of all exorcism, insinuated himself into every spiritual endeavor. The life of the knight from which Hutten came, from which he was never emancipated, offers examples in abundance.

Eck later denounced Hutten before the Curia precisely on account of his Italian epigrams,[15] and the Curia did well to be on its guard against the author of these incendiary utterances. In comparison with Luther, who soon was to attract all eyes, Hutten's writings seemed calculated to disintegrate the Roman hierarchical system of the Middle Ages but not to bowl it over. The spiritual

15. Hutten, *Opera,* I, 317.

residue of his pilgrimages was not comprehensive or potent enough to demolish the structure of centuries. It remained to be seen how far during the struggle he would become aware of this, how far he would have the power to seek deeper spiritual sources.

At any rate, a more aggressive tone was acquired through acquaintance with the exposure by Lorenzo Valla of the forged Donation of Constantine, which Hutten, on the point of returning to Germany, found at the house of Cochlaeus.[16] Ulrich at once resolved to put out in Germany a new imprint of this Italian who so excelled his time in critical acumen and enlightenment.[17] But something else, too, is recorded of Hutten's last days in Italy. He might have taken ship from Venice with some cousins on a pilgrimage to the Holy Land had not Crotus laughed him out of it.[18] There could not be a better illustration of the dichotomy of his spiritual personality. Who can fail to see how far the ideals of medieval piety and the ideals of a universal world order continued to influence him?

The second Italian period was likewise disturbed and in a measure insecure. In Rome he had a severe attack of that frightful disease which he had sought in vain to cure before leaving for Italy.

He wanted to go to the baths of Tuscany, but in Viterbo he had a serious mishap. In a quarrel with several Frenchmen he killed one of them. The exact sequence is obscure.[19]

16. *Ibid.*, p. 142.

17. P. Kalkoff has proved that the preface to Hutten's edition of the *Donatio Constantini* could not have been written in 1517 as the fictitious date *Steckelberg Calen. Decemb. Anno MDXVII* would make us believe. The "in libellum Laurentii contra effictam et ementitam Constantini Donationem ad Leonem X. Pontificem Maximum praefatio" was written early in 1519. The book itself did not reach the public before the beginning of the year 1520. Compare P. Kalkoff, *Huttens Vagantenzeit und Untergang,* pp. 223 ff. See in addition *Luthers Werke, Kritische Gesamtausgabe,* L, 65, and O. Clemen in the *Briefwechsel,* II, 48 ff.

18. Hutten, *Opera,* I, 141.

19. *Ibid.*, III, 280 ff. The report of Sauermann has been published by G. Bauch in "Hutteniana," *Vierteljahrsschrift für Kultur und Literatur der Renaissance,* I, 491 ff. In the appraisal of the report and the whole incident I disagree entirely with P. Kalkoff, *Huttens Vagantenzeit und Untergang,* pp. 277 ff.

He himself says that they provoked him by slurs upon the Emperor Maximilian, who had just made an ignominious retreat from Italy. There appears to be no doubt that the dispute, which plainly took place in an inn, became heated and issued in blows because the political situation and national passions kindled the tempers of the participants. There is nothing contradictory in the highly partisan account of a Silesian, George Sauermann, a fellow student of Hutten in Bologna, who declares that the trouble started because of Hutten's resentment when the host served the Frenchmen first. Hutten bombastically asserted that he, as a knight, would not endure such a slight, and in the ensuing scuffle, with the help of a companion, he killed the Frenchman. Probably the affair did start, as Sauermann says, through some trivial pretext and became heated only through political passions, as Hutten continually insists. He is probably right, too, that he was outnumbered in the end—though we may doubt whether he was in the beginning, and also how far his companion helped him. Certainly the fight did not proceed as he felt called upon to portray it in later epigrams. Here he exalted himself in the rôle of the hero, a Christian knight who, outnumbered, in self-defense and indignation against the slurs of the Latins, fought to the finish, leaving the issue to God and praising Him for the victory. Really it was a soldiers' saloon brawl and would merit no further attention were it not typical of the way in which Hutten liked to idealize himself in his writings. Because of the tension between the actual man and his picture of himself, he has been stigmatized as a moral degenerate. But this is to miss the real problem which he sets his biographers.

Hutten had a consuming desire to identify his own existence with great political and spiritual struggles. Thought and fancy moved for him on the stage of decisive events. To imitate them and build his existence around them was an inner necessity. But in comparison with these far-reaching projects his daily life was straitened and pathetic. He chose it and rejected a better lot, certainly not merely because he hoped in that way to experience more of the life of his time, but because his ambition dreamed of a fairer prospect at the end of a humanist career. As a result of this pursuit, though partly through his own fault, he came into such extremities that his life was filled with continual sickness, intermittent harrying, and all too daily vexations, so that his career could scarcely supply the model for a significant literary production. Just as his early publication was greater in many regards than the occasion which called it forth, so in larger measure was his own self-portrayal. He wanted to appear as he delineated himself because in this guise he could influence men. On this picture his fame depended as well as the possibility of emergence from his present straits. That is why his astonishing industry in publication did not flag, for he well saw that if his pen weakened he could not maintain his reputation as a distinguished knight and scholar.

Yet without doubt also he desired not merely to appear great before men but to find justification in his own eyes. The picture which he offered his readers was not so much a deceptive mask as an ideal of himself for which he strove. That he did not entirely attain it in his personal career was not due altogether to the dangerous environment in which of necessity he moved, nor to his material impoverishment, but also to a certain incapacity arising from his knightly origin. The dominant morality of the knights by which Hutten was affected was not of the best. The ideal of the knight was most potent in engendering class consciousness rather than moral integrity. When Hutten's acquaintances all portrayed him as wild, undisciplined, blunt, and belligerent, when he paraded before the poets in the armor of the knight, and swaggered before the knights with the laurels of the poet, one cannot avoid the impression that the humanist emancipation of individuality, coupled as it was with moral discipline, served in his case to produce a strong tension. In thinking and writing, to be sure, he reached after new ethical standards and recognized their obligation, but in his personal conduct the outlook on life underlying his ethic served to unloose rather than to regulate and bind the unruly elements. The new ideas did not obliterate the knight's incapacity for persistent effort and desire to "gather rosebuds while ye may," and at one point there was an intensification of the knightly legacy, in that class arrogance survived as a tendency to precipitant self-justification.

But here, too, one must recognize the residual vitality of the cultural patterns of the Middle Ages, in spite of much disintegration. As we have seen, humanist ideals in the political sphere might issue in schemes for the restoration of earlier cultures. Likewise in the personal sphere they might intensify the corresponding faults of the old days. In Germany, at any rate, the world of the Middle Ages was still sufficiently potent to enlist tendencies essentially incompatible with itself.

Hutten did not emerge from the average mores of his environment. One ought by no means, therefore, to characterize him as morally inferior. He might readily pacify his conscience with regard to his occasional escapades and fail to display here the same capacity for the realization of the new ideas as in the political sphere. One may call him average in this regard, but scarcely common. Apart from the fact that his life came nearer to the moral ideal in the years when his fortunes were on the mend, we must also recognize that in such periods of historical transition there is a certain cleavage between man's spiritual grasp and moral attainment. Thought outruns achievement.

After the occurrence in Viterbo, Hutten had to hurry over the frontier of the papal states. He may have gone to the imperial army at Verona. Then in July he went to Bologna, where, after a fashion, he completed his juristic study. Here, too, he was engaged in brawls.[20] The "nations" quarreled at the university. The German nation blew off gunpowder at the Lombards. There was street rioting in Bologna, which the *podestà* suppressed after the

20. Hutten, *Opera,* I, 146. Allen, *Opus epistularum Erasmi,* Ep. 611, III, 25 ff.

second day. The outcome of the affair was not flattering to the prestige of the Germans, who lost the right to carry arms; and Hutten, who was the syndic of the German nation in the system of student self-government, found himself arraigned as the fomenter of the riot. How far the charge was justified cannot be determined. At any rate, he complained that in exchanging Viterbo for Bologna he had escaped Scylla to fall upon Charybdis. Nevertheless, in spite of disturbances, the fall of 1516 and the spring of 1517 were filled with legal and humanistic studies. Here in Bologna were composed the first and second *Exposures of Ulrich of Württemberg*[21] and the dialogue *Phalarismus*,[22] directed likewise against him, and the *Epistles of Obscure Men*. The dialogue was composed under the influence of Lucian, whom Hutten came to know through the Greek studies so enthusiastically prosecuted at Bologna.[23] Other and better dialogues followed. The Lucianic form of question and answer offered a congenial mode for the expression of his inner thought and feeling, and the mould of *pro* and *con* stamped his polemic and exhortation with greater verve.

These linguistic studies constituted a favorable counterbalance to his political compositions. He gained stylistic maturity which was to be evidenced in later studies. We should like to know what he absorbed from the literary output of Italian humanism. He may have read, though perhaps not then, not only Valla's *Donatio Constantini* but also other critical works in theology by which Erasmus, too, was influenced. We must assume that of Petrarch's works he knew at least the *Fortuna*. Later he shows an acquaintance with Aeneas Sylvius. Of the his-

21. Hutten, *Opera*, V, 23 ff. 22. *Ibid.*, IV, 1 ff.

23. See G. Niemann, *Die Dialogliteratur der Reformationszeit nach ihrer Entstehung und Entwicklung* (Leipsic, 1905). A. Bauer, "Der Einfluss Lukians auf Ulrich von Hutten," *Philologus*, LXXVII, 437 ff. O. Gewerstock, *Lucian und Hutten* (Berlin, 1924). Compare also R. Förster, *Lucian in der Renaissance* (Kiel, 1886). N. Caccia, *Note sulla Fortuna di Luciano nel Rinascimento* (Milan, 1914). M. Heep, *Die Colloquia Familiaria des Erasmus und Lucian* (*Hermaea*, XVIII, Halle, 1927).

torical writings of the Italians, he came in Venice to know the work of Egnatius, *De Caesaribus,* which confirmed his views of the struggle between Papacy and Empire. What other books he may have read we cannot determine with precision because dependencies apart from a direct citation may be at second hand.

After Hutten had made a further residence in Bologna inexpedient—or thought he had—by the tart speech which he delivered before the *podestà* in defense of the German student rioters, he left and went to Ferrara, whence a few days later his cousins invited him to Venice. In both places he received a warm reception at the hands of the Italian humanists, who honored him especially because of his relations to the great Erasmus. Egnatius, for example, wrote to Erasmus, "Greetings from you have been conveyed to me by Ulrich von Hutten, a man, so far as I can judge from a single meeting, of such distinguished manners and literary ability that one recognizes him as a disciple of Erasmus. I received him at first, as was appropriate, with open arms on your account. Then his quality and graciousness caused me to value him not merely because of your recommendation but also for his own sake."[24] The solidarity of humanism could not be better exemplified than by this cordiality at Venice, against which he had already taken some sharp digs, even if he had not yet published the two sharpest, *The Venetian Fishers* and the *Marcus,* both composed at Bologna.[25] His feeling for the supernational solidarity of humanism was deepened. At the same time the general Italian contempt for German culture hurt his national pride and put him on the defensive.

24. Hutten, *Opera,* I, 135. Allen, *Opus epistularum Erasmi,* Ep. 588, II, 587.

25. "De piscatura Venetorum," and "Marcus," Hutten, *Opera,* III, 289 ff.

VI
POET LAUREATE
1517–1518

FROM Venice he passed momentarily through Bologna again, and then returned to Germany at the end of June. This time he was not a "nobody." Erasmus had recognized him as one of the most gifted and promising of German authors, with a large number of writings already to his credit and many more on the way. News of these projects had infiltrated to the homeland through fellow students together with accounts of the author's personal intrepidity. Hence he was received with attention. In Augsburg he lived with the humanistically trained city secretary, Conrad Peutinger, a relative of the great commercial house of Welser. Peutinger belonged likewise to the intimates of the emperor and was able to secure an audience for Hutten with the monarch then resident in Augsburg. Ulrich had already broken several literary lances for the emperor and his Italian wars. These writings were now brought together into a sizeable compilation augmented by new materials and published a year later.

On the fifteenth of August Hutten appeared before the aged monarch to be crowned as poet laureate.[1] The young daughter of Peutinger had braided the crown with which henceforth the artists and printers portrayed him. The ceremony of coronation was no innovation. The custom arose in Italy as a symbol of the restoration of classical Latinity. The Emperor Charles IV seized upon it eagerly in order to place the German emperor in the center of the

1. See Hutten, *Opera,* I, 173. Also in Konrad Peutinger, *Briefwechsel,* edited by E. König (Munich, 1923), pp. 301 ff. Hutten's diploma in Hutten, *Opera,* I, 143. Compare also K. Schottenloher, "Kaiserliche Dichterkrönungen im Heiligen Römischen Reich," *Papsttum und Kaisertum. Festschrift für P. Kehr* (Munich, 1926), pp. 645 ff.

movement as the successor of the Caesars and Augusti. For Maximilian, too, the laureate was a device to enlist humanism in the literary exaltation of the throne. His selections were sometimes undiscriminating. Nevertheless the coronations of Hutten now and of Celtis in 1487 and Cuspinian in 1500 were refreshing signs of the interest awakened in political circles by the German humanists. Under Charles V the ceremony became an empty gesture. Humanism sank to the level of a rare and undistinguished guest at court.

The honor conferred upon Hutten entitled him to give lectures in all schools and universities, but his ambition was not directed in academic channels, but rather to a broader practical activity. The statement to Erasmus that he would rather perfect himself in scholarly attainments under his tutelage than reside at court, certainly envisaged also a common effort on behalf of the reform. The decision for court service was based on the same grounds. For a time he hesitated whether to follow his Augsburg friends in the train of the emperor, or to pursue the old plan of going to Mainz. Also in Bamberg and Würzburg openings developed. The primary question for Hutten throughout was where he could strike the most telling blows for the reform in the next few years.

Connections with German humanism had been formed while he was still in Italy. Of these the most important was with the city councillor of Nuremberg, Willibald Pirckheimer,[2] who had sent two nephews under the tutelage of Cochlaeus to study in Bologna. With them Hutten read Lucian and Aristophanes. To their uncle he wrote from Italy, and now on the journey from Augsburg to Bamberg he visited him in person and derived an ineradicable impression of the glory of the German towns, of which

2. F. Roth, *Willibald Pirckheimer* (Halle, 1887), is only a superficial sketch. E. Reicke has prepared a critical edition of Pirckheimer's correspondence. The best treatment of the humanist circle of Nuremberg is to be found in H. von Schubert, *Lazarus Spengler und die Einführung der Reformation in Nürnberg* (Leipsic, 1934).

Nuremberg was then one of the finest examples. Hutten, knight that he was, with all of his antipathy for the big business of the town, could not escape a measure of admiration for the power and character of urban culture. Something of this feeling, despite the conventional mode of treatment, came to the fore in the *Lötze Philippics* in praise of Frankfort-am-Main.[3] A year later he celebrated the excellencies of the Nuremberg of the Reformation period, the city of art and learning, the city of the best brains in Germany. She gave due honor to her men of genius. Here was undoubtedly the basis of the Venetian proverb, "All German towns are blind. Nuremberg alone still sees out of one eye."[4] In this connection we have the only reference in Hutten's works to the fine arts, which otherwise left him cold. Here again he introduced the subject really only from the point of view of national "gloria." The art of the Italian Renaissance apparently seemed to him to be a phase of Roman "luxuria," whereas Albrecht Dürer received praise as the "Appelles of our time" because he had contributed so largely to raising German prestige in Italy. The measure of his influence appeared in that many Italian artists would attribute their works to him in the interest of a readier sale.

In the late summer of 1517 Hutten entered the service of Archbishop Albert of Mainz. The court prefecture after the death of Eitelwolf von Stein was held by Frowin von Hutten, who utilized his high governmental post to the full in the interests of the neighboring knights. The literary works of his nephew scarcely interested him any more than the humanist tendencies of his predecessor. But the political plans of Ulrich did not leave him cold particularly after Franz von Sickingen, the mightiest knight of the day, was enlisted on their behalf. But that came later. In any case Ulrich enjoyed family support as he entered the service of the elector in the capacity of a learned counsellor. Two types of counsellors were distinguished at

3. Hutten, *Opera,* III, 38. 4. *Ibid.,* I, 199.

Mainz.[5] There were "court counsellors" or "daily counsellors," who were always at the prince's side. Then there was a second and much more numerous group of "nonresident counsellors and servitors," who were called on only for specific assignments and commissions. Hutten came to Mainz in this rôle. Archbishop Albert, by thus patronizing him, undoubtedly sought not merely to show favor to one of the noble houses, but also to ingratiate himself with the humanists. The young primate and archchancellor of the *Reich* wished to appear before the world of European scholarship as a Maecenas of humanist learning. Hutten had a hand also in the attempts of Albert to induce Erasmus to come to Mainz, there to write the lives of the saints in humanist style. Erasmus declined, leaving Hutten as his humanist representative at the court of Mainz.[6] The praise bestowed upon him by Erasmus enhanced him in the eyes of Albert and gained for him exemption from court duties, that he might devote himself to his studies.

The commissions entrusted to him by Albert were limited to the period from the winter of 1517 to the summer of 1519. In December, 1517, he was sent to the court of France to exchange the ratifications of a treaty between Albert and Francis I. In the spring of 1518 he was in the train of the archbishop at Halle, and in the summer at the Diet of Augsburg. Then Hutten had a breathing spell at Mainz and Steckelberg, and not until March, 1519, was he again with Albert. Next came the campaign against Duke Ulrich of Württemberg, until July, 1519. On Hutten's return Albert in June commissioned him to deliver a golden goblet to Erasmus, and on the ninth of that month took him with him to Frankfurt for the imperial election. Thereafter Hutten was not to see Albert again.

5. H. Goldschmidt, *Zentralbehörden und Beamtentum im Kurfürstentum Mainz* (Berlin, 1908).

6. See Erasmus' letter to the archbishop of December 22, 1518, in Hutten, *Opera,* I, 231 ff. Allen proposed to read 1517 instead of 1518 which seems to me very unlikely. Compare W. Kaegi, "Hutten und Erasmus," *Historische Vierteljahrsschrift,* XXII (1924), 213, n. 1. Allen, *Opus epistularum Erasmi,* Ep. 745, III, 175.

The duties of the new post, however irksome in themselves, left more freedom for study than did the lean days of the strolling scholar. When freed from the responsibilities of the position at Mainz he loaded himself with enterprises of his own and inaugurated his campaign against Rome for German liberty. He was already disposed to this course on his return to Italy, but the post at Mainz laid on him certain inhibitions. Not until the fall of 1518 did he begin again to write on Church and State, and after the summer of 1519 the impression of world events and the development of his own personality caused him to be completely engrossed in this endeavor. The brief respite at Mainz served to clarify his own purposes and his attitude to Humanism. Pausing for a moment in the intimate circle of the German humanists, he became for the first time aware of his own distinctive will and objective.

He had not gone to court without the expectation of advancement. His hope was not simply for a post that would provide leisure for literary pursuits, but also for a vantage point from which to sponsor humanism at court in a practical political way. He dreamed of persuading Albert to throw the full weight of his influence as a prince into the balance on the side of humanism. Apart from illusions as to Albert's personality—for he was no real humanist and had bound himself to the Roman system—Hutten was unrealistic also in that he looked upon Albert too much as a Maecenas and too little as a prince bishop whose entourage must of necessity be colored by preachers and especially officials and lawyers. For their administrative work Hutten's juristic studies had left him no taste. What he wanted to attain politically was on another level. His ambition was to prove himself a man in the struggle of humanism against barbarism. This objective overshadowed all others, and in this cause he still entertained hopes of assistance from Albert. As soon as they became manifestly illusory, and Sickingen appeared on the horizon as a protector, Hutten asked to be relieved of his service at Mainz.

To be sure, he was not without reservations and misgivings before. He could never have found the environment entirely congenial. Such a free lance would find it hard to feel at ease among courtiers and officials. However bovine, they could scarcely miss the point of his barbed and pungent jibes, and more than once he must have rubbed them the wrong way. His own reactions found expression in the dialogue *Aula,* written in the weeks of the Augsburg Diet at the instigation of friends at Mainz. The stylistic model was Lucian's *Dialogue on Court Life,* with which Hutten became acquainted at Mainz through a friend, Dr. Stromer von Auerbach.[7] The content owed more to the tract of Aeneas Sylvius on the *Vexations of Court Life.*[8] Hutten's work, however, is not mere plagiarism; there is the stamp of his own genius. The conversation between the two interlocutors, Misaulus, the depreciator of court life, and Castus, the defender, can scarcely be identified with Hutten before and after he accepted the post at Mainz. Both are Hutten, and it is Castus who comes closest to what Hutten had written to Pirckheimer on October 25, 1518.[9]

The letter shows that he was still minded to stay at court, however much he might play up the less attractive side. Pirckheimer, on receiving the Dialogue, had suggested, a trifle ironically, that it seemed to him somewhat premature in view of so short an experience at court. He advised him, however, to drop the court and devote himself completely to humanist studies. Oddly enough, Hutten made this bantering letter an occasion not for a defense of the Dialogue but of his whole manner and aim in life. Here again a trifling stimulus awakened all his powers. The delicately insinuated reprimand would have embittered him had it come from some one other than Pirckheimer,

7. On H. Stromer, a Leipsic physician and the founder of "Auerbachs Weinkeller," see G. Wustmann, *Der Wirt von "Auerbachs Keller"* (Leipsic, 1902). G. Bauch, "Aus der Geschichte des Mainzer Humanismus," *Archiv für hessische Geschichte,* Neue Folge Vol. 5 (1907).

8. Compare G. Monacorda, in *Archiv für das Studium der neueren Sprachen und Literaturen,* CXVIII (1907), 140 ff.

9. Hutten, *Opera,* I, 195–217. "Ad Pirckheimerum epistola vitae suae rationem exponens."

but to him Hutten disclosed his inner self with passion and warmth in the hope of persuasion. The idealization of his own personality and objectives is unmistakable, but one feels a primal and immediate power becoming self-conscious in contact with the environment. Seldom is Hutten so thoroughly himself as he is here. Seldom is his very being so powerfully disclosed, and through him the fullness of the individuality of the epoch. One finds here the dark note of anxiety and insecurity so characteristic of the sixteenth century. "To me instructed and disillusioned by long travel all things seem commingled and full of disorder and inquietude, misery and tragedy. Wherever I turn I see nothing secure, nothing tranquil: here are obligations, clients, debates, meetings, obsequies, cares, disturbances, labors, and then calamities, the ever imminent shocks of fortune and disease and sorrow."[10] But into this unlighted background breaks through all the more radiantly the knowledge and power of the new endeavor rising to the rhapsodic cry, "What a century! What studies! It is a joy to be alive."[11] One can understand how the young Goethe was captivated by this letter from the age of Faust.

Vita contemplativa or *vita activa?* This is the theme of the letter, even if the contrast is not so sharply expressed. For if Hutten defends himself for remaining at court, he concedes that he is simply compelled to stay in order to live. Necessity constrains him, he tells Pirckheimer. He is not free to choose. At the same time he rises above necessity and expressly casts his lot with the active life. "I will try out court life, which I counsel others to flee." He confesses that the decision is not due altogether to outward compulsion, but also to inner desire.

It is no accident that he addressed his confession to Pirckheimer, who was perhaps the least retiring of the German humanists. The Nuremberg patrician from whom Maximilian himself sought counsel had his own ideas

10. *Ibid.*, p. 204.

11. *Ibid.*, p. 217.

about the great world and its affairs. Undoubtedly he was veering from the Middle Ages, driven by his delvings in antiquity, but his practical work and his humanist efforts were segregated spheres. As a humanist one was not obliged to take part in public life, only as a citizen. Humanism taught such men as Pirckheimer in Nuremberg and Peutinger in Augsburg to endure the distasteful outward realities with Stoic indifference, but the temple of learning which they erected and in which alone they could breathe in perfect blessedness stood aloof from the turmoil of rough and uncouth life. There was a vestige of medieval forsaking of the world in the humanism of the urban patrician.

Hutten likewise sought the ideal condition of life for the humanist outside of the active sphere. He too wished to find rest after labor and defended his resolve to participate in practical activity in part on the ground that he intended to amass sufficient means for such a humanist existence. He denied, however, that court life left no time for humanist studies. On the contrary, he had never studied more, for the prince had given him sufficient leisure. "My friends in Germany were deceived who thought I should have to give up my learned pursuits on accepting court service."[12] But his attempt to find an ideal justification for his decision shows that he was far from Pirckheimer's dichotomy, though perhaps not fully aware of the difference. "You have already heard," he wrote to this friend, "how I loathe a life of irresponsibility and that I proposed to achieve something before taking refuge in such retreats. Not that I have resolved to live only from day to day, to commit my life to chance and plunge through haphazard incentives into the unknown, but because I have not yet amassed enough to preserve the even tenor and be myself. I cannot at present endure repose, or rather inertia. I have not yet disciplined myself and cooled the hot blood of my youth. I am not yet worthy to retire with Epicurus. He

12. Hutten, *Opera,* I, 196.

invites to repose, but, I doubt not, only those who are capable of repose. If he were alive today and accepted me as his disciple, he would not invite me to retirement before I had learned something and done something. You must know that I do not vacillate and fluctuate. To something I hold firm and by something I try to steer the ark of life, toward something I strive freely and deliberately, though I despair of attaining apart from the aid of others. . . . If I seem to you to change my state and alter my condition, I do not change my mind. I try always to be Hutten, never to desert myself, but to walk with equanimity through the unequal scenes of life."[13] And in another passage Hutten writes: "When you summon me so readily to secluded and sedentary study, I do not know whether you take account of my nature and age, which are not capable of repose. Should I, at my time of life, shut myself up within four walls and withdraw to calm seclusion before acquiring experience of the storm and tumult of the world? Should I refuse the requests of my relatives and friends for the services which I can render them, and instead give myself over, as you advise, to the Muses? If I immure myself in scholastic quietude and drive myself to study and writing for which, I know not why, you think me capable, how, I should like to know, could I enjoy the comradeship of my literary colleagues? What stories could I tell? About what could I talk? That I have experienced so little? During my long years of travel I saw much and learned much, but did nothing, accomplished nothing, and this does not yet suffice. The time has come really to live. So far my days have been only the prelude to life, the prologue of the drama."[14]

Here is a different attitude to life and knowledge than that of Pirckheimer. He had had more of a taste than Hutten of realistic thinking and practical experience of the world, but he had not connected all this with humanism. Rather, he regarded as a disturbance to his studies

13. *Ibid.*, p. 205. 14. *Ibid.*, p. 195.

the clamorous world so ardently craved by Hutten. The discrepancy in age in part explains the difference, but there is another temper in the young man, distasteful to the quietistic humanism of the elder. The humanist Kingdom of Heaven lies not in withdrawal but in participation in the *melée*. "All the knowledge which we philosophize in the shade,"—he means apart from the active life—"without doing something is no knowledge at all," says Castus in the dialogue *Aula*.[15] And again, in more general terms: "He does not seem to me to live at all who lives apart, as our humanists say."

Hutten seems to me to be making a gracious concession to his honored patron, rather than expressing a genuine doubt, when he refuses to decide whether his age or his nature drives him to the active life. He writes to Pirckheimer: "My nature and my age cannot settle down to domesticity and quiet obscurity, or at least not yet. Wait until the fire has burned itself out; wait until my restless and turbulent spirit flags, until it merits the repose which you seem to me to counsel prematurely."[16] And again, more clearly, in another passage, where he says: "You scarcely understand me if you would withdraw me from the society of my fellows. My aptitude for studies is not such as to breed misanthropic distaste for honorable intercourse even with men of another type, and, if you would understand me rightly, know that I prefer to actual solitude the jostling of the alien crowd, in which I can attain complete detachment. So do not think of me as altogether unhappy in my present situation. I may accomplish a little something in the world of letters, nor do I despair of winning fame in great enterprises. I offer myself freely for the discharge of affairs though I have nothing less in mind than to say farewell to my delightful studies which will engage me so long as I am in my right mind, not merely for the moment but forever and uninterruptedly in the midst of these distractions."[17]

15. Hutten, *Opera*, IV, 49.
16. *Ibid.*, I, 201.
17. *Ibid.*, p. 196.

Not even a Hutten could discover in the new humanist philosophy a direct ethical justification for the active life. For this he was driven to have recourse to a class morality. Yet the reflections which humanism had developed on bearing the common lot had a much greater significance for him than for Pirckheimer. Hutten's febrile spirit achieved a deeper fusion of the spiritual and the real world than German humanism had been able to do, living, as it did, in the four-walled study of a patrician residence. Hutten's humanism continually tried and proved itself in the confusion of the great world. Above the sphere of the pure and absolute worth of the world, he could never forget blind Fortune. "I may not be so wise as to expect no more from Fortune. I am clinging to her wheel, waiting to be lifted. She may carry me up. She cannot let me farther down—how can she?—since I care so little for what she confers, and what I really possess she cannot take from me." Thus he rejected the tendency of humanism to flee the world. In the world he must work; else would his contemporaries despise not only him, but humanism along with him. In the world he would work, for only if he achieve something here would he deserve to be called noble. "I do desire honors, if possible without arousing envy, but if not, then in any case. I have no little thirst for glory that I may be a noble so much as in me lies, but woe to me, Willibald, if I regard myself as noble although the son of such a class, family, and parents unless I deserve the name by my own industry. I have a loftier work in hand. I am conceiving greater plans. Not that I may advance my family. Elsewhere I seek to find and drink from the spring of nobility. Think me not content with an ancestor gallery or family inheritance. I would enhance it for posterity. So, though Fortune does not control all things, yet she weighs heavily, perhaps very heavily. You see on what slender grounds some become famous. If their virtue be not wholly tarnished at least they escape common accusation. This entirely fortuitous nobility is frivolous. I do not crave it. Sometimes capacity does not come to light because Fortune is adverse. I wish the wheel may be turned. I know she is a blind goddess, an unreasonable director, a fickle queen, unstable, vacillating, volatile, mobile, changeable, unreliable, inconstant, uncertain, wandering, and whatever else may be said to her discredit. There I must cast, there I must give the wheel a second turn, that I emerge, that I advance. To this end I labor. To this end I strive. I am not of those who acquiesce in any lot. For me nothing satisfies. Just as I have given you a frank and unsolicited confession of my ambition so I do not envy those who outstrip me. From those of my class indeed I dissent who prey on men of humble origin but native endowment. They who put to use the stuff of glory which we neglect are certainly to be preferred to us, be they but sons of fullers and cordwainers. They wrestle with greater difficulties than we. Not only is he who sits off and envies the man of letters an illiterate fool, but pitiable and thrice pitiable. Our nobility in particular suffers from this vice of obstructing these adornments. But what sort of envy before Christ is this to covet in another what we ourselves neglect? Why do we not devote ourselves to laws, letters, and arts, lest these tailors, fullers, and carpenters outdo us? Why do we cede a place, why relegate liberal disciplines to servitude and indignity (for shame)? With good right, therefore, does an industrious student capture the task of nobility by us deserted. We, alas, neglect so much and another from the bottom is able to outstrip us. Let us then undertake that which, to our great shame, has become the enterprise of others. A lost article belongs to everybody and all may look for it. And how much more easily we might have occupied ourselves with it than they, had we not deliberately renounced the paths of glory, occupied with lesser things, committed to torpor and lethargy. Glory is a legitimate ambition for all. Every struggle for great deeds is laudable, and to each his own species of honor is becoming. Family portraits are not to be altogether despised. They do give a certain embellishment. But whatever they confer is not strictly ours unless we have made it such by our own efforts."[18]

This need for recognition frequently appears in Hutten's character and explains the way in which he rationalized his outward situation. He had a political nature and was more radical because as a humanist he could despise the outward reality which he sought to mould and the success which he tried to achieve. This is why his political activity could inspire enthusiasm while his political ideas were unsuited in the main to immediate realization. He remained "a statesman from Utopia."

In Hutten's exchange with Pirckheimer there is a reflection of the difference in the outward status of their lives. If Hutten's attitude is to be explained in part as due to the inner urge of his character, it is due also to external necessity. "You city folk live not only comfortably but even cozily if your tastes are so inclined. Do you think I shall ever find repose among my knights? Are you unmindful of the disturbances and disquietudes to which the men of our class are subject?" he writes Pirckheimer.[19] Hutten's rejection of tranquillity springs from the soil of chivalry. The urban culture of the time had reached a sufficient point of development to vouchsafe to a little group the peace of a contemplative existence, whereas the life of the knight, whether in the castle, on the road, or at court, did not suffer one to "live apart" but plunged one into a struggle for existence demanding every resource. No segregation of the spheres of life was possible here. There was but one stage, on which they must be pursued undivided. Whether the noble was more concerned for the common good or to maintain the ancient privileges of his caste, whether new political conceptions could germinate in the soil of chivalry—these are questions immaterial to our purpose, because it was not the gross materialism of the wars of the knights which influenced Hutten so much as the readiness of knighthood to assume public responsi-

18. Hutten, *Opera,* I, 208 ff.

19. *Ibid.,* p. 201.

bility. If his knightly origin inhibited him at many points, his knightly temperament enabled him to entice humanism more deeply into the world. We feel already that Hutten was not going to be content to abandon humanism to a little aristocracy of culture. This amicable interchange is a friendly prelude to the controversy with Erasmus four years later. Unity still dominated the humanist camp. Differences of temperaments and interests enhanced the joy of the common enterprise. Above all there was still agreement as to the common enemy. All of the humanists regarded themselves as reformers of the previous state of affairs.

VII

POLITICS AND PAMPHLETEERING
1518–1519

ON the mission which Hutten undertook for the Elector in 1517 to the French Court he found an opportunity to enlarge his conception of the scope of the humanist republic of letters. As an Erasmian he found *entrée* among the leaders of French humanism, a Guillaume Budé, a Ricius, a Lefèvre. Budé praised Hutten to Erasmus as "a man thoroughly courtly and polished, distinguished by nobility and generosity."[1] And a little later Hutten characterized the French as the most polite and hospitable people of Europe.[2] Not the French but the Italians were the hereditary enemies. The feeling that he belonged to this new cosmopolitan society enhanced his self-esteem and stimulated him at the same time to strive to achieve for this spiritual aristocracy an impregnable position in the world without. On this ground he had justified to Pirckheimer his entry into the court service. As the theologians had achieved power and influence by the assumption of civil posts, so the humanists should commend themselves to princes. Some of them were already showing signs of favor to humanism. They should be encouraged by literary eulogy. Let them be hailed as Maecenates and Augusti, even if they did not deserve it. Humanism should achieve political power and its enemies in Church and State be brought low.

Hutten's desires to elevate humanism by the conquest of the courts of princes were accompanied as early as 1518 by threats to root out the tares of scholasticism, but such outbursts are not to be taken too seriously at this time, for service with Albert of Mainz naturally imposed many re-

1. Hutten, *Opera,* I, 171. 2. *Ibid.,* V, 400.

strictions. Hutten thought, too, that the humanists might now await a favorable turn of events, since their opponents were consuming each other in hairsplitting. Thus in 1518 he characterized the dispute which had begun in Wittenberg. At the court of Mainz, to whose diocese Hutten belonged, he would doubtless have heard early of the indulgence controversy. On the fifth of April he expressed his mind for the first time to Count Neuemar with regard to the occurrences at Wittenberg. "One faction attacks the authority of the pope, the other vindicates papal indulgences. There is great excitement and heated controversy with the monks as captains on both sides. These leaders are violently agitated. They cry out, bellow, sometimes weep and upbraid fortune. Recently they have turned to writing. The booksellers are busy. Propositions, corollaries, conclusions, and articles with which many have broken their necks are on the market. I hope they will devour one another. When I was recently informed on the matter by one of the brethren I told him, 'Eat and you will be eaten in turn.' I devoutly hope that our enemies will cockfight to the last feather."[3] In October of the same year he could still write: "Luther's many controversies show with what virulence the theologians attack one another."[4] Over against this, Hutten's acquaintance with the great leaders of European humanism filled him with confidence that the movement was on the up grade. When a humanist like Budaeus was addressing himself to Roman law, a Faber Stapulensis to Aristotle, and theologians of the standing of Oecolampadius were aiding Erasmus in the purification of Holy Scripture, here was proof enough that humanism was embracing all fields and was on the point of introducing a purer world. This reflection could make him well-nigh forget that the world was full of "excitement and turbulence, misery and woe," and enabled him, as he contemplated the lot of man and the tasks of the times, to exult, "What a century! What scholarship! It is a sheer joy

3. Hutten, *Opera,* I, 167. 4. *Ibid.,* p. 216.

to be alive, even though not yet in tranquillity [that is, in the contemplative life]. Learning flourishes, men are spiritually quickened. O Barbarism, take a rope and prepare for extinction!"[5]

Hutten's belief that inner relationships were making for the eventual triumph of humanism enabled him to feel that the time was ripe for outward political action. Christendom was menaced by the expansion of the Ottoman kingdom through the victories of Selim I. The pope endeavored to foster a European crusade against the Turk. Maximilian had long cherished a similar plan in the interests of his hereditary dominions and he needed the pope's help to straighten out the succession of his heirs. For this reason he was ready to combine with Leo X in a common campaign. The succession to Maximilian and the Turkish war were the two most important matters up for discussion at the Diet of Augsburg in the summer of 1518.

Ulrich von Hutten, too, was affected by the general impression of the disquieting news of the Turkish menace. Momentarily, when the opponents of humanism were agitating, the Turkish question could recede into the background and the progress of humanism would appear as of prime importance. When a preacher at Mainz openly apostrophized him in a sermon, Hutten commented: "If Germany would hear me I would advise that, necessary as the Turkish war may be, we should first cure this internal cancer before embarking on an Asiatic expedition. What good will it be to wipe out the Ottomans, who fight us for imperialist reasons, when at home we have the subverters of universal piety?"[6] At the same time Hutten brought out *A Speech on the Turkish War*, prepared in the spring of 1518, with the hope of delivering it before the Diet itself.[7] Nothing came of that. The speech is interesting, not

5. *Ibid.*, p. 217. Compare J. Huizinga, *The Waning of the Middle Ages*, Chapter II.

6. Hutten, *Opera*, I, 166.

7. "Ad Principes Germanos ut bellum Turcis inferant exhortatoria," *ibid.*, V, 98 ff.

for its influence on events, but as a means of determining the development of Hutten's political views. On a previous occasion he had found it easy to idealize the Italian politics of Maximilian because of an underestimate of the outward obstacles which shattered the emperor's plans. Now Hutten still looked to the emperor for leadership, but pointed out more expressly the actual presuppositions of success and concerned himself with plans to overcome the inner disunity which crippled the organism of the Empire.

Outward events, naturally enough, affected the tone and the objectives of the *Speech on the Turkish War*. We can scarcely assume that the government at Mainz had requested it,[8] but a general call for such efforts from the court of Maximilian may well have been the stimulus. Hutten certainly thought he had done the emperor a service and hoped to be paid for it. Apart from a few places where divergent views gained the upper hand, Hutten's speech accorded with the intentions of the emperor and of Archbishop Albert of Mainz, who had espoused the imperial cause at Augsburg and abrogated the treaty with France. We must not assume, however, that the agreement was merely a forced accommodation to political interests, because Hutten's own opinions were by no means suppressed.

While the emperor had really submitted to the pope this time and was willing to follow his initiative in the Turkish war, even though leadership really lay with the Church, Hutten had not abandoned his firm conviction of the superiority of the imperial power. He shared the mood of the German estates at Augsburg. Seldom had there been such an anti-papal diet as in 1518. The estates bitterly complained of the ancient grievances of the German people against the exploitation of the Roman system and the fulfilment of the wishes of emperor and pope alike was made dependent on the correction of the "Grievances of the German Nation." Hutten appropriated the complaints of the estates and ran the gamut of papal financial exactions.

8. P. Joachimsen, *Historische Zeitschrift,* CXXV, 489.

But he was not willing to obstruct the Turkish war, seeking rather to entrust the leadership to the emperor instead of to the pope. For that reason he was very much irritated with the papal legate, Thomas de Vio, who presented a completely worked-out plan of campaign. This was enough to make him suspicious of the whole project, and he insinuated that the Turkish war was merely a subterfuge of the Curia to mulct Germany of gold. The conduct of war was the office of the emperor as the representative of Christendom. Because Hutten took so seriously the position of the Empire within Christianity, he could not doubt that the emperor, as the head of Christendom, was obligated to ward off the Turk.

In his defense of the imperial politics in Italy he had already injected a new note into the pretensions of the emperor, in spite of all retention of the medieval universalism, by introducing the humanist idea of the integrity of peoples. Now in the Turkish question he went a step further and endeavored to find a nationalist basis for the imperial policy. To be sure, the speech was addressed only to Germans. Nevertheless it is significant, even taking anticurialism into account, that the conception of the universal European crusade for which Leo X had appealed at the close of the Lateran Council in 1517 here drops out of the picture. For Hutten the Turkish war was really a German affair. The outward prerequisites for success were to be found in Germany. She was now at peace with her neighbors. She had enough unoccupied soldiers who should be employed, all the more because the recent crop failures made their support difficult. An ideal goal lured the Germans in that they had an opportunity to regain their world importance and to display the ancient German virtues. "Make war! Up! Then will our former glory revive, our ancient German valor gleam like the plough in the furrow."[9]

But he has no illusions with regard to the capacity of the Germany of the moment even to defend its own borders

9. Hutten, *Opera,* V, 110.

against the Turks. The probabilities were rather that "Germany will be consumed by its own powers," as he remarks in the language of Horace.[10] The reason lay in the constant internal dissension occasioned by the egoistic politics of the territorial princes. "German manhood is not deficient, but leaders are lacking. Youth is virile, valorous, ambitious. No one takes the lead, no one directs. Thus vigor vanishes, virtue languishes, and flaming zeal for great achievements sputters out." Here we have the motives which actuated Hutten in his campaign against the German princes. He was right in reproaching them with indifference to the interests of the Empire, which was prevented all too often by particularistic tendencies from playing a distinctive rôle in world affairs. It is questionable, however, whether at this time the clock could be turned back on the century-old emergence of the German states. Hutten talked as a knight, and the knights were imperial precisely in the interests of their particular class. Nor was Hutten fair to the princes in his *Speech on the Turkish War* when he laid at their door the sole responsibility for the failures of Maximilian, who must himself share a large measure of the blame. What the princes contributed to peace, order, and legal security Hutten did not recognize. When he called the princes tyrants—Ulrich von Württemberg was to serve as a glaring example—Hutten was giving vent to the hate which the knights felt so cordially for those who curbed their buccaneering and crushed their feuds. He was himself a scion of that political libertarianism which had grown up amid the ruins of the medieval Empire. The emperor was for him primarily the *conservator libertatis*, but the freedom of the individual was not so much intended as the conservation of the rights and privileges of groups whose independence encroached alike upon the community and individuals. Hutten's national ideas looked in a different direction. He would have liked to see the local powers eliminated in fa-

10. Hutten, *Opera,* V, 116. Horace, *Epod.* 16.

vor of a stronger national unity. By way of absolute centralization this was not indeed then capable of attainment in Germany, nor without amputations. Here Hutten was lacking in that realism which he displayed later only in the ecclesiastical sphere. To politics in the stricter sense he had little to offer beyond the current concepts. At bottom he was more of a national awakener than a practical statesman. For the most significant reformatory creation of the era of Maximilian, the Cameral Tribunal, Hutten, like the knights, had no feeling. Here again, as in his judgment of the territorial princes, he was dominated by his prejudice against Roman law and its representatives, the princely counsellors and judges.

Since Hutten's ideas on imperial reform were vitiated by class limitations, his propaganda in this direction was stillborn, but when he summoned all resources to united effort for the exaltation of German influence in world affairs he was saying something of permanent significance. A little later, in the *Arminius*, he was able to give a new turn to the conception of freedom by transferring it from the independence of the estates to the independence of the nation from foreign influences.

The dialogue *Fever the First*[11] may have been composed while Hutten was still in Augsburg. The attack on the Curia shows affinities with the *Speech on the Turkish War*. In other respects, however, the pamphlet belongs to the purely humanist works of this period. The contrast of the rich man and the poor, of the bane and blessing of sickness, is the subject of this pungent broadside, but the problem of Church and State is always in the offing. In the *Speech on the Turkish War* the relations of the Papacy and the Empire had been touched upon with reference to the spuriousness of the Donation of Constantine, here for the first time proclaimed in Germany. Now in the dialogue the contrast was presented to a larger circle in the form of vivid caricature. Cardinal Cajetan was made

11. "Febris Prima," Hutten, *Opera,* IV, 27 ff.

the object of satire, portrayed as a pampered sot, a genuine example of the irresponsible ecclesiastic. Hutten wished the fever upon him because he had come to Germany to swindle the people out of their money, so that the Romans might again have something to squander.

This picture of Cajetan has little resemblance to the real man, who was one of the most distinguished and serious of the Roman theologians. No breath of scandal touched his life, but the way in which he paraded his office and sponsored the interests of his master over against the emperor and the estates of the *Reich* aroused Hutten thoroughly. Besides, Cajetan was a former general of the Dominican Order which conducted the campaign against Reuchlin. In Cajetan Hutten saw an enemy of humanism and of independent imperial policy. That was enough. To try to discover a portrait of Cajetan in Hutten's dialogue would be nonsense. He wished to inflame passions, to inspire hate against a system of exploitation, to provoke action. In *Fever the First* he restrained himself in a measure, with an eye to his position at Mainz. In this form he might actually hope that his polemic would meet with favor from Archbishop Albert, who felt that his personal wishes had not been sufficiently regarded by the Curia. At the same time, *Fever the First* is a thinly veiled version of Hutten's later pamphleteering. He was not capable of faithful delineation of living individuals. Few were in his day. The great German artists Dürer and Holbein have left us genuine portraits. Among literary men the only one comparable to them is Erasmus, detached and impartial. Though Hutten had the capacity for sensing the peculiar power of great individuals, and could sketch a recognizable profile, yet he had no ability to achieve a literary portrayal. He lived in a moral world and saw in his controversies the battles of good and evil rather than the tension of personal energies. His public pronouncements naturally give this impression more than his confidential correspondence, but when, in order to create such an impression, he squeezes his opponents into a stereotype and attributes to them low motives, he remains a man of his times. In order to demolish scholasticism and shatter the chains of the hierarchy he is employing—albeit in a new way—the old technique for dealing with heretics. To be sure, Hutten was more unscrupulous than most of the pamphleteers of the Reformation, but the newly invented device for moulding public opinion, the printed word, subjected authors to a great temptation. Hutten had succumbed as a young man in the *Lötze Philippics*, employing the new weapon for personal and unworthy ends. He was not to do that again, but even the tracts which served a better cause were not free from the sort of demagoguery which in the long run defeats its own ends.

Fever the First was published in February, 1519, in Mainz, where Hutten had gone from Augsburg. In March he joined in the campaign against Ulrich von Württemberg, exchanging the pen for the sword. On the twelfth of January the Emperor Maximilian died. Ulrich von Württemberg saw in the interregnum an opportunity to incorporate the free city of Reutlingen into his duchy. He had not expected serious opposition so long as there was no emperor, but the Swabian League assembled troops to prepare for action under the leadership of Duke William of Bavaria. Ulrich von Hutten joined this army. The campaign turned out to be easier than had been expected, for it proved possible to detach the Swiss from the side of Württemberg. Almost without opposition the Swabian League was able to occupy the territory. One senses how Hutten gloated in his military environment. His craving to do something was at last satisfied. The opponent so long resisted was now brought suddenly to the ground. Hutten saw here the hand of destiny and the proof, too, that wishes and prayers are not enough. There is a place also for work and the sword.[12]

During the preparations for the Württemberg campaign Hutten became better acquainted with Franz von Sickingen, whom he visited and to whom he read from

12. Hutten, *Opera,* V, 84 ff.

Fever the First, resolving to turn it for him into German, though he considered it "more appealing and artistic in Latin."[13] Hutten now shared Sickingen's tent and thought to make him a convert to his ideas. In Stuttgart they paid a visit together to Reuchlin. The old man was debilitated by the harrying of the inquisitor and a new war threatened his possessions. Sickingen promised him help and protection. Hutten was overjoyed. To have won the most outstanding man of his class for the cause of Reuchlin and humanism awakened great expectations.

Sickingen was then at the high water mark of his career.[14] Hutten was the incarnation of German chivalry on the spiritual side, Sickingen on the political. In the next few years his person was of extraordinary political significance. His adherence was more decisive than the resources of mighty German princes. His greatness had been achieved through canny business ability to conserve and increase the family inheritance. This German *condottiere* knew how to sell his services at a high price and was able to take advantage of the chaotic state of affairs. He had made a great reputation with the mercenaries and the knights, so that they were glad to trust themselves to his leadership. He had enough ready cash to provide kings with arms in advance of pay. At the same time he was not endowed with preëminent political gifts, as he showed when he came to act independently. He was not equal to the cunning and reckless diplomacy of Charles V. Sickingen easily allowed himself to be deceived, and his sodden nature disqualified him from differentiating between the fixed and the movable stars. Probably if he had been a legitimate prince he would have maintained his place with more honor and success than did many, but to win a principality as a knight required an extraordinary capacity and less attachment to the class from which he sprang. Only for a short time was he a meteor on the political horizon.

But Hutten had found in him the personality for which

13. Hutten, *Opera*, I, 247.

14. Compare H. Ulmann, *Franz von Sickingen* (Leipsic, 1872).

he sought. To Erasmus he wrote: "Franz is a man such as Germany has not had for many a day and who deserves to be immortalized also in your letters. My hope is that great glory will accrue to our land through this man. Nothing which we admire in the ancients does he fail studiously to imitate. He is wise and persuasive, grapples with every situation with the alacrity and the indefatigability of a genuine leader. Nothing does he say or do in a servile manner, and at the moment he has a grand enterprise under way."[15] Here was a leader to clarify the sultry atmosphere and realize the new ideas.

The first move in this direction was the intervention of Sickingen in the Reuchlin affair. We mentioned that the trial had gone through several stages, ending in an indefinite postponement by the pope. This feeble conclusion of the affair was interpreted by the humanists as a victory for their side. Hutten so regarded it, and when one considers the means employed by the Dominicans probably it was. But Reuchlin had won only at the cost of his private fortune, for the expenses of a trial protracted over several years reached unheard-of proportions. Here Sickingen sought to help. On the twenty-ninth of July, 1519, he declared a feud with the Upper Rhine province of the Dominican Order in a letter demanding that they reimburse Reuchlin. He based his action upon the decision at Speyer, which had not been exactly annulled, though actually superseded by the action from Rome. The Dominicans were afraid to offend the dreaded *condottiere* and went so far as to remove Hochstraten and to petition the pope, with a deferential reference to Reuchlin, to drop the case. In May 1520 Reuchlin received his money.

The Dominicans, however, were intimidated only for a moment. Secretly they conspired together. The emergence of Luther and the orthodox zeal of the young emperor gave them the preponderance. Hochstraten pointed out to the Curia that Luther would never have dared to challenge

15. Hutten, *Opera,* I, 276. Allen, *Opus epistularum Erasmi,* Ep. 986, III, 613 ff.

papal authority had he not been encouraged by the mildness of the pope toward Reuchlin. Hochstraten was successful in having himself reinstated and in securing the condemnation of the *Augenspiegel*. At the very moment when the bull was launched against Luther, the sentence was pronounced on Reuchlin's tract and the decision of Speyer was annulled. An appeal to Charles V would be futile. Reuchlin submitted. He, who had been reared in the old faith, had no mind to throw in his lot with Wittenberg, nor did he accept the invitation of Sickingen to take refuge at the fortress of Ebernburg. He studied and worked at the house of the violent anti-Lutheran John Eck in Ingolstadt and publicly condemned Luther's teachings. That brought Hutten into the lists. He now bitingly characterized his former hero as craven. "You are so intimidated and enfeebled that you even indulge in curses on those who sought to save you. . . . I am ashamed to have written so much, to have done so much on your behalf, when you allow the case for which we have struggled so valiantly to peter out in this ignominious fashion. . . . But even if you oppose, we will shake off the yoke of turpitude and liberate ourselves from base servitude."[16] So ended Hutten's campaign for Reuchlin. The matter was more important than the man. When Hutten said farewell to him on the twenty-second of February, 1521, the fight for Reuchlin had become the larger struggle for German liberty. Hutten was led from the Reuchlin feud to greater issues.

Acquaintance with Sickingen in the summer of 1519 and his entry on the side of Reuchlin had brought these plans to definitive expression. The vindication of Reuchlin which had not been obtained through the Emperor Maximilian had been accomplished easily by the boldness of Sickingen.[17] Hutten was the counsellor of this redoubtable warrior and preferred the life of the camp to that of the insufferable court. He had all the more joy in the defeat of

16. Hutten, *Operum Supplementum,* II, 803 ff.
17. Hutten, *Opera,* I, 320.

the tyrannical Ulrich von Württemberg in the summer campaign because physical health at the same time seemed to be restored. His enervating disease was apparently cured through a remedy recommended to him by an Augsburg doctor. His whole being now flared up against court life. "I hate it," he wrote to Erasmus.[18] He really never had been where he belonged, in between untutored courtiers and tutored jurists, both of whom he despised. His unmitigated frankness was scarcely the proper dower for one who would spend his life in the entourage of princes. Albert of Mainz gave leave of absence from court, on pay, to Erasmus' *protégé* in the late summer of 1519, that he might have leisure for humanist studies.

When one reads the letters referring to this release and the dialogue *Fortuna* of the summer of 1519,[19] one receives almost the impression that Hutten desired no other existence than that of Erasmus or Pirckheimer. The quiet life of the scholar seemed so enviable that all the praises of the active life to Pirckheimer of the year before appear to have dropped out. One scarcely recognizes the Hutten who in the Württemberg campaign at the side of Sickingen had found the outlet for his activist urge. One is inclined to suspect that the longing for a quiet life of learning was merely a pretext to be free from the court at Mainz. Perhaps there were such ulterior considerations, but they did not predominate. There was always an undercurrent pulling him to tranquil labor in the European republic of letters, in the Platonic fellowship of the new representatives of culture, and weaning him from his thirst for daily activity. We recall that in the famous letter to Pirckheimer he fell somewhere short of describing his devotion to the common calling as an ideal. He could never quite emancipate himself from the aristocracy of culture, a feeling of superiority to average society, which, combined with the disillusioning experiences at Mainz, might well provide

18. Hutten, *Opera,* I, 248. Allen, *Opus epistularum Erasmi,* Ep. 923, III, 501 ff.

19. Hutten, *Opera,* IV, 75 ff.

the material for the literary picture of the "tranquil" humanist existence portrayed in the *Fortuna.* But this was not his whole mind, however much he might toy with the notion of securing tranquillity through prosperous matrimony. Even leisure was desired not for philosophical or aesthetic enjoyment, but for the maturing of political projects. These should be emancipated from outward dependence and given freer course. He had no mind to spend his life in a distasteful service to the detriment of his activist calling. He would abandon the court, not the kingdom of *Fortuna.* His bow was drawn, his plan and objective determined.

In the same letter of the third of August, 1518, in which he informed Eobanus Hesse and Peter Amerbach that he had been granted a leave by Albert of Mainz, he told them, too, that he had under way a dialogue of unexampled sharpness against Rome. He summoned even his friends at Erfurt to "risk something for German liberty."[20] The dialogue of which he spoke is the *Roman Trinity,* also called the *Vadiscus,*[21] a declaration of feud with Rome, the great manifesto of his campaign for German liberty. What emboldened him appears between the lines of the letter. "You will see that I mean to enlist people of great resources who have not known how to utilize their strength and now are glad to accept my guidance," he informed his friends. The enlistment of Sickingen in the Reuchlin affair brought Ulrich out of the retirement from which he had been watching the course of events since his return from Italy.

Further circumstances also contributed to unchain his agitation. The death of Maximilian and the election of Charles V had inspired the best of the nation with confidence for the future. Hutten in 1518 had attended the Diet when Albert of Mainz dissolved his treaty with France and instead promised his electoral vote to the grandson of Maximilian, provided Charles of Spain should

20. Hutten, *Opera,* I, 302.
21. "Vadiscus sive Trias Romana," Hutten, *Opera,* IV, 145 ff.

first be approved by the pope—a condition which was not actually fulfilled when Charles was elected in 1519. Hutten cared little for the diplomatic intrigues. He was pleased by the election of a Hapsburg, for Maximilian had personified to him the glory of the German Empire and his anti-papal stand was now being renewed during the election, inasmuch as Charles V had to circumvent the pope in order to secure the imperial throne. In the *Fortuna* Hutten manifested enthusiasm for the choice of Charles. The displeasure of the pope was fraught with promise, and the victory already attained by the Spaniards over the African Mohammedans was of good omen.[22]

Hutten had just been sponsoring the Turkish war as an exclusively German affair. Now the Spanish victory was a favorable sign. Here is the measure of the degree to which he identified the person of the emperor with the German nation. If Maximilian's policy was by no means so national as Hutten supposed, nevertheless the emperor's nature had a human relationship to the consciousness of the German people. This was not to be true of Charles V; he was and should remain an alien.

Strange that no one thought of this in Germany at the time of the election and that the popularity which Maximilian had won for the House of Hapsburg was transferred unsuspectingly to his grandson. There was little realization of how genuinely disheartening were the political relations of the nation, although the national consciousness was in some measure disturbed. No one wanted Francis I, the Frenchman. Especially among the knights of the Rhenish and Franconian provinces there was vigorous protest. Hutten himself warned Francis I when Ulrich von Württemberg sought to involve him in Germany's internal affairs. "He who would lose the war should fight the Germans," says the old proverb. "No one has ever reaped any good from a victory over the Germans," wrote Hutten.[23] On the other hand, Germany ought to have been more dis-

22. *Ibid.*, p. 92.

23. *Ibid.*, I, 246.

tressed that Hapsburg gold played so large a part in the election. Hutten, of all people, had seen enough of this.[24] He had witnessed the army of the Swabian League, which he thought strong enough to expel the Turk, enlisted by the Hapsburgs at the close of the Württemberg campaign and directed to the vicinity of the place of election. He knew, at any rate, that the Elector of Mainz sold his vote for a high price, and certainly did not suppose that the other electors were any better. This traffic shocked him no more than his contemporaries. He was glad of the outcome and pinned his political dreams to the person of the young monarch. So also did the majority of the German nation, who during the days of the bitter decision built castles in Spain with an energy seldom displayed elsewhere in their history.

Charles was for the people the legitimate heir of Maximilian. To be sure, the Empire was elective, but the choice was largely conditioned by the dynastic feudal conceptions of the people. What one did not like in Maximilian was attributed to his age. From the youth of the unknown Charles one expected a rejuvenated and vigorous Maximilian. Even Martin Luther entertained expectations from the "young noble blood," and allowed himself to be carried along with the fresh flower of national consciousness. All of these expectations were destined to speedy and frightful disillusionment. Nothing else could have happened in 1519. Had the choice fallen upon Frederick the Wise of Saxony, the hope that such a territorial prince could found a strong German Empire would have been a greater Utopia than the national expectations attached to the coronation of Charles V.[25]

24. Hutten, *Opera,* I, 259.

25. Compare K. Brandi, "Die Wahl Karls V.," *Nachrichten der Gesellschaft der Wissenschaften zu Göttingen* (1925), pp. 109 ff.

VIII

EXPECTATION AND PREPARATION FOR THE REFORM IN 1520

IN an address to Charles V in September, 1520, Hutten, looking back, declared that embitterment over the opposition of the Curia to the election of Charles had driven him to the publication of his sharp invective against Rome.[1] At the same time there was a certain contact with Luther. To Eobanus Hesse, on the 3d of August, 1519, Hutten wrote, "there will be more authors for this cause than you suppose."[2] And again on October 26 he wrote in a letter to Eobanus: "I do not venture to associate with Luther on account of Prince Albert, who is wrongly persuaded that he is involved. I do not think so and I am sorry to lose an opportunity to vindicate my fatherland. Yet I am doing nothing other than that, and perhaps better in my own way. Besides, Luther has an excellent assistant in Melanchthon."[3] Luther's stand now had taken on a different color. At first the indulgence controversy appealed to Hutten as a monks' squabble, as a rift between his opponents. Now he saw in Luther a welcome comrade in the war against Rome, though, to be sure, only one among many. Nevertheless the shift is significant. While in Augsburg, he still took no notice of Luther and he probably would not have done so even had he not been completely separated from society by the drastic treatment of his disease. In the very days when Luther appeared before Cajetan, Hutten probably composed the long letter to Pirckheimer. Noteworthy is the distinction already being drawn between one theologian and another. Hutten recounted a visit of Oecolampadius: "A young theologian

1. Hutten, *Opera,* I, 379, and similarly, IV, 176.
2. *Ibid.,* I, 302.
3. *Ibid.,* p. 313.

with sharp teeth, who so thoroughly chews the literature of all three languages that those well known toothless chaps envy him."[4] What brought Hutten into closer spiritual alignment with Luther cannot be determined with perfect confidence. Perhaps Pirckheimer or Peutinger gave him fuller accounts, for they had seen Luther in connection with his appearance before Cajetan at Augsburg. Probably the decisive moment was Luther's Leipsic disputation from the twenty-seventh of June to the thirteenth of July. A theologian who dared to call papal authority into question, and to appeal like a humanist to the primary sources, was a welcome comrade to Hutten. A deeper acquaintance with the religious probings of Luther cannot be inferred from this recognition of comradeship. Hutten was still reserved in his attitude to one more of the company of those whom he would incite against Rome. Luther was not yet important enough to warrant imperilling the post at Mainz for his sake; or perhaps he was already too influential and independent for Hutten to be willing to become his disciple and renounce leadership in the campaign against Rome, now that the preaching of the monk was already stirring the people.

But before the writings were published on which Hutten was working—not until February, 1520, did the *Roman Trinity* appear, and with it the dialogues *Fever the Second* and *The Onlookers*[5]—he had an opportunity to break a lance for Luther. The tie between Hutten and Erasmus was not dissolved during the period at Mainz; on the contrary, it had become more intimate. Erasmus, to be sure, had some misgivings over the increasing bitterness of Hutten's polemic, and also the participation in the Württemberg campaign was not to his taste. An intimation of the later feud and separation appears in a letter which Erasmus sent Hutten. With ironic admiration he

4. Hutten, *Opera,* I, 216.

5. "Vadiscus sive Trias Romana," "Febris Secunda," "Inspicientes," Hutten, *Opera,* IV, 101 ff.

speaks of Ulrich as one who fights not only with "pen and tongue, but also with the weapons of Mars." "I praise your valor, but if you will listen to me you will consecrate Hutten to the Muses. For where shall we find such a genius if anything goes wrong?—which may the gods avert! But you know that Mars is fickle and unpropitious to the gifted, and of all the gods most stupid. May all turn out well, but if anything happens you have already erected in yourself and your writings a perpetual memorial."[6] Both were by this time aware of the difference of their natures. Hutten in presenting the *Fever the First* and the *Phalarismus* had already written, "I know that you will reprove my audacity more than you will praise my courage."[7] Erasmus was spending most of his time in the orthodox scholastic Louvain and was sufficiently uneasy to be at pains to assure his ecclesiastical opponents that he had had nothing to do with the *Obscure Men* and the *Nobody;* in fact, as the *Praise of Folly* showed, he eschewed personal affronts.[8] Erasmus was compelled to be discreet because he was himself under scrutiny on account of the *Julius Exclusus,*[9] the authorship of which he strenuously denied. His real opinion is better expressed in a letter directed to Cardinal Wolsey on the eighteenth of May, 1519. Germany, the letter says, has some young publicists such as Hutten of which the country will someday be proud. Granted that they are audacious. They have been severely

6. Hutten, *Opera,* I, 260 ff. Allen, *Opus epistularum Erasmi,* Ep. 951, III, 553.

7. Hutten, *Opera,* I, 248. Allen, *Opus epistularum Erasmi,* Ep. 923, III, 501.

8. Hutten, *Opera,* I, 265. Allen, *Opus epistularum Erasmi,* Ep. 961, III, 573 ff.

9. The discussion on the authorship of the *Julius Exclusus* has been summed up by Wallace Ferguson in his excellent edition of *Erasmi Opuscula, A supplement to the Opera Omnia* (The Hague, 1933), pp. 38 ff. Out of the number of studies devoted to the question mention may be made of P. S. Allen in his *Opus epistularum Erasmi,* note to Ep. 502, and his *Age of Erasmus* (Oxford, 1914), pp. 184 ff. J. B. Pineau, "Érasme est-il l'auteur du Julius," *Revue de Littérature comparée,* V (1925), 385 ff. and the same author's *Érasme et la Papauté* (Paris, 1924).

threatened and provoked. "They are Germans and they are young. They have pens and they have brains. . . . I can advise them, but I cannot compel them."[10]

Erasmus saw the recklessness of Hutten and rejoiced in it to some extent as a sign of exuberant youth. Yet more he admired the genuine learning and ability of this man of thirty years. At bottom however, he still hoped that Hutten would come back completely to scholarly and poetic work. With this in mind he erected to him in June, 1519, the greatest public memorial of his esteem in that he couched the literary portrait of his most intimate and famous friend, Thomas More, in the form of a letter to Hutten.[11] This was no gesture of superficial humanist courtesy, for he had already remembered him amply in dedications, but a sign of personal gratification shared by Thomas More.

The whole circle of English humanists, not only More but Bishop Fisher, Colet, Linacre, Grocyn, Hugh Latimer, Tunstall, had early taken an interest in the Reuchlin affair and their relish for the *Obscure Men* made the work more at home in England during the next two centuries than in Germany. Equally the author of the *Utopia* would be interested in the dialogues which Hutten had written after 1517 in the manner of Lucian. Erasmus and More were the sponsors of this author north of the Alps and More had taken a lively part in the new edition of Lucian which Erasmus published after long preparation in 1515 in Paris. The two were concerned not so much for the restoration of the text as for the recovery of a literary form. And here Hutten's dialogues were the demonstration that their effort had not been in vain. "Lucian reborn" was the title bestowed upon him by the distinguished editor of

10. Hutten, *Opera,* I, 269 ff. Allen, *Opus epistularum Erasmi,* Ep. 967, III, 587.

11. Hutten, *Opera,* I, 278 ff. Allen, *Opus epistularum Erasmi,* Ep. 999, IV, 12 ff. An English translation of the letter to Thomas More, *Selections from his English works and from the lives by Erasmus and Roper,* edited by P. S. and H. M. Allen (Oxford, 1924).

ERASMUS OF ROTTERDAM, 1523

HVLDERICHI HVTTENI EQ. GERM. DIALOGI.

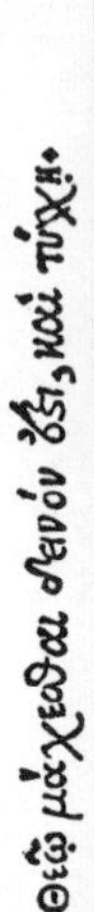

πᾶσιν γὰρ εὖ φρονοῦσι συμμαχεῖ τύχη.

FORTVNA.
Febris prima.
Febris ſecunda
Trias Romana.
Inſpicientes.

Cum priuilegio ad ſexennium.

TITLE-PAGE OF HUTTEN'S *DIALOGI*, 1520

MARTIN LUTHER, 1521

A Engel
TRIVPHV
Das grab der hey-
ligen schrifft.
E Aposteln.
C Patriarchen.
D Propheten.
B Danckſagung des gemeynen volcks.
Hutten.

TRIUMPH

RITATIS.
Reuelatus ẽ homo,
pcti, filius pditiōis, & abominatio, quē
percussit deus virga oris sui.
Regi autē sclorū
imortali inuisibi
li, soli deo honor
& glia in scla se
culorū Amē.
Ego sum via veritas
& vita. Iohan. 10.
Euangelistae.
Carlostat.
Saluator.
Luther.

RUTH, 1521

Martinus Lutherus.

Vlrichus ab Hutten.

Gespräch büchlin herr Vlrichs von Hutten.

Feber das Erst.
Feber das Ander.
Wadiscus. oder die Römische dreyfaltigkeit.
Die Anschawenden

Veritatem meditabitur guttur meum.

Perrumpendum est tandem, perrumpendũ est.

*

Odivi ECCLESIAM malignantium.

Erasmus and of More's *Utopia*, John Froben, when in November, 1518, he sent a copy of Hutten's *Aula* from Basel as a lightsome consolation that More had been called away from the muses to the court of the invincible Henry.

No doubt that Erasmus' introduction to his work on More is to be taken at face value: "Your unbounded admiration for the genius of Thomas More and your enthusiasm for his writings, which, as you properly say, are unexcelled for learning and charm, I assure you are not limited to yourself and are reciprocated by More. He in turn is so delighted with your writings and your genius that I almost envy you." Hutten was accepted among the leaders of European humanism and Erasmus was glad. At the close of the sketch on More, which is the most important contemporary literary portrait, he comes back again to Hutten's conflicts. Not only the *Aula*, but also the *Fever the First*, with its disparagement of Cajetan, is mentioned with praise. Even the name of Sickingen appears, due to Hutten's commendation. Ulrich could still feel himself in accord with Erasmus, even though he began to sense the difference. But if this be true, the letter of Erasmus on the nineteenth of October or the first of November must have made all the greater impression.

Erasmus was penetrating and sensitive enough to perceive early the significance of Luther's stand.[12] Probably he never entertained any illusions with regard to the difference in their objectives. Nevertheless he saw in Luther a great force for the realization of the reform of the Church and endeavored to shield him as long as there was hope that he might be moderated. The letter to Albert, entrusted for delivery to Hutten, made an attempt at once

12. See P. Kalkoff, "Die Vermittlungspolitik des Erasmus und sein Anteil an den Flugschriften der ersten Reformationszeit," *Archiv für Reformationsgeschichte*, I, 1904. *Erasmus, Luther und Friedrich der Weise* (Leipsic, 1920). M. Richter, *Die Stellung des Erasmus zu Luther* (1920). E. König, "Erasmus und Luther," *Historisches Jahrbuch,* XLI (1921), 52 ff. A. Renaudet, *Érasme, Sa pensée religieuse et son action 1518–1521* (Paris, 1926). *Erasmi Opuscula,* edited by W. Ferguson (The Hague, 1933), pp. 304 ff.

to help Luther and at the same time to ward off the frequent accusations of fully endorsing his program. Luther, he wrote, is not to be condemned lightheartedly. We must seek to win him for the Church. "Sparks of evangelical teaching" are bright in his breast. His protest is intelligible when one recalls scholasticism, monastic traffic in indulgences, and "more than Jewish ceremonies." Over against the harsh aspersions heaped upon Luther's person and cause, this letter of Erasmus must have fallen heavily in the opposite scale, even though Luther was right in the main when he said: "He defends me, but in such fashion that he seems to do anything but defend me."

Hutten was to have delivered the letter to the archbishop in a propitious moment. Instead of that, he printed it. The indiscretion he committed did not make so much difference in that age. Erasmus expected it to become public eventually and for that reason did not take Hutten's action amiss. Only after the breach did he reproach him on this account. More significant for our interests is the fact that Hutten should find a letter in which Erasmus showed some feeling for Luther of sufficient importance to publish. A closer approach to Wittenberg does not appear until the letters of Hutten to Melanchthon of the twentieth of January and twenty-eighth of February, 1520.[13] It is noteworthy that he turned to Melanchthon, whose call to Wittenberg in 1518 he had welcomed as a sign of the progress of humanist studies. These letters, the first of which did not reach its destination, transmitted to Luther an offer of protection from Sickingen. Here, too, out of consideration for Albert, Hutten endeavored to veil his own share, though he could scarcely conceal the fact that it was he who had persuaded Sickingen. Hutten recalls Sickingen's gesture for Reuchlin. What he had done for the great Hebraist he might do also for Luther, who, if persecuted, might find a refuge with Sickingen. On the way he could visit him in Steckelberg and there common

13. Hutten, *Opera,* I, 320, 324.

plans could be matured. For Erasmus, too, Hutten sought to enlist Sickingen, who should use his influence with the brother of the emperor, Archduke Ferdinand. All the new forces should coalesce in a campaign against Rome and find a focal point in the outward power of Sickingen.

The offer to Luther was the fruit of a visit of Hutten to Sickingen's fortress, Landstuhl, in 1520. At the same time Sickingen must have promised to try to obtain for Hutten a post with the younger brother of Charles V, Ferdinand of Austria, whom Erasmus also regarded as a friend of humanism. Thus one hoped to influence the imperial court, to acquire a lever with which to alter the whole political situation. Hutten therefore dedicated to Ferdinand in March, 1520, a polemical tract discovered at Fulda and emanating from the period of Henry IV and Gregory VII.[14] From the preface one can see how he would counsel the imperial court. Everything which Hutten had gleaned against Rome was now garnered into a greater unity. For Ferdinand the political side was played up. The popes were charged with usurping lordship. Temporal dominion over Rome no more pertained to them than over Germany, which they were bleeding of gold and crippling in its national development. Therefore the war for German liberation must be started. The Hapsburg brothers, Charles and Ferdinand, should take the lead. Hutten did not contemplate a revolution, but a resumption and extension of the policy of Maximilian through the heirs of his legitimate authority.

But the ground was apparently already too hot in Mainz. In the preface to the *Roman Trinity* of the thirteenth of February, 1520, Hutten says that he counts on the protection of the German nation if he should be persecuted for his declaration of the truth.[15] Sickingen travelled to Brabant in March to meet Ferdinand. Hutten's next moves are obscure. We know of a trip to Bamberg which brought a closer approach to Luther; then of

14. *Ibid.,* p. 325.

15. *Ibid.,* p. 322.

a move to the Netherlands in response to news from Sickingen that a post awaited him with Ferdinand.

In Bamberg Hutten met Crotus Rubeanus, just returned from Italy. Crotus had previously been his guide in theology, and even more now that he had obtained his doctorate in the subject. The Leipsic disputation had opened Crotus' eyes. His fine critical sense could look at the situation objectively. Because he realized how deeply the Roman system was buttressed by faith and force, he had a feeling for Luther's unparalleled courage. Crotus understood Luther's position in the main, though he underestimated his steadfastness when he exhorted him to stand fast, while counselling him at the same time to tread softly.

Crotus and Hutten had more than ever in common when they met in Bamberg. Crotus wrote Luther how together they waxed both merry and indignant over his persecutors,[16] and the tone of the remainder of the letter indicates that Crotus was beginning to have an inkling of the national importance of the movement of Luther, whom he now describes as the "father of his country." Hutten may well have influenced Crotus in this letter, and even more in the tracts which were soon to follow. If so, the conversation in Bamberg marks a further stage in Hutten's approach to Luther. A few days before his departure for the court at Brussels, Hutten prefaced a new edition of some tracts from the period of the papal schism, with an appeal *To All Free Germans* in which he came out openly for Luther.[17] There is no mention of the name, but the reference is obvious. The former reservations are abandoned. Now he desires a personal connection with Luther.

Probably he informed the Wittenbergers of his plans in the Netherlands before the twenty-seventh of May, because we have a record of two letters of Luther to Hutten in that month.[18] The first, on May 5, 1520, was the ac-

16. Hutten, *Opera,* I, 337 ff. M. Luther, *Werke, Kritische Gesamtausgabe, Briefwechsel,* edited by O. Clemen, II, 87 ff.

17. Hutten, *Opera,* I, 371 ff.

18. *Ibid.,* pp. 345, 354. M. Luther, *Werke, Briefwechsel,* II, 98, 111.

knowledgment of the invitation of Sickingen. The second, on the thirty-first of May, appears to have been an answer to a new letter from Hutten, both of which have been lost. The brief remark of Hutten at the close of his letter of June 4, that he was going to the court of Ferdinand to do his best for the common cause, and the letter of Melanchthon to Johannes Hess that Hutten was going there to enlist the great princes in the struggle for liberation,[19] presuppose an earlier exchange with Wittenberg of which we are not informed. Perhaps Hutten's letter to Luther of June 4, 1520, is not the first.[20] The disconnected character of the content would fit in well with that assumption, though the outward circumstances may be a sufficient explanation. On the way to Ferdinand Hutten learned of Luther's excommunication. This news convinced him that he must make public profession of his adherence to Luther. Now he felt that the battle was common and he began also to subordinate himself to Luther in view of the influence which the latter was exerting over the German masses. "For Christ we stand. We dispel the mists of papal obscurantism which had beclouded His teaching and we bring it into the light. You with greater success, I to the best of my ability." Now that Luther was persecuted by the Romanists, he took on for the first time the proportions of greatness. "Eck accuses me of being on your side. He is right. In so far as I have understood you I have been with you, though we have never discussed our plans. Eck lied to please the Roman bishop when he said we had conspired together before. The impudent scamp! He will receive his deserts. May you be steadfast and firm. Do not falter. But there is no need that I should urge you. I will stand by you, whatever comes. You can trust me with your secrets. Let us vindicate the common freedom; let us liberate the fatherland, so long oppressed."

But what did Hutten understand of Luther's teaching? Wherein did he see the agreement? Hutten's reform pro-

19. Hutten, *Opera,* I, 358.
20. *Ibid.,* p. 355. M. Luther, *Werke, Briefwechsel,* II, 115 ff.

gram is contained in the three dialogues, *The Roman Trinity*, *The Onlookers*, and *Fever the Second*. No essential alteration took place in his objectives to the end of his life, however varied might be the means employed for their realization. In the *Roman Trinity* (the form of which, by the way, is again borrowed from Crotus[21]), we find combined the two angles from which the young Hutten had criticized the Roman system. There is the political polemic which would vindicate for the Empire its proper place in Christendom, and the humanist polemic which would vanquish scholasticism. From the outset he called for the subordination of the Papacy to the Empire, and if, to begin with, the warrior Pope Julius II appeared exceptional, historical studies and especially acquaintance with Lorenzo Valla's *Donatio Constantini* convinced him that in the early days the Papacy had no temporal power. This recognition on the one hand served to provide a theoretical justification for the imperial pretensions, and on the other hand reënforced his humanist view of Christian piety and culture. That these might have free course he set himself to achieve a just political structure. This meant for him, in the first place, a reform with reference to the position of the Church in public life as well as an inner reform of the Church itself. Both should take place through an alteration in the relations of the Roman see and through a curtailment of ecclesiastical possessions. The treatment to be meted out to Rome was perfectly clear. All contributions should be forbidden and the Curia should be denied the right to fill German benefices. The result would be the extermination of the "courtesans,"[22] and Hutten used this term not merely in the current sense of the Roman *cortegiani*, but also with reference to the Germans, who owed their churchly revenues to Rome, and in the still wider

21. J. Freund, *Huttens Vadiscus und seine Quelle* (Dissertation, Marburg, 1899).

22. The word "courtesan" was used in the English and German of those days as an equivalent to the Italian *cortegiano*. It connoted especially a courtier at the court of Rome. It changed its meaning in the last quarter of the 16th century.

sense of those who defended the Papacy. But this was only one aspect of the reform of the clergy. The civil government should undertake to employ Church goods directly and indirectly to better ends. At that point he had in mind a war tax, which should make possible the establishment of an army and the execution of a stronger national policy. The government should concern itself also with the problem of poverty and thereby quiet the general social unrest. Finally it should foster the new spirit in society by the support of humanism. The central point, however, was the reform of the clergy. A new priesthood, consecrated to its original purpose, should preach and exemplify German simplicity and purity. The restoration of Christian piety and of primitive German manliness went hand in hand for Hutten.

But the ideal of national character and greatness predominated over the tendency to religious enlightenment in the sense of Erasmus, whose ideas Hutten unquestionably attenuated. His criticism of contemporary sacerdotalism was colored more than that of Erasmus by the ideal of apostolic poverty. Nevertheless, although Hutten was actuated in his attack on the dominant system more by national consciousness and political desires than by religious discrepancies, one ought not therefore to call him an irreligious nature. For him, as for his time, divinity was an indisputable reality with which man must make his peace. Likewise the Church remained an indispensable form of society. One is tempted to say that the religious presuppositions were so predominantly theological that even a heathen—and Hutten was often so described—would have to take account of them if he wished to accomplish anything in the political sphere. But is there really any point in trying to shell out the timeless kernel from a personality which receives its stamp from the interplay of the forces of its time? Have we not seen that Hutten's personality was profoundly stirred by all the woes and the pangs or the longings and the hopes of this period? Was this simply a rôle imposed upon him by destiny? Did he not rather inwardly appropriate the spiritual strivings of his time with a high degree of impressionability? One ought not to call his political interests heathen—the more so because his religious position underwent a distinctly personal development, which shows that for him religion was not simply a means to political ends. We recall that Hutten had praised Erasmus as the prophet of a new piety and theology, and had been kindled to reformatory zeal in the ecclesiastical sphere by contact with his personality and teaching. And even after the commencement of the war on Rome his criticism of the Church, in spite of the assumption of some Lutheran elements, remained essentially humanist. There are, of course, some personal traits in Hutten's attitude to the Roman Church. We have seen already that his position with regard to the Papacy from the outset differed from that of Erasmus, for whom the bad popes were only personal exceptions in the succession of the honorable heads of the Church. He would not have it forgotten, moreover, that many bad popes were no worse Christians at least than many of the laity. The conception of the apostolic commission of the head of the universal Church was dear to him and here he looked for leadership in the new age of culture and peace. On the accession of the Medicean Leo X, successor to the pope pilloried in the *Julius Exclusus*, Erasmus began to dream of a great movement toward peace. The general political situation appeared favorable. In England foreign politics were controlled by his friend and patron, Cardinal Wolsey. Charles had ascended the throne of Spain and had appointed him a counsellor. Now was the chosen moment when the pope would arbitrate in great international disputes and would lead the people in the ways of peace and in the appreciation of the works of peace. In this period he wrote most of his political works, the *Institution of the Christian Prince*, the *Complaint of Peace*, and the *Adages* were expanded with political maxims. More significant was the dedication at just this time of the new edition of the New Testament in Greek to Leo X. In the preface this work for the reconstruction of Christian piety is compared to the construction of the new church of St. Peter.

Hutten's epigrams against Julius II are not originally altogether irreconcilable with the position of Erasmus. He, too, treated Julius II as an exception and directed his satire not against the institution of the Papacy as such. At the same time there was an undertone of German patriotic disgruntlement at the slight cast upon the German monarchs and the hurt done to the welfare of the people, and there was the realization, confirmed by later studies, that the conflict of the spiritual and civil powers—Hutten would have said the spiritual and secular arms—was historically older than the period of Julius and always disadvantageous to the German people. Hence Hutten was early driven to the question of the position of the Papacy in the structure of society. The publication of Valla's *Donatio Constantini* brought to a head the conviction that the Papacy had not merely recently made use of devious ways, but had been guilty of usurpation for many a day.

Hutten, too, had dedicated his work to Pope Leo.[23] He, too, had celebrated him as a prince of peace and restorer of Christian piety. Contact with Erasmus is discernible even here and we must not forget Leo's position in the Reuchlin affair. However, the immoderate language of Hutten with regard to Leo X shows that he expected nothing more from popes. He demanded from Leo as proof of sincerity in the rôle of *Restaurator Pacis* the absolute renunciation of the temporal power of the Papacy, which had been unjustly usurped, "for you are the restorer of peace, but there can be no peace between robbers and robbed without restitution. You would not declare such intentions if you did not intend to fulfill them, for you are not the kind to impose upon us with vain words." The step is only slight from polemic against particular popes to an attack upon the Papacy itself.

23. Hutten, *Opera,* I, 155 ff.

Luther found it hard to renounce the Papacy.[24] He wrestled with the problem between 1518 and 1520 very seriously and Hutten's literary work, as we shall see, played a part. When Luther was persuaded that the popes were corrupted beyond redemption he attempted nevertheless to save the institution, whose decline could not have occurred, so he said, apart from the will of God. While we must uphold the word of God against all outward power, we should endure the dominance of the pope as a trial sent by the Lord. Not until after the clearer formulation of the principle of the priesthood of all believers, as developed in the reformatory tracts of 1520, was he ready to reject the Papacy entirely. The Church was for him now no longer a hierarchical institution, but a community of convinced persons.

Hutten seized the idea of the priesthood of all believers with avidity. He was one of the first to follow Luther in saying that the Church needed no head, for Christ is her head. The political implications of the idea interested Hutten more than the theological premises. Luther's conclusion agreed perfectly with his own political passion and his historical studies. On that account he neglected a deeper reconciliation of the Lutheran theology with the ethic of humanism. The Church of the Middle Ages had divided society into two classes and had assigned different standards to each. Only the clergy were called upon to fulfill completely the commands of Christ and they, too, only in finely differentiated degrees. Lesser demands were imposed upon the laity. Celibacy and the Sacrament of Ordination most obviously set the clergy apart. This medieval division of society was not essentially contested by the humanists, who frequently allegorized the churchly sacraments and even regarded celibacy more from the point of view of expediency than of faith, and the segregation of the faithful into the more and the less perfect corre-

24. Compare K. Holl, "Die Entstehung von Luthers Kirchenbegriff," in his *Gesammelte Aufsätze zur Kirchengschichte,* I (2/3d edition, Tübingen, 1923), 288 ff.

sponded only too well with the humanist separation of the learned from the unlearned. We see this also in Hutten, who, while utilizing Luther's ideas on the Papacy and the priesthood of all believers, yet missed the logical implications. He did not see that the humanist division of society was thereby destroyed. Hutten attacked the clergy primarily because they did not fulfill the higher righteousness, the evidence of which was to be found in the exemplification of apostolic conduct rather than in the acceptance of evangelical truth.

He did go on, however, to apply his reformatory views to the other ranks of society in a measure, though the emphasis here was not on primitive Christian piety, but on primitive German virtue. The two were inseparable for him. Here he cut deeper than Erasmus, who saw his Christian renaissance in the seeds sown by the example of a cultured and segregated aristocracy. But humanist ideas so weighed upon Hutten's conscience that he could not be content to cultivate them in retirement. He might forgo criticism of the sacramental system, more readily in fact than Erasmus, but he would not abandon the propagation of reformatory ideas among the masses, though at this point, as we have seen, he had some inhibitions. Yet national romanticism was not the only factor inducing him to participation in public life—had this been all, he might have been a historian—but also the state of his own character and his need for theoretical justification. We may even go further and say that his political zeal cooled when he could discover for it no theoretical warrant. Particularly indicative for Hutten is the prominent place occupied by *Fortuna* in his thinking, more so than for any other German humanist. In his reflections on the problem of fate he broke no new ground, but his constant outreaching for a solution is noteworthy for his thinking on the relation of the individual to the course of history. The use of classical forms is not to be interpreted as an attack on Christianity as such, but merely as an attempt to escape from scholastic restrictions. Erasmus was endeavoring in the theoretical sphere to vindicate a larger place for reason, and Hutten was now making the same effort in the practical realm. This attempt, however, was of necessity restricted on German soil. A Machiavelli could compress his whole philosophy of life in the problem of Fortune and could discover the meaning of history in her conflict with *virtù.*[25] He was thus able to coördinate in a significant context the evil spirits of the political life. Whether he went too far need not now concern us. But Hutten was unable to discover in the combination of man's power and reason a sufficient counterbalance to Fortune. He would check her by reason, as he wrote to Pirckheimer on taking up service at Mainz, but reason none the less plays a minor rôle. "Yes, I have been borne along, but not against my will. I am led, but with reason's consent. Nor am I so led that at a signal from reason, the guide of life, I cannot retrace my steps, and when satiety sets in retrieve myself and take refuge from the voyage in some harbor."[26]

Reason, then, cannot prevail against the power of a blind and arbitrary Fortune to shatter its plans. Reason can merely indicate the point at which to withdraw from the *vita activa;* she cannot supply the means of victory. The world of Fortune remained for Hutten, in spite of all allurements, bad. Here he was not unaffected by the pacifistic longings of the humanists. This explains why he does not hearken more to Fortune and try to attain greater realism in his ideas. Utopian he knew they were, but he preferred to keep them intact and oppose them to the world. He did not suffer himself to enter fully into the sphere in which *virtù* and Fortune are at war. He was not this-worldly enough to treat the realm of outward events without more ado as the world, nor had he enough self-confidence to wrestle with it, relying only on his own resources. At the close of his dialogue *Fortuna* he turned, disillu-

25. E. W. Mayer, *Machiavellis Geschichtsauffassung und sein Begriff virtù* (*Historische Bibliothek,* Vol. 31, Munich, 1912).

26. Hutten, *Opera,* I, 205.

sioned, from the Goddess of Chance to a Christian chapel to seek the fulfilment of his wishes from the "Redeemer Christ."[27] This artistic scene is symbolical of his deep dependence upon the Christian view of Providence. One might say, paradoxically, that he appealed to the classical deity in order not to blaspheme the Christian, for he was unwilling to make God responsible for the evil and extremity of the world. He could explain earthly misery and earthly injustice only if God had divided His lordship over the goods of chance with a demoniac goddess. He comforted himself somewhat with regard to injustice by the ancient preaching that every outward blessing awakens the longing for more, whereas misfortune is a spur to moral improvement. He wished rather that the exploited might be compensated and the bad punished, and when that really happened, as in the case of Ulrich von Würtemberg, he suggested that this might be the work of Divine Providence, though only with hesitancy, for the theologians had overdone this sort of thing. The belief in divine justice he retained: we can also say, the belief that justice is divine. His dynamic attitude to life, which drove him to activity, was at once enlarged and restricted by a moralistic view. Only that man, he held, can venture into the dread realm of Fortune who knows that she is not the supreme arbiter in human life. She may indeed possess outward glory and power, but she does not determine the justice of the idea. Only as a humanist was Hutten prepared to be a statesman, for only humanism, which is identical with justice, armed him against Fortune. He would appeal to her, but he would not commit his judgment to her.

A logical, consistent formulation he never found for the problem which continually distressed him. All of these attempts at systematization whirled through his brain without being tied down, but they reveal, nevertheless, a constancy of aim and attitude. If he sometimes worshipped

27. *Ibid.*, p. 99.

Fortune more than he could justify, he was in the main steadfast when persecution overtook him. "When Fortune gives me the opportunity I will make a valiant effort," he wrote to Erasmus in November, 1520, though the statement is prefaced by the assertion, "I do not contest the outcome."[28] During the fight he always retained the hope, as he expressed it to Luther on April 17, 1521, that "God can no longer tolerate such vileness. He is a just and mighty judge."[29] With such a conviction he was willing to dare the uttermost and would not suffer himself to be daunted by external misfortune and the collapse of all outward expectations. He saw in his cause not God's cause, like Luther, yet a just cause. In persecution he found consolation not in a vital communion with God, as did Luther, but also not—as we might perhaps have expected—in a hope of personal reward. He was content with the simple consciousness that in what he did he was true to the idea which led beyond Fortune, and, let it be said once and for all, would continue to live. This mood inspired the verse of his poem.

Though sore to press my will
The "courtesans" be bent
The heart they cannot kill
That is of sound intent.[30]

This will-power to maintain the integrity of conscience did not plumb the profound spiritual depths of Luther's unruffled force of conscience, but it was enough to give Hutten a high degree of understanding, if not for Luther's cause, at least for his personality.

28. Hutten, *Opera,* I, 423. Allen, *Opus epistularum Erasmi,* Ep. 1161, IV, 380 ff.
29. Hutten, *Opera,* II, 55. M. Luther, *Werke, Briefwechsel,* II, 301 ff.
30. Hutten, *Opera,* II, 93.

IX

HUTTEN AND LUTHER

DEEPLY significant for the total development of Christianity in the West is the fact that Luther undertook his spiritual revolution not as an outsider to the Roman Church but as one who sought to fulfil the demands of the Catholic faith.[1] What drove him to the cloister was nothing other than the fundamental query of Western monasticism, "How can I serve God perfectly?" The unqualified purity of his conscience and the strength of his religious grasp left him discontented with the answer which the Church of his day gave to the question. When he squarely faced the terrors of God's judgments, the cleavage began to widen which separated him from his times. The unbridgeable chasm between the moral demands of Christianity and their actual realization, between the Christian man and the natural man—a chasm which the medieval Church had not obliterated but had tried to fill up with its system of penance and grace—this chasm yawned before Luther with sheer precipitance. When in the cloister he tried to love the Lord his God with all his heart he realized that human effort cannot obliterate sin, and the laws of the Church only make things worse by regarding a turning to God as meritorious. When the holy and absolutely exacting God seems to turn away from sinful man, how then shall man dare to seek fellowship with God?

But here, where despondency was about to undo him, he found a way out. God does not suffer Himself to be compelled by human conduct or human work, but He works, He acts. He awakens the consciousness of human imper-

1. Compare K. Holl, "Was verstand Luther unter Religion?" in his *Gesammelte Aufsätze zur Kirchengeschichte,* Vol. I: *Luther,* (2d edition, Tübingen, 1923), pp. 1 ff.

fection, and precisely because He wishes to call man to Himself. As a just judge He rejects man utterly; as a loving God He grants him complete forgiveness. In faith in the just and forgiving God one may realize the truth of Paul's words, "The just shall live by faith."

A consideration of this source of Luther's piety suggests at once that his experience and the thinking of the German humanists lay in different spheres. One may doubt at the outset whether humanism ever could understand Luther. That Catholicism should reject him as a revolutionary was natural, for his repudiation of good works and sacramental grace struck at the very vitals of the Catholic system. But humanism also stood at a different level, because it, too, had endeavored to bridge the gulf which Luther broke down between the Christian man and the natural man. If no one in Germany had gone so far as to demolish the transcendence of the medieval cosmic hierarchy in the interests of this-worldliness and immanence, none the less humanism had gone a long way toward reduction and simplification of the gradations. Religious impulses were moralized and man was thus exempted from the frightful antinomies of Christianity, and his conscience no longer shuddered before titanic spiritual forces. Between Luther's religious experience and the efforts of humanism there was no inner affinity.

Was it, then, a mere illusion when humanism and Lutheranism felt so close to each other in Germany after the Leipsic debate? One might think so in view of the fact that the majority of the humanists after a few years returned to Rome and made their peace with the Church. But although this outcome was symptomatic of the character and ideas of the humanists, nevertheless Luther did have certain affinities with humanism, and there was, besides, the possibility of a league of good omen because of the spiritual, political, and social constellations in the heavens at the moment.

We may take for granted that Luther was not influenced by humanism in his decisive years.[2] He was not an intimate of the Erfurt circle of humanists, and we must not so interpret the letter of Crotus after adherence to Luther in 1520. At the university Luther had found teachers who emphasized linguistic studies, but they were none the less scholastics. His release from distress of conscience is explicable only in the light of a monkish, scholastic environment. That is why his preaching had the power to combat successfully the Catholic faith and the Roman system. This, too, is partly the reason why any tendencies in Germany to a movement of enlightenment were stifled. There was in Germany widespread discontent with scholasticism, but the force of religious impulses was too strong to allow the intellectual emancipation to take root. Even humanism moderated its tone in Germany and lost something of its cutting edge. Only on the graves of the wars of religion could the Enlightenment raise its head in Germany and even then was compelled for a long time to share the leadership with orthodoxy and pietism.

But humanism did help to disintegrate scholasticism. The pretensions of the Church were discredited by its criticism and the way thus far prepared for the Reformation. A common enmity strongly enticed humanism to come over into the Lutheran camp. At least this was true for Hutten. The outward similarity blinded him to the inner cleavage, and the opening of his eyes was rendered the more difficult by the fact that humanism had something to contribute to Lutheranism at one point. It was not merely "languages," as Luther said, but the grounding of salvation in Scripture which constituted a deep affinity between Protestantism and humanism.

Luther had not arrived at his new faith through the authority of Scripture, but rather through his own spiritual experience. Nevertheless he attained this new knowledge of Christian truth through the study of the Gospels, to which he had been more and more driven by perusing the

2. See O. Scheel, *Luther* (Tübingen, 1917), I, 229 ff.

Church Fathers. The fact that his faith rested on common cultural ground made it intelligible. For Luther was no visionary. Not for his own sake but for others unconsciously he became a reformer, first as a shepherd of souls, then as a doctor of theology and Biblical exegete. Here was the point at which alliance was made between the languages and the Gospels, an alliance of the highest significance for the future of Protestantism. A concrete expression of it is found in the coöperation of Luther and Melanchthon, and the emergence of the Lutheran clergy as a learned class.

To be sure, this is the only common element of humanism and Lutheranism which survived the century. What attracted the humanists to Luther's exegesis and made them regard him as one of themselves was the fact that they were on the way to a better understanding of primitive Christianity. Usually they stopped with the Church Fathers, from whom to the Gospels the step was but short. Hence the difference of their exegesis from Luther's readily eluded them. Significant is it not only that they did adopt him but that he could talk of "our Erasmus."[3] A common opposition to scholasticism served to overcome any misgivings. And need we wonder that Luther was attracted to humanism, which before him had ventured to launch such vigorous criticism against the Church? He allowed himself to go a step with the humanists, while at the same time struggling consciously to work out his teaching in that he tried to think through the religious implications of the empirical data supplied by his forced entry into the great arena. Not until after 1521 did sharp differences begin to manifest themselves with the knights, with the "heavenly prophets," with Erasmus, and with the peasants.

Just as the indulgence controversy brought Luther into line with the nationalist movement, so here we can say what we have said in general with regard to his development in these years. He took over from his environment

3. M. Luther, *Werke, Briefwechsel,* I, 361 ff. Allen, *Opus epistolarum Erasmi,* Ep. 933, III, 516 ff.

whatever he could combine with his religious position. His attitude to political life, however, had undergone a certain modification due to the rapid course of events. The objective was always the same: to create sufficient room in the world for Christian freedom. He tried at first to combine diverse approaches to the realization of this idea. New men should be awakened by his preaching. But was not a change also necessary in the general scheme of things? Luther could have denied this flatly had he considered only that the world is bad and the Christian is inwardly emancipated from all law by his justification. Luther had to wrestle with the question, however, because he grounded his Christian principles not only on the love of God but also on the love of man. Here again he renewed one of the fundamental antinomies of primitive Christianity. This experience of tension compelled him step by step to enter upon the discussion of public relations and the development of his own political and vocational ethic.

This is not the place to pursue in detail the development of Luther's political thought.[3a] Suffice it for our purpose that from 1519 to 1520 Luther had not attained clarity at many points. His fight was for the "freedom of the Christian man." But he could employ many of the particular criticisms which the opponents of Roman Catholicism in Germany had elaborated with other presuppositions and purposes. There were many points in which the German and the Christian struggles against Rome coincided. Hutten could rightly see a comrade in Luther in so far as his Christian reform broke some of the bonds of the German people; and Luther, too, could approve of the national movement in a measure because the dominance of the pope weighed upon no people so heavily as upon the Germans. The mood which he came to know in Augsburg in 1518 had influenced him markedly and from that time forward he had an eye for the political needs of his people. National expectations moved him also. He, too, greeted the young emperor in the eager hope that Charles

3a. Cf. H. Holborn, *A History of Modern Germany: The Reformation*, pp. 175-6, 186-91, 193-4, 209-10.

would not renounce the Gospel and would resist the usurpation of the Papacy. With all this in mind he was able to compose his great reform program in 1520, which he published in the *Address to the German Nobility.*[4] Here as never afterwards Luther appropriated the national aspirations and made the national powers responsible for a comprehensive church reform. He came so close to Hutten that some assumed this tract to have been written under the influence of Hutten's dialogues of April, 1520. Some even went so far as to suppose that Luther had been emboldened to make this vigorous attack on the Papacy because of the protection offered him by the knights, von Sickingen and the Franconian, Sylvester von Schaumburg.

Such assumptions will not bear examination, for the tract has all the earmarks of the Lutheran spirit, which, as we have seen, departed from current conceptions and even here moved along its own religious lines. If Luther made himself the spokesman of the nation against the Roman Court, and if he incorporated in his tract the ancient grievances, nevertheless his polemic acquired its peculiar quality from the undergirding of religious assumptions. This is all the more apparent in the tract *On the Freedom of the Christian Man* published shortly after, for it was only through an abolition of the sacramental system and the development of a vocational ethic, rooted in his view of God, that the way was opened for the reform of the internal relations of the *Reich.* The arguments by which he justified the right of the civil magistrates—the appeal in the *Address to the German Nobility* is not merely to nobles in the limited technical sense—to take a hand in the affairs of the Church constituted something quite new. Just as every Christian is bound to use his calling in the service of

4. M. Luther, *Werke,* VI, 381 ff. Compare in the first place W. Köhler, *Luthers Schrift 'An den christlichen Adel deutscher Nation'* (1895), and "Zu Luthers Schrift 'An den christlichen Adel deutscher Nation,'" *Zeitschrift für Rechtsgeschichte,* 44, *Kanonistische Abteilung,* VI, 1 ff. E. Kohlmeyer, *Die Entstehung der Schrift Luthers an den christlichen Adel* (Gütersloh, 1922), and "Noch ein Wort zu Luthers Schrift an den christlichen Adel," *Zeitschrift für Kirchengeschichte,* Neue Folge, VII (1925).

his neighbor, so the magistrate uses his sword out of Christian love for his fellow men. If now he sees his duty to lie in the purification of the spiritual order he is fulfilling the obligation laid upon him by God.

In view of this fundamentally different treatment of the subject, any particular borrowings from the nationalist polemic are not of primary significance, though the verbal reminiscences in Luther's writing from Hutten's *Roman Trinity* are not unimportant. Nationalist complaint against Rome might easily have been derived from other sources. Yet the lingering of language betrays the impression which Hutten made upon him from a distance. The national demands were not the staple of Luther's message, and their very character was altered through his conception of the freedom of the Christian man. Nevertheless they had a deep hold upon his thinking in this period and Hutten was involved.

The inference has been made from Luther's tardy answer to Hutten's letter to Wittenberg of February 28 that the reformer was indifferent. But the letter to Capito of April 30, 1520[5] reveals the cause to have been lack of a messenger, and this is probably no polite evasion, for we know that the channels of communication between Hutten and Luther were not always open. Unfortunately Luther's reply to him at the end of April is not extant. Certainly Luther did not mean to relinquish the protection of the Elector of Saxony. Nevertheless we know from other letters[6] that the offers of protection from Sylvester von Schaumburg, Sickingen, and Hutten did not leave him cold, for they demonstrated that his word had reached not only the theologians and the simple laity, but also the holders of power, who exercised an influence beyond his range. To the political directors of Germany he resolved to dedicate his great plan of public reform. Hence we may

5. M. Luther, *Werke, Briefwechsel,* II, 93.

6. *Ibid.,* pp. 146 and 162. An English translation of the two letters in *Luther's Correspondence and Other Contemporary Letters,* edited by P. Smith (Philadelphia, 1913), pp. 339 ff.

interpret the gestures of Sickingen and the Franconian knights and the letters and agitation of Hutten as belonging not exactly to the causes, but to the historical background of Luther's *Address to the Nobility*.

Nor is this all. The Leipsic debate in which Luther was trapped by Eck into unpremeditated admissions necessitated a rethinking of the idea of the Church.[7] In the midst of extensive studies over the theological and legal bases of the Roman Church Hutten's edition of the *Donatio Constantini* fell into Luther's hands at the end of February 1520.[8] Premonitions now took on the guise of facts. The pope became Antichrist, the demonic forerunner of the approaching cataclysm. Luther was deeply imbued with late medieval apocalypticism and in view of the menacing calamities of the time was not infrequently shaken to the depths by the expectation of the imminent judgment of God. This was his mood when, in the summer of 1520, the papal bull reached him.

Yet Luther could easily leap from the frightful scenes portrayed in Dürer's woodcuts of the Apocalypse to the picture of the civil authorities as the scourge of God sent to wreak vengeance on the antichristian abominations. Hutten, the knight, may well have been more impressive to Luther as one of the four horsemen than as the author of the *Roman Trinity*. In any case, in November 1520, he could break out with the despondent sigh, "if only Hutten had captured the papal nuntios."[9] This was at the moment when the legates were travelling throughout the various portions of Germany and consigning Luther's tracts to the pyre. Then it was that he resolved by a public and revolutionary act to proclaim the results of his studies in the canon law by committing to the flames before the gates of Wittenberg not only the bull of Leo X banning him

7. See K. Holl, "Die Entstehung von Luthers Kirchenbegriff," in his *Gesammelte Aufsätze zur Kirchengeschichte*, I, 288 ff., especially pp. 317 ff.

8. M. Luther, *Werke, Briefwechsel*, II, 48 ff. Hutten, *Opera*, I, 324. *Luther's Correspondence*, ed. by P. Smith, p. 291.

9. M. Luther, *Werke, Briefwechsel*, II, 213 ff. Hutten, *Opera*, I, 426.

personally, but also the law books of the See of Rome. In all this antipapal campaign of 1520 there were contacts with Hutten enough.

Even his political plans evoked an interest in Wittenberg. The analogy of the Reuchlin affair with that of Luther did not escape Reuchlin's nephew, Melanchthon, nor Luther either. His reply to the condemnation of his teaching by the universities of Louvain and Cologne occurred in March, 1520, just after the reception of Hutten's letter to Melanchthon and directly following the reading of Hutten's edition of the *Donatio*. Was it a mere accident that he threw in a remark to the effect that the two theological faculties could not damage him since their reputations had been so sadly damaged in the Reuchlin feud?[10] Hutten must have seen this response just before going to the Netherlands[11] and the reference to Reuchlin would please him, as it did Erasmus.[12] The Wittenbergers in turn were following Hutten's projects in the Netherlands. Would he attain his object of winning over the imperial court?[13]

We may grant that in the second half of the year Luther was more inclined to give a purely religious interpretation to Christian freedom. The hopes entertained in Wittenberg for Charles V waned together with the expectation of the reform of the Church through the constituted authorities. But Luther had no mind to see his cause furthered by such disorders as the student riots at Wittenberg. In the *Freedom of the Christian Man* and the *Babylonian Captivity* he had sharply segregated Christian freedom from the world and thereby paved the way for the position that the soul does not depend for rejuvenation on outward circumstances, but only on the working of the pure word of God. This was the faith in which he went to Worms and made his heroic stand before the emperor and the estates. But it was the faith of his own pro-

10. M. Luther, *Werke,* VII, 183.
11. Hutten, *Opera,* I, 340. M. Luther, *Werke, Briefwechsel,* II, 87.
12. M. Luther, *Werke,* VI, 171.
13. Hutten, *Opera,* I, 358.

phetic calling which he was not inclined to make a norm for others, and which, from now on, should under no circumstances be compromised by even a casual approval of Hutten's resort to violence. The knight's other political plans, however, were not thereby ruled out. His writings of this period, in particular his complaint to the Elector of Saxony, are mentioned in Luther's correspondence and without any apparent disapprobation.[14] Hutten's keen and caustic annotations to Leo's bull must have given him real delight, and his advice to Hutten in January, 1521, to abstain from his projected declaration of war against the Papacy does not indicate any real breach, in view of the fact that at the moment Hutten himself had indicated to Luther a readiness to wait.[15] On February 9 Luther wrote: "Hutten and others are writing courageously for me and just now are preparing songs which will not be especially pleasing to this Babylon."[16] Luther's friendliness toward Hutten had suffered no change through the events of that year.

But before the Diet of Worms opened on the day of the Three Kings in 1521 great changes had taken place in Hutten's life. The journey to the Netherlands realized not a single one of his innumerable expectations. The trip and the residence appear to have occupied about two months. In Louvain he met Erasmus[17] and disclosed to him the far-reaching plans to be achieved through the Hapsburg brothers. Erasmus did not take these schemes seriously enough even to stand in the way and was quite willing to give letters of introduction to humanist friends at court. Hutten's departure was precipitant, for the ecclesiastical court was on the scent. On the way back from Brussels—

14. Hutten, *Opera,* I, 345, 354, 369/70, 420, and 437. M. Luther, *Werke, Briefwechsel,* II, 98, 111, 184 ff., 190 ff., 235 ff.

15. Hutten, *Opera,* I, 435 ff., II, 5 ff. M. Luther, *Werke, Briefwechsel,* II, 230 ff., 248 ff.

16. M. Luther, *Werke, Briefwechsel,* II, 258 ff., 262 ff. Hutten, *Opera,* II, 6, 9.

17. Hutten, *Opera,* II, 317 ff. Compare W. Kaegi, "Hutten und Erasmus," *Historische Vierteljahrsschrift,* XXII (1924), 226.

we do not know whether he actually reached the court of Ferdinand—he met on the open highway the terrified Hochstraten. Hutten was sufficiently controlled not to run him through.[18] The restraint must have been an effort in view of the blast which he had just blown on the eve of his departure from Germany. On the fourth of June, the day on which he wrote to Luther, he had sent the following letter to Mosellanus: "I have started the war on the papal tyranny. . . . I have made up my mind to go on, whatever the outcome. The wretches should burn. Burn they shall, even if I burn with them."[19]

On his return to Mainz he discovered that here, too, he was no longer secure, for the complaints previously lodged against him by Eck at Rome had had their repercussions here. Hutten had not taken them very seriously. He was foaming for the fight. If his opponents wished it, all the better. Nor had the danger to his person inhibited him from adherence to Luther. But on Hutten's return the archbishop was already informed through his diplomatic representatives at Rome that the Curia would take action.[20] Hutten withdrew to Steckelberg. His printer, Schöffer, was arrested shortly afterwards in Mainz, while a hint was dropped to the knightly publicist that he might retrieve himself on easy terms.[21] This happened in the beginning of August, when the news reached Mainz of the instructions entrusted by the Curia at Rome to the nuntios, Aleander and Caracciolo, on their departure for the imperial court.[22] The Curia had resolved at last to expend every effort to quench the fire of heresy in Germany. One may wonder that they had taken so long, but general political considerations had dragged Luther's trial through-

18. Hutten, *Opera,* I, 434.

19. See G. Bauch in *Vierteljahrsschrift für Kultur und Literatur der Renaissance,* I (1886), 489 ff. Hutten, *Opera,* IV, 689.

20. Compare Hutten, *Opera,* I, 362 ff., 408.

21. Hutten, *Opera,* I, 367 ff. Allen, *Opus epistularum Erasmi,* Ep. 1135, IV, 328 ff.

22. The instruction edited by P. Balan, *Monumenta reformationis Lutheranae* (Ratisbonae, 1884), pp. 8 ff.

out two years at Rome and the spiritual lords of Germany were too feeble and unreliable to put out the blaze on their own motion.[23] Highly characteristic is the position of the Archbishop of Mainz. His tolerance for the antipapal campaign conducted at his court by Hutten after 1518 shows that he had his own ideas with regard to his position as a bishop of the Roman Church. As a matter of fact he carried on an entirely ruthless and egoistic policy throughout these years. His ambition was the primacy of the Roman Church and he utilized his vote as an imperial elector without a qualm to displace the Curia in the holding of German benefices and revenues. An anti-Roman publicist, under certain circumstances, might be used in the interests of such a policy. But even in Luther's case, too, he was tepid so soon as he saw that public opinion was warming for Luther. One would have expected the archbishop to exert himself to the utmost to lay hands on the obstinate monk, since Wittenberg belonged to the ecclesiastical province of Mainz. And if this was impossible because of the intervention of the Elector of Saxony, Albert might, at least, have taken measures in the lands under his direct princely jurisdiction.

But little happened, partly because he was not averse to utilizing this affair as a means of bringing pressure to bear on Rome and more because the structure of the ecclesiastical principalities was too feeble. During the first ten years of the Reformation it is a safe generalization that the spiritual territories were far behind the secular in battling for the faith. The weakness of the government displayed itself especially in Mainz. The nobility in the ecclesiastical foundations had to be taken into account and

23. For the history of Luther's trial see Karl Müller, "Luthers römischer Prozess," *Zeitschrift für Kirchengeschichte,* XXIV (1903); P. Kalkoff, *Forschungen zu Luthers römischem Prozess* (1905); and *Zu Luthers römischem Prozess* (Gotha, 1912), and a host of special articles by the same author chiefly in *Zeitschrift für Kirchengeschichte* and *Archiv für Reformationsgeschichte.* Kalkoff's studies on Luther's trial need, however, a critical examination throughout. Compare E. Stracke, *Luthers grosses Selbstzeugnis 1545* (Leipsic, 1926).

were an uncertain quantity. The councils of the princes were infected with secret Lutheranism. A personality such as the court preacher and later counsellor, Capito, may serve as an example.[24] He was genuinely interested in both Hutten and Luther. So long as Erasmus tilted cautiously for Luther, Capito, in counselling Albert, could appeal to the authority of the prince of the humanists. To the influence of Capito, and men like him, we may attribute the fact that Albert not only remained inactive, but even wrote to Luther in February, 1520, that the responsibility for inciting him lay with his opponents.[25] The difference between curial and conciliar theory was treated as a matter of religious indifference. Luther was indeed urged to moderation, but only with the word of Gamaliel that his cause might be of God. Furthermore the highest ecclesiastical dignitary of Germany did not blush to say that during the course of three years he had not been able to find time to read Luther's writings.

High time it was for the Curia to take up again the reins which had so long been dragging on the ground. Even though the results of the imperial election did not satisfy the Church's political aspirations, in the religious sphere the best could be expected from Charles V. Under these auspices the definitive stage of Luther's trial opened in January, 1520. By the end of May the essential outcome had been reached and on the fifteenth of June the bull *Exsurge Domine* was published.[26] The harsh tone was not incompatible with certain concessions. Luther was not condemned outright, but was given sixty days in which to recant. Only forty-one propositions out of his works were excerpted and condemned. This was a highly questionable and undiscriminating procedure and constituted one of the objections employed in Germany to hinder the publication and execution of the bull.

24. See J. W. Baum, *Capito und Butzer* (Elberfeld, 1860), and P. Kalkoff, *W. Capito im Dienste des Erzbischofs von Mainz* (Berlin, 1907).

25. M. Luther, *Werke, Briefwechsel,* II, 53 ff.

26. See P. Kalkoff, *Die Entscheidungsjahre der Reformation* (Munich, 1917), pp. 128 ff.

Eck, who had had a large influence in the composition of the document, crossed the Alps shortly thereafter as papal nuntio to care for the publication of the bull in the western portions of the Empire from Bavaria to Brandenburg, while Aleander was to represent the pope at the court of the emperor in the Netherlands and at the Diet of the Empire at Worms, in order to secure the publication of the bull together with executory mandates from the civil authorities in the western and Rhenish territories.

The bull was expressly directed against Luther and his adherents. Whether Hutten was meant, too, was left deliberately ambiguous. Aleander was empowered to decide on the expediency of pronouncing him a disciple of Luther, but left the weapon in the scabbard, since it would be possible to proceed against Hutten directly on the basis of the regulations of the Lateran council visiting severe penalties upon the authors of tracts against the pope or the dignitaries of the Church. In any case the decision had been reached to act with vigor. Eck, too, had denounced Hutten at Rome and Aleander's instructions as Roman legate applied to the burning not merely of heretical writings, but also of political manifestoes such as "Hutten's preface to Ferdinand, the *Roman Trinity*, and the like." In the papal brief to Archbishop Albert on July 12 the preface was again singled out.[27]

The question was whether the papal nuntios in Germany would succeed in publishing the bull against Luther without too great difficulty. Then the future would have to decide in what manner to commence the process against Hutten. One point was obvious that the extradition of a German nobleman was more difficult of attainment than that of a heretical monk and, since the Lutheran question was more important and more pressing, all of Aleander's efforts were concentrated here. The complications of the German constitution slowed up his activity markedly. In the imperial Netherlands the case was easy. The land for the moment was not greatly touched by Lutheran teach-

27. Hutten, *Opera*, I, 362.

ing and the civil government in conjunction with the ecclesiastical authorities had the necessary power to proceed against every heresy. Here there was readiness to go ahead at once. But in other territories the execution of the papal instructions was difficult in view of the popular temper and the impotence of the magistrates. When on November 28 the papal legate witnessed the burning of Lutheran books in Mainz, during the foregoing celebration of the mass he was almost mobbed and barely saved his dignity, and on the way out from the church, when Luther's books were piled up in the public place prior to burning, the headsman asked the crowd whether the books had been properly condemned. On the booming of a many-throated no, he jumped down declaring that he would not discharge an improper sentence. The next day, on the authority of the elector, a grave-digger was impressed and finished off the nasty business. But the legatine dignity was scarcely saved in this fashion. The German bishops alone were not in a position to create respect for the papal orders, and the civil princes and lords were too divided. Only through the support of the imperial power could the representatives of the Curia hope to erect an obstacle to the spread of the conflagration of evangelical preaching.

To this end Aleander bent his efforts, seconded by his predecessor as papal legate at the imperial court, Caracciolo. Shortly after, in the last weeks of October, the young emperor had taken the oath of the German kings in the cathedral of Charlemagne at Aix-la-Chapelle. The most important part of the oath referred to the protection of the faith and the Church. At the close of the ceremony an emissary of Leo X proclaimed him the "elected Roman Emperor." At once the legates presented him with the draft of a mandate against Luther and the Elector of Saxony was compelled to make strenuous representations to the emperor that he would alienate public opinion in the *Reich* should he yield to the inducements of the legates. His attention was also called to the fact that the electoral constitution contained the promise that no German should be delivered to Rome without a trial. The counter assurance was demanded of him that Luther should be summoned to the diet at Worms.

This demand, of course, met with bitter opposition on the part of the legates. Luther had been legally condemned by the Roman Church. The case appeared to be purely religious and theological. Should the civil power exercise in this case any judgment at all, let alone a dissenting one? The diet might indeed be given an ecclesiastical caste by the preponderance of the bishops, but would be thereby threatened, on the other hand, with becoming a national church council independent of the pope.

The bull *Exsurge Domine*, with its forty-one wrenched extracts, was no longer an adequate basis for papal action now that the document had been subjected on all sides to critical inspection. When, then, the sixty days of grace expired the Curia set to work to give the prosecution fresh impetus and a new bull appeared on January 3, which unequivocally placed Luther and his sect under the papal ban. A brief accompanied the bull appointing an inquisitorial board with the necessary authority to pursue or absolve the sinner. Only three persons besides Luther were singled out for specific mention and their cases reserved for the pope, namely the two Nurembergers, Lazarus Spengler and Willibald Pirckheimer, along with Ulrich von Hutten.

The fluctuations of these tangled months may the better enable us to understand Hutten's personal fortunes.

At Mainz also Hutten's case was not at first regarded as a question of faith, and for that reason light conditions could be laid down: if he stopped his anti-Roman polemic he might have peace. But he spurned the proposal. On the eighth of August he wrote to Capito: "This fire is already kindled and I should not be surprised if it could be put out only by my ruin; but in this fight the consciousness of rectitude gives me more strength than they derive from outward power. Break through the ranks; now is the time to strike."[28] And in similar words, on August 28, 1520, he formed his resolve not to recant his publications.[29] A reconciliation was henceforth practically out of the question.

It was a great and honorable decision, in spite of a possible touch of obstinacy and pride not to appear as a deserter before the world. But he drew to himself the lightning of the ecclesiastical and imperial ban, without the assurance that he would not be hit. He was incomparably brave, even though he could still count on strong support. Hopes for the emperor were not yet abandoned and lively expectations were entertained for a popular movement and especially for Sickingen. To him at Ebernburg Hutten went in September, lest his parents at Steckelberg be involved in the affair. Though he had deliberately taken the offensive in the political struggle, at the same time he was now willing to portray his opponents publicly as the aggressors. He would arouse sympathy by crying to all the world that he who struck a blow for the common good and for the truth was being excluded from all fellowship. But his person came to connote a political program the moment he repudiated the way of ease. He had a right to associate himself so closely with the cause and without doubt the picture of the German knight prosecuted by Rome exerted a potent influence.

This is the figure displayed in the many "manifestoes" issued in September from Ebernburg and addressed to the emperor, the Elector of Saxony, and all the estates.[30] Significant is the legal treatment of the case. The constant complaint is that he had been condemned without a hearing. As a matter of fact he had the right to a hearing, and that before the emperor, so long as his case was not treated solely as a question of faith; and at the outset it was not. Charles V was obligated by his electioneering promises to grant such a hearing. Hutten was therefore right in de-

28. Hutten, *Opera,* I, 367.

29. See P. Kalkoff, *Ulrich von Hutten und die Reformation* (Leipsic, 1920), p. 241.

30. Hutten, *Opera,* I, 371 ff.

manding a legal trial. At the same time the manifesto to Charles V intimated that Hutten was ready and able to defend his cause with the sword. Nevertheless he would surrender everything into the hands of the emperor. The passionateness of his polemic was intensified as he felt his person to be openly and secretly persecuted by Rome. In the main he adhered to the plan of reform through the legal authorities, that is, the estates under the direction of the emperor, as announced the year before. Even then he had envisaged the possibility that the reform might issue not in peace but in war and bloodshed. Precisely this unruly tendency in his war on the Romanists began now to dominate his thinking and coalesced with the intention to resist the persecutors with his own sword. In November he strode down the Rhine to Cologne, where the papal nuntios were gathered at the court of Charles V. Among Hutten's associates—and he was not squeamish as to the company he kept—threats were disseminated against the papal nuntios so that their friends might find it necessary to warn them. The Elector Frederick, who was also at Cologne, brought the news to Saxony that Hutten had prepared a direct attack on the nuntios, and Luther was by no means incredulous, since Hutten had informed him in August of his intent to strike the Romanists both with books *and with blades.*[31] Nothing beyond words actually occurred, however, though every one pricked up his ears at the knight's fulminations. Hutten correctly informed Luther on the ninth of December that thus far no force had been employed.[32]

Apparently Sickingen took the lead in keeping alive his hopes for the emperor, and Sickingen's judgment must have seemed warranted in Hutten's eyes, for he it was who elicited from Charles V at Cologne a promise that Hutten would not be condemned without a hearing.[33] It was the

31. Hutten, *Opera,* I, 369. M. Luther, *Werke, Briefwechsel,* II, 190. Compare P. Kalkoff, *Ulrich von Hutten und die Reformation,* pp. 262 ff.
32. Hutten, *Opera,* I, 435 ff. M. Luther, *Werke, Briefwechsel,* II, 230 ff.
33. *Ibid.*

same promise made in fulfilment of election pledges to the Elector of Saxony in the case of Luther. Besides, Sickingen's stock with the Emperor seemed to be going up. The *condottiere*, who already had a claim for his share in the imperial election, now made a further contract of mercenary service with the House of Hapsburg. In November the emperor was especially gracious to him at Cologne and reenforced the political bond by borrowing from him twenty thousand Rhenish gulden without security or interest. Sickingen came away from Cologne with the impression that the friendship between the pope and the emperor would not last forever.[34] He even entertained hopes for a reform of the Church at the initiation of the emperor, the more so because Hutten strengthened his conviction that the Church was in need of a drastic reform. Luther's writings, which Hutten had read and explained to him at Ebernburg, captivated the lord of the castle. On the ninth of December Hutten wrote about it to Luther, that Sickingen was so filled with his teaching as to have exclaimed recently: "No one will dare to overturn this building, or, if he dare, will he be able." There were attempts to detach Sickingen from Hutten's influence by warnings and insinuations from the Catholic side, but he stood his ground and kept a wing over Hutten so long as he confined himself to a "legal" program—if one may say so—and to an appeal for a hearing before the emperor.

The attempts to detach Sickingen from Luther and Hutten are nevertheless of historical importance. The arguments apparently used to this end at the Ebernburg by Sickingen's brother-in-law, Philip von Flersheim,[35] reflect the view dominant among the nobles. The knights were on the point of rupture. The inevitable estrangement from Charles V was not the only argument used to dissuade the imperial captain from protecting the rebel. More important were the points which Hutten set himself to refute. He was being reproached with treachery to his

34. H. Ulmann, *Franz von Sickingen,* pp. 161 ff.

35. P. Kalkoff, *Ulrich von Hutten und die Reformation,* pp. 253 ff.

class because the ecclesiastical reform or revolution would have a drastic effect on the position of the nobles. Did he wish to "reduce the Church from the splendor of its present eminence to the degradation of its miserable origins?"[36] He was inciting the people against the Church with his petticoat slogans. In other words he was a defeatist.[37] The spiritual lords, and that meant the nobles, would be robbed of many comfortable berths. We hear the reverberation of the cry of the bloated nobles in Hutten's tract: "Bishops who do not fight? We in Germany would be ashamed of them! Bishops who live in simplicity as examples of virtue? How much more agreeable to live under the paternal complaisance of the Roman Church![38] And what good fortune that a change in Germany appears hopeless!"[39]

As a matter of fact the ecclesiastical reform, as Hutten conceived it, would affect the nobles and Hutten made no bones about it. Although the especial object of his attack was the pope and the "courtesans" no one acquainted with the situation could miss the point that the "courtesans" meant also precisely the spiritual lords drawn from the German nobility, "for the power of Christian bishops not only at Rome but in all places should consist in apostolic virtue. . . . Such an one, whoever he be, will not exercise worldly authority, but will display the works of an apostle."[40] And more directly: "Though a well trained man could be obtained, thoroughly versed in the Scriptures, nevertheless a swashbuckling *Junker* is assigned as shepherd of souls. Perhaps he lives outside of the country and never pays any attention to his flock, but leaves them to some hireling at threepence."[41] Again in the *Robbers:* "Our clergy have learned the trick from Rome. Note how they carry on among us with fraud and plunder. They squat on the most fertile places of Germany, the most productive fields, for they hold both sides of the Rhine." Frederick III had called this stream the "priests' lane"

36. Hutten, *Opera,* IV, 337–338.
37. *Ibid.,* II, 144.
38. *Ibid.,* IV, 345 ff.
39. *Ibid.,* IV, 346.
40. *Ibid.,* IV, 340.
41. "Einn freyer stoltzer junckherr," *ibid.,* II, 148.

because its banks from the source to the ocean were ruled by the German bishops. The noble young canons likewise elicited jibes at their unchristian conduct.[42]

It is characteristic of Hutten's courage and intellectual integrity to have looked from the outset straight into the eye of the difficulties into which the nobles would be precipitated by the reformation of the Church. Naturally he hoped that they would retrieve themselves through positive contributions in other directions. The educational reform of the nobles had long exercised him. Nor did he intend to expropriate all Church property. The new bishops might possess more than they used, but they might not use for themselves more than they really needed.[43] One feels that Hutten was concerned not merely for the other classes of society, but regarded himself as the renewer of his own group, and he faced unflinchingly the consequent enmity and mistrust. He was indeed to learn like Sickingen that here a momentous rupture had taken place.

The compositions of Hutten emanating from this period, especially the *Apology*[44] and the two dialogues, the *Monitor First and Second*,[45] show how hard Hutten had to work to carry Sickingen with him and how difficult it still was to undermine the deep and widespread reverence and fear of Rome. Hutten may be responsible for injecting into Sickingen's political position the Lutheran tone which later manifested itself in his feud with Trier, when he did not hesitate to clothe his political egoism with an evangelical garment. Did the captain really hope that the emperor would trust the reform of the Church to him, as Hutten intimated in the second *Monitor?* Did he just toy with the idea? Or did Hutten merely lead him on with such pictures? We cannot tell. At any rate the class consciousness of the knight, which always permeated Hutten's reform program, could intrigue Sickingen on the political side

42. *Ibid.,* IV, 402.
43. *Ibid.,* IV, 403.
44. "Endtschüldigung wyder etlicher unwarhafftiges aussgeben, als solt er wider alle geystlicheit und priesterschafft sein." *Ibid.,* II, 130 ff. P. Kalkoff has shown that this tract was already written at the end of 1520. *Ulrich von Hutten und die Reformation,* p. 269.
45. "Monitor Primus, Secundus," Hutten, *Opera,* IV, 337 ff.

and offer him something. The way in which he attained power was scarcely national in Hutten's sense. But since the imperial election he had been sailing in these treacherous waters. He had abandoned the service of the French king and had become the right hand man of the emperor. Would not the ideas of Hutten enhance the prestige of the emperor? Hutten in the second *Monitor* had sowed in Sickingen's mind the suggestion that disobedience might often be the highest form of obedience.[46] Sickingen would hardly have thought so, but if the emperor should pass him by and not summon him to his service, might not Sickingen, as a member of the Estates, enter a vigorous remonstrance? So far he would go, but the more drastic part of Hutten's program he sought at first to moderate.

And Hutten, too, at the beginning had reason to look for the success of his writings and to await the development of events. If now and then he was inclined to take immediate vengeance on his enemies, the great manifestoes of August and December are by no means dominated by these intentions. He was profoundly grateful to Sickingen for the security which gave him free scope and enabled him for the first time to mature his conception of German freedom. The new year's greeting and the dialogues express his thanks in words reminiscent of the Pirckheimer letter: "I wish you, not as we often wish our friends, an agreeable and enjoyable leisure, but plenty of serious, hard, and strenuous work, by which, for the benefit of the many, you may exercise and test your own proud and heroic mind."[47] To be sure, Hutten was not emancipated completely from the limitations of the Middle Ages, from the conception of a Christendom incorporated politically and spiritually within the framework of the Roman Empire. His ultimate aspiration was for the dominance of the German emperor over the Empire, but he would not purchase it at the cost of subserviency to the Papacy. In the *Remonstrance* addressed to Frederick the Wise, he wrote: "Servitude of any sort is distasteful to all men, but espe-

46. Hutten, *Opera,* IV, 360 ff. 47. *Ibid.,* I, 449.

cially objectionable is subjection to others in the case of those who ought to rule. We Germans ought either to refuse to subscribe to the title of the Roman Empire and elect for ourselves an emperor—who would be such, however, only in name—or else we ought stoutly to reject the papal tyranny and liberate ourselves before helping others."[48] He knew, however, how little the nation was "conscious of itself,"[49] how deeply in Germany the authority of the Pope was rooted by faith and protected by material interests. For that reason he sought to disparage the court and the "courtesans" and to disintegrate the current conceptions. Whether in the glosses on the papal bulls against himself and Luther, or in the dialogue *The Bullkiller*,[50] where the papal bull locks horns with German freedom, in all the compositions of this month, we meet character and courage, understanding and pungency, not the world-compelling spirit of a Luther shaping up raw stuff out of the deepest sources, but the colorful style of an author very much alive and highly gifted, and a warrior trying to hammer things into his own mould.

Although Hutten's trial naturally predominates in the *Remonstrances*, the figure of Luther stands out significantly in the dialogues. He was associated now with German freedom. "Not Luther alone is attacked in this affair, but every one of us. The sword is not pointed at one only, but every man of us is menaced."[51] So he cried in the winter of 1520. By that time he was trying to reach every one with his word; he had begun to write German.[52] We saw that in 1519 he had translated *Fever the First* for Sickingen into the German tongue. The revision and editing of a German translation of Cicero's *De Senectute* was an attempt to turn a philosophical work of antiquity into a lan-

48. *Ibid.*, I, 391. 49. *Ibid.*, I, 430.

50. "Bulla Decimi Leonis contra errores Martini Lutheri et sequacium cum Hutteni glossis," *ibid.*, V, 301 ff. "Bulla vel Bullicida," *ibid.*, IV, 300 ff.

51. *Ibid.*, I, 430.

52. Compare S. Szamatólski, *Ulrichs von Hutten deutsche Schriften* (Strassburg, 1891).

guage as yet sparse in philosophical terminology.[53] Here was a good preparation for the translation of his own dialogues. He showed that he had grasped the differences between the languages in the construction of words and sentences. His translations are not wooden reproductions, but apart from a few Latinisms, to be found likewise in Luther, they are a new creation out of the spirit of the German tongue. This is the more noteworthy because the adoption of German as a literary medium was undoubtedly affected by political considerations.

In the meantime he had really found out that the support of unlearned men was not to be despised. Composition in German was adopted for the sake of a wider audience. But not without a pang did he wrench himself from the spiritual heritage of his student years, of which he was proud, and resolve to make no more use of it. Yet there before his eyes stood the mighty working of Luther's tracts. So he began to translate his dialogues and increase his literary output by new works in the German tongue. Latin epigrams and hexameters made way for German verses in rhyme. In September he published his first German tract, entitled *A Remonstrance and a Warning against the Presumptuous, Unchristian Power of the Bishop of Rome and the Unspiritual Spiritual Estate.*[54] It is an extensive work of more than fifteen hundred verses. One is astonished to see the accomplished master of Latin verse and prose in the rôle of a gifted child essaying clay modelling. Although the medium is refractory there are already the warm tones of popular feeling and some perfect lines which may be imperfectly rendered.

> *He who for the truth will stand*
> *With bans is hounded from the land.*
> *This is not godly and not right.*
> *He who against it will not fight*
> *Will be with God in dire disgrace.*
> *I warn him of his evil case.*[55]

53. Hutten, *Opera,* II, 152.
54. *Ibid.,* III, 473 ff.
55. *Ibid.,* III, 509.

In the year 1632 when Gustavus Adolphus sought to rally all of the Protestant forces against the threat of the Counter-reformation this tract was reprinted with the title *An Awakener of the German Nation.* And it may be that its passionate cry for the union of the land on behalf of spiritual freedom may yet awaken another echo.

In November followed the *Complaint against the Lutheran Bonfire at Mainz,* a powerful summons to resist the burning of Luther's writings.[56] A little later appeared the *Disclosure of How the Roman Bishops or Popes have Acted against the German Emperors.*[57] With like intent and in popular fashion he gathered up the results of his humanist historical studies, pointing out with a dogmatism equal to that of the papalist historians on the other side that Leo X and Julius II were not the first to oppose the Empire, but that this abuse went back to the balmy days of the Middle Ages.

Wholly apart from the political context, these works as literary achievements demonstrate that Hutten overtopped contemporary publicists by more than a head. As a writer of Latin no one in Germany surpassed him in his own day and perhaps we may say that no German before or since ever so fully mastered the genius of the Latin tongue. As a German author he had but one peer, Martin Luther, who drew directly from the rich storehouse of popular imagination as no one ever had or would. That is why he is the father of modern German speech.

To be sure this language, rich and profound as it is, remains somewhat sprawling and a trifle formless. Religious and philosophical ideas here find garments and wings as scarcely anywhere else, but precise distinctions tend to be blurred, and centuries were required to obliterate the coarseness from which the earth-born Luther was not emancipated. What German humanism meant or might have meant at this point Hutten's works demonstrate. The Germany of these years was fertile in talented satirists and polemicists, but brought forth only one Hutten. His

56. *Ibid.,* III, 455 ff.

57. *Ibid.,* V, 363 ff.

works are so deftly executed, his characters so personal, his invective so telling, his wit so human. There is a disciplined power, a classical balance in spite of the stormy rhythm and the clamor of strife. We feel in the clinching of his arguments, in the quest of concise diction the influence of his Latin education. Often he lacks the German genialness, but also the German discursiveness and pointless vulgarity. The German genius, however, has found better expression at his hands because of the richness of emotion conveyed through chastened speech.

By his revival of the dialogue he gave a deep impulse to German literature, the force of which was unhappily soon spent. The late Middle Ages had not made the attempt to portray actual people in relation with each other. In Hutten's mimicry actual figures are set before the public in real situations. The German drama might have found here a point for development, but the artistic and human capacities of the next generation were not able to pursue the lead.

The last great tract of the year 1520, *The Apology of Ulrich von Hutten against Some Lying Reports that He is Opposed to any Spiritual Estate, Any Priesthood Whatever*, is a definitive declaration of war. He was constantly preoccupied with the thought of acting on his own initiative, more and more dubious whether the emperor would give him a hearing. In spite of Sickingen's optimism, he had reason to be dubious. But what should he do, were he denied? Already on December 9 he had written to Luther to know whether there would be a refuge in Saxony in case the situation called for "a fair deed," that is, a blow on the part of the knights, since "hope in the emperor is slight."[58] He was right. Eight days later Charles V repudiated the promise he had made to Frederick the Wise in Cologne, that Luther should have a hearing at the Diet of Worms, summoned for the following January.[59]

58. Hutten, *Opera*, I, 435 ff. M. Luther, *Werke, Briefwechsel*, II, 230 ff.
59. P. Kalkoff, *Entscheidungsjahre der Reformation* (Munich, 1927), pp. 202 ff.

Under this impression Hutten wrote his *Apology*, which has been incorrectly described as a retrenchment.[60] It is directed against insinuations which had been lodged with Sickingen against Hutten. If he denied that he ever contemplated revolution—rather he had urged the magistrates to step in and thus prevent revolution—he did not now repudiate for himself the right to combat force with force. And nothing short of that was the rule of the Romanists. For on that account every one at every time not only might but should combat them, for they were simply "enemies of the fatherland" and "breakers of the peace." As for himself, he would not await the decision of the emperor but, wherever and however he could, would smite the "courtesans."

He was combining personal vengeance on his enemies, who threatened him with death by poison and dagger, with the idea of a root-and-branch reform of the Church. The war of the Romanists must come. If the emperor and the princes would not move, then he as a knight would serve the common good and at the same time vindicate his honor, if not in a court of law, then by the law of feud. He hoped that his resolve would attract followers. When he put in Sickingen's mouth the description of disobedience as the highest form of obedience, there is a reminiscence of Ziska and the popular Hussite revolution.[61] Hutten had become, however, more indifferent to success. Since August he had reckoned squarely with the possibility of his own defeat. Now he made his ultimate declaration of faith: "This is infidelity: to shift according to the turn of fortune and allow one's loyalty to be fickle. The justice of my cause moves me to withstand even outrageous fortune."[62]

60. P. Kalkoff, *Ulrich von Hutten und die Reformation*, pp. 269 ff.
61. Hutten, *Opera*, IV, 354. 62. *Ibid.*, IV, 417.

X

WORMS, 1521

IN January, 1521, while Hutten was trying to find out how far he could count on his own kin,[1] the Diet of Worms opened, almost in the shadow of the Ebernburg.[2] The mood of the estates at the outset was obviously highly unfavorable to Rome. Even so convinced an adherent of the old Church as Duke George of Saxony wanted reforms and limitations of the Roman administration in Germany. The hopes of Frederick the Wise for an intervention on the part of the Estates seemed to be not unwarranted, and Hutten would have to grant that Sickingen's expectations for the improvement of the political situation had something to be said for themselves. Ulrich was pleased with the opening of the diet but he waited to see what would happen next—the more so because he was not as yet able to foresee even whether his family would help him in his personal feud. Would the emperor, after all, take the German side in the end and dismiss Hutten's pet aversion, the jurists and the theologians who had exerted such a sin-

1. S. Szamatólski, *Ulrichs von Hutten deutsche Schriften* (Strassburg, 1891), p. 157.

2. The main sources for the history of the Diet of Worms have been conveniently gathered in *Deutsche Reichstagsakten, Jüngere Reihe,* Vol. II, edited by A. Wrede (Munich, 1893). See also T. Brieger, *Aleander und Luther 1521* (Gotha, 1884), and P. Kalkoff, *Die Depeschen des Nuntius Aleander vom Wormser Reichstag* (2d edition, Halle, 1897). Part of these letters have been rendered into English by P. Smith in his edition of *Luther's Correspondence and Other Contemporary Letters* (Philadelphia, 1913). Compare P. Kalkoff, *Die Entstehung des Wormser Edikts* (Leipsic, 1913), *Die Entscheidungsjahre der Reformation* (Munich, 1917), *Der grosse Wormser Reichstag* (Darmstadt, 1921), and *Der Wormser Reichstag von 1521* (Munich, 1922). For a critical examination of Kalkoff's methods and results see J. Kühn, "Zur Entstehung des Wormser Edikts," *Zeitschrift für Kirchengeschichte,* Vol. 35. A recent treatment based on partly new materials is in Chapter VIII of H. von Schubert, *Lazarus Spengler und die Einführung der Reformation in Nürnberg,* edited by H. Holborn (Leipsic, 1934).

ister influence upon the emperor's grandfather?[3] If even a suggestion of a move in this direction on the part of Charles V loomed on the horizon there flared up in Hutten again, as in 1519, the longing for a genuine German emperor.

He began once more to scan the general trends and was all aflutter with eagerness over the changing scenes at Worms. Never was he personally more in the foreground of general interest. His writings had placed his name in many mouths as the assailant of the Romanists and the comrade of Luther. A popular cartoon portrays them together. Hutten, on horseback, introduces the "*Triumph of Truth*," the introduction of the Gospel. To the tail of his steed is bound a horde of wicked bishops and priests. Then follows Christ, his chariot drawn by four allegorical figures representative of the evangelists in medieval art, the eagle, lion, calf, and man. Karlstadt and Luther walk alongside. The period was fond of such mythological constructions, in which also Hutten's own thinking was deeply immersed. He was the object likewise of literary adulation by his friend Crotus, and particularly Eberlin von Günzburg, a popular writer, as well as the Strassburg humanist, Nicolaus Gerbel.

The impression produced by Hutten's publications was more than literary. Worms was buzzing with the most varied rumors with regard to him. On the twelfth of January Bernhardt von Hirschfeld, an electoral counsellor and an old hand at politics, wrote to a friend: "Luther is much spoken of here, and Herr von Hutten has put out so many astounding tracts that he is much more incensed and the Romanists much more infuriated against him than against Luther. The scholars tell me that he writes miraculously."[4] If the politicians took him so seriously the explanation is not to be found altogether in his literary activity, but perhaps more in the connection with Sickingen, then at the zenith of his influence. The continual reports of the papal

3. Hutten, *Opera,* II, 43.
4. See *Theologische Studien und Kritiken,* 1882, p. 697.

nuntio Aleander to Rome, however much they exaggerated the menace of Hutten's plans in order to magnify the services of the reporter in the eyes of his commissioners, are none the less indicative. When the new papal bull *Decet Romanum Pontificem* reached Aleander on the tenth of February with its specific mention of Hutten, Spengler, and Pirckheimer, the nuntio feared grave danger from these personal references and sent back for a revised version, which came in the beginning of April. Hutten, protected by Sickingen and widely idolized by the people, was a political force with which the Curia had to reckon. Now at last the goddess *Fortuna* smiled on him. By his own fault the trumps slipped out of his hands.

At Worms there was unfolding before Hutten's eyes—and he was watching with passionate interest—the picture of a kaleidoscopic diplomatic struggle fraught with immense issues for the future. Though well and quickly informed of what was taking place, Hutten was not able to penetrate the veil which the emperor and his counsellors drew over their plans. Charles V never for a moment doubted that Luther's teaching was manifest heresy and he was inwardly ready to salve his conscience by delivering the monk to the Roman Church, for the emperor had a conscience, not a German conscience indeed, nor a Spanish, but a Burgundian. He had grown up in the Burgundian Netherlands, was at home in its speech and in its pious, credulous religiosity. In the French tongue he informed his estates of the German *Reich* that he "would risk his kingdoms, lordships, friends, body, life, and soul" rather than be responsible for the spread of heresy.[5] The spiritual air of Burgundy here blew about him. He was as yet scarcely at home in Spain, which at that very moment was in full revolt against him. Only in the long years following did he convert the country from a source of weakness into a pillar of strength. Only then did the tradition of the land of his mother take deeper hold upon him.

5. *Deutsche Reichstagsakten, Jüngere Reihe,* II, 594 ff.

But a high sense of the dignity of the imperial office had been engendered in him by blood and breeding, though he was still far from mature. Development was slow and emancipation from the Burgundian environment very gradual. All in all he was more a monarch of the confessional period with its absolutism and strict orthodoxy than a typical Renaissance despot like the Italians or Francis I of France. Charles was a pious ruler even if his religion did not exceed the conventional. Though not irreproachable as to worldly enjoyments, he was nevertheless more industrious, serious, and self-controlled than the monarchs of his day. With what contempt he must have regarded his German "cousins" at the diet, the guzzlers and gluttons, whom Hutten also scorched. There was something in this seriousness and aloofness particularly impressive to the serious observer such as the representative of Nuremberg, Lazarus Spengler.[6] Such hauteur, however, chilled the relations between the emperor and his estates and evoked nostalgia for the gay familiarity of his grandfather. No one was intimate with Charles.

His policy in Luther's case at Worms would have been straightforward had not so many other considerations entered in. The first necessity was the granting of a tax to make possible an active foreign policy. Otherwise all Charles really wanted was peace in order to concentrate his attention upon Spain and Italy. But the German estates made their consent for the "Roman months," a tax in support of the army to accompany the German monarch to the coronation in Italy, contingent upon serious consideration of the "Grievances of the German Nation." In this respect the majority of the German princes were united. The bitter enemy of Luther, Duke George of Saxony, was one of the most vigorous in pressing these claims and Aleander was insistent in his warnings to Rome

6. *Ibid.*, pp. 886 ff. H. von Schubert, *Lazarus Spengler und die Einführung der Reformation in Nürnberg* (Leipsic, 1934), pp. 255 ff.

not at any price to provide fuel for German complaints. Rome took the advice to heart.

Also the pressure for the participation of the estates in the imperial government was lively. The princes were urging the establishment of a Council of the Empire. The imperial cabinet had the greatest difficulty to extract the worst teeth from this project. Under such circumstances the emperor had to be all the more considerate of the estates in dealing with Luther. Their position was not simple. The majority was conservative and ready to sacrifice Luther. But were not distinctions to be made? Was not his campaign against indulgences and church finances essentially sound? And could not the stormy response which he had evoked among the masses be directed into useful channels for the eradication of ecclesiastical abuses? Nor were the police measures against Luther and his party capable of execution unless it were shown that he had been condemned as a result of a fair trial.

These considerations worked together in the end to persuade Charles V after all to give Luther a safe conduct to Worms, but only on one condition with which the majority of the estates were in full accord. There should be no public discussion. Luther should simply be asked whether he acknowledged his books and was prepared to recant. Even this seemed to the emperor a great concession. What would happen if Luther made a partial recantation and appealed before the diet to a general council? In that case he might induce the estates to bring strong pressure on the emperor and the pope. The attempt was worth making, therefore, either to terrify Luther from coming to Worms at all, or else to get the matter out of the hands of the estates by committing it to the imperial cabinet.

Aleander tried the first method and secured the publication at the end of March of the so-called "Sequestration Mandate," which meant an open violation of the truce between the emperor and the estates. In accord with this order Luther's books were to be confiscated, though for the moment not burned. Such procedure indicated that his case was prejudged as heretical. The attempt to work on him directly was made from the imperial side over the Ebernburg through Hutten, Sickingen, and Bucer. That the unruly elements in Sickingen's entourage could thus not only be held in hand during these decisive months, but even utilized on behalf of the imperial policy was a masterpiece of diplomatic intrigue.

One understood quickly in Worms that an author of Hutten's rank could do no end of damage, in view of the anti-papal mood of the diet. Aleander tried to pacify him by informing him, through Capito, that he was not excommunicated.[7] On the imperial side, also, attempts were made to quiet the dangerous man. Sickingen had made emurgent representations on Hutten's behalf with the emperor on the nineteenth of February, and hopes were now held out that he might enter the imperial service.[8] He could then be released from the ban, the more readily because his case could easily be dissociated from that of Luther. Pirckheimer and Lazarus Spengler, Nuremberg's representative, were working to this end[9]—all the more remarkable in the case of Spengler who undoubtedly had been genuinely and deeply enlisted by Luther's teaching. Hutten, however, treated the question of his own trial with sovereign indifference. If he restrained himself in the following period it was only because he saw in the imperial offer an indication that Charles V had not yet entirely sold out to the Romanists. Had Hutten been concerned merely for security and gain, he might easily have accepted an invitation to enter the service of Cardinal Lang,[10] as Stau-

7. Hutten, *Opera,* II, 113. The right date is, however, 1521, as P. Kalkoff has shown in his *Hutten und die Reformation,* p. 310, n. 1.

8. T. Brieger, *Aleander und Luther* (Gotha, 1884), p. 92. Christoph Scheurl, *Briefbuch,* edited by F. von Soden and J. Knaake (Potsdam, 1867 ff.), II, 126.

9. See H. von Schubert, *Lazarus Spengler und die Einführung der Reformation in Nürnberg,* pp. 201 ff.

10. Hutten, *Opera,* II, 340. G. Bauch, "Hutteniana," *Vierteljahrsschrift für Kultur und Literatur der Renaissance,* I, 490.

pitz, Luther's confessor and intimate friend, was notoriously not ashamed to do. But Hutten did not wish to betray Luther's party and continued to work on the *Invectives* against the nuntios, commenced when one of them provoked general murmurs of resentment at the meeting of the estates by threatening civil war in Germany. And, when on the twenty-sixth and twenty-seventh of March the mandate was proclaimed against Luther—he had been summoned to the diet on the sixth—subjecting him to the treatment of one under the ban and thus prejudging his case, Hutten could no longer restrain himself but published his *Invectives against the Nuntios and the Priests who mistreated Luther.*[11] Hutten correctly discerned that the mandate was intended to frighten Luther from going to Worms, for Charles V also bestirred himself on behalf of Luther's appearance at the diet in the interests of ingratiating himself with the estates. Likewise Hutten saw that the emperor meant merely to lay before Luther the question of recantation, and this, as Lazarus Spengler observed, meant no trial at all. Hutten now, on the one hand, threatened the nuntios and the priests with a feud in his *Invectives* and thereby threw down the gauntlet for a war against the Romanists, while, on the other hand, he petitioned the emperor once again for a full and fair hearing for Luther.[12] This was the last cry of a deeply disillusioned believer, for his conception of the emperor's obligations was more than a party doctrine. "Fulfil at last the hopes of Germany to which you have committed yourself. Allow no doubt of justice to arise. . . . Has Germany then deserved to perish with you instead of for you? Lead us into open danger, war and conflagration. All nations may work against us, all peoples may fall upon us. We would rather test our power in danger than in this unmanly fashion to lie down like women and be slaves. And

11. "Invectiva in Lutheromastigas sacerdotes," Hutten, *Opera,* II, 21 ff.

12. "Ad Carolum Imperatorem pro Luthero exhortatoria," *ibid.*, pp. 38 ff.

we hoped that you would liberate us from the Roman yoke."

Shortly thereafter Charles V gave signs of such intentions. At least Hutten thought so, and perhaps no other interpretation was possible. Charles, indeed, had something else in mind. Aleander, on receiving the *Invectives*, had gone to him and lodged a protest over the threat of a diplomatic representative. But Charles was not in a position to control Hutten. Sickingen could not be counted on. Apparently the events of Worms had provoked him to playing with the thought of desertion from the imperial service. The shadow of Charles V's war against France already cast itself across the land. Sickingen had exhibited his displeasure with the imperial policy by refusing to fight Robert von der Mark, the lord of Sedan, who had fallen upon Burgundy. A representative of Robert was staying with him at Ebernburg.[13] Sentiments favorable to Luther and regrets that the emperor was ill-disposed to reform were floating about. The course of wisdom seemed to be not to push penal measures but to unloose the purse strings and render innocuous the turbulent German knights. The wily Paul von Armstorff, counsellor of the emperor, was entrusted with a commission to Ebernburg. Glapion, the confessor of the emperor, accompanied him.[14]

The plan was not merely to win Sickingen and Hutten but also to try to prevent Luther from entering Worms. Glapion has been regarded with dubious right as a mediating theologian of the Erasmian school. We do not know enough about him to venture a more precise characterization. Had he not already, in February, made a similar attempt with the chancellor of electoral Saxony, we could scarcely reconstruct the arguments which he now used at Ebernburg to ensnare Sickingen and Hutten, as well as the theologian Martin Bucer. In any case Glapion went beyond any Erasmian reconciliation, as we learn from his

13. *Deutsche Reichstagsakten, Jüngere Reihe,* II, 150.

14. See F. Walser, *Die politische Entwicklung Ulrichs von Hutten während der Entscheidungsjahre der Reformation* in *Historische Zeitschrift, Beiheft 14* (Munich, 1928), pp. 72 ff.

later account to Aleander. Everything indicates that he was rather an ambitious politician than a devout theologian. He succeeded in giving the knights the impression that the emperor was inclined to reform. He knew also how to quiet their fears for Luther's fate. Nevertheless he recommended that Luther should not go to Worms but should come to Ebernburg and thence put himself in touch with the imperial government. Glapion informed them that a more exact discussion of Luther's teaching was necessary. Even though one might endorse the reformatory trend of his German writings, his Latin compositions went too far. Luther's tract on the *Babylonian Captivity of the Church* was obviously laid before them and passages pointed out with which neither Sickingen nor Hutten could agree. We have seen that Hutten's anti-Roman attitude all along the line stopped short of the sacraments.

Glapion's plan began to intrigue the knights and undoubtedly they thought the emperor was behind him in everything. The discussion of the particular theological questions they were content to leave to the young Bucer, who, whether out of weakness or inexperience, saw in the proposals of Glapion a basis for a discussion with Luther. Since Hutten fell sick, Bucer started out to invite Luther to Ebernburg. He met him in Oppenheim on the fifteenth of April. Luther refused.

Hutten's attempt at mediation has been interpreted as a lapse from his previous position,[15] the more so because he accepted an imperial pension. He could scarcely have done otherwise. What sort of an impression would have been made upon the emperor if Hutten had pretended to be in accord with his policy and yet had rebuffed him at the same time by refusing the grant? The pension might be used as a basis for judging his position only if it could be shown that he had not allowed himself to be persuaded of the good intentions of the emperor. In spite of lingering doubts he composed an apology to the emperor in Latin

15. P. Kalkoff, *Hutten und die Reformation*, pp. 358 ff.

and German,[16] and did he not have more ground for hope than in the months preceding? The reason for venturing one last throw was that misgivings as to a fair hearing for Luther had been satisfied. But when the news came of the actual hearing—in reality it was no hearing at all—Hutten began to recoil from the emperor, and on learning that a severe edict was to be launched against Luther, repudiated the imperial services. This was on the twenty-second of May, hence before the emperor had signed the law. Indignant over the intrigues of the imperial counsellors by whom he too had been duped Hutten now turned to the execution of the plan which had been so long maturing. Feud was unleashed against the Romanists and the "courtesans."

We must remember, too, that while still bound to the emperor Hutten had refrained from an urgent warning to Luther to adopt the course proposed in the interchanges with Glapion. When Bucer returned on the seventeenth of April and reported Luther's refusal, Hutten at once acclaimed the decision. To Luther he wrote: "You need never doubt of my constancy. So long as you are true to yourself I will cleave to you to my last breath."[17] In Hutten lived the ineradicable passion to live up to his high ideals. For the unswerving stand of Luther, who had committed himself to the hand of God, he felt the highest admiration. From the outset he expected that Luther would make no concessions and would maintain his cause without qualification. In a letter addressed to Luther on the eve of the "hearing" at Worms he expressed his own and Luther's position in these words: "Here is the difference between us. I look to men. You, who are already more perfect, trust everything to God."[18] In similar vein, on the first of May, 1521, looking back on the events of the diet,[19]

16. Hutten, *Opera,* II, 47 ff.

17. *Ibid.,* p. 55. M. Luther, *Werke, Briefwechsel,* II, 301 ff. Compare his letter to Spalatin of March 25, 1521, in *Zeitschrift für Kirchengeschichte,* XL (1930), 181.

18. Hutten, *Opera,* II, 55.

19. *Ibid.,* pp. 59 ff.

he wrote to Pirckheimer: "It is clear as day that he was directed by divine guidance. He disregarded all human considerations and threw himself utterly upon God." For that reason, when Luther turned to him (we do not know why —perhaps because of some negotiations with Glapion or the estates) Hutten would not venture to influence Luther's decisions.[20] He was sure "that Luther would do the right thing and stand by it." But he was so distressed over Luther's situation at Worms and over the conduct of the others that on the seventeenth of April he wrote to Jonas in Erfurt: "If only I could be there to push things along . . . . but one must tread softly now."[21] And when all the hopes which he had entertained for the emperor and the estates were blasted and shattered, he forswore his allegiance. His reputation had suffered because in these decisive days he did not resort to action as one might have expected from his earlier words. Taunts of bragging came from his old friend Hermann von dem Busche, who was most zealously campaigning for Luther at Worms. There were references to dogs whose bark is worse than their bite.[22] Such jibes prompted Hutten the more to indulge his propensity for action. Apparently at the close of the diet he made an attempt on Aleander, but was then confined by illness in Sickingen's castle. Not until late summer was he able to open his war on the Romanists, which he hoped would be the signal for a general rising against the "courtesans." In the weeks before the commencement of the campaign is to be placed the composition of the poem in which posterity has seen him at his best. A distinguished critic has characterized it as the one great German poem in secular literature between Walther von der Vogelweide and Klopstock.[23] The tone is unaffected and genuine, and there is a clear eye for the political importance of his venture. In these decisive months he was outwardly true to his inner nature. That helped him to forget

20. Hutten, *Opera,* II, 58. M. Luther, *Werke, Briefwechsel,* II, 303 ff.
21. Hutten, *Opera,* II, 56. 22. *Ibid.,* pp. 62 ff.
23. F. Gundolf, *Hutten, Klopstock, Arndt* (Heidelberg, 1924).

the gnawing sense of having been duped by uncanny folk. What he knew and sang he had himself lived through:

I counted well the odds
And still have no regret.
Though beaten by the gods
Know I am faithful yet.
The risk I ran
Not for one man,
But, if you wish to know,
For Fatherland
I took my stand,
Though dubbed a mere priests' foe.

So let them lie and slander
Malign me as they will.
Had I but stooped to pander
I'd have defenders still.
So was I banned
From out the land.
I cry to all true men,
'So far I go,
But farther, no,
And may come back again.'

I will not sue for grace,
I do not own my guilt.
I would have shown my face
And answered to the hilt,
Could they but wait
To try my fate,
As men were wont of old.
Perhaps 'tis God,
Or Fortune's rod
Hath made them overbold.

XI

HUTTEN'S WAR ON THE ROMANISTS

THE Diet of Worms had blasted most of Hutten's hopes. The expectations which he had set upon Charles V had proved illusory, and if Hutten thought to influence the action of the estates by his publications he had been grossly deceived. No opposition had ventured to lift its head against the edict of Worms, with its sharp condemnation and persecution of Luther. Even Frederick the Wise had thought it discreet to conceal Luther in the "Patmos" of the Wartburg. We may grant that Luther, by his stand at Worms, had not made it easy for his friends to intervene on his behalf. He might have enlisted a general following had he been willing to drop his theological polemic and confine himself to the social and economic program outlined in the *Address to the German Nobility*. We can understand that many of Luther's contemporaries supposed this to be his primary purpose. Few, indeed, were those who had the remotest conception of the full import of his doctrinal teachings. Hutten, too, had approached Luther because he sensed in him a comrade in political reform. The measure of Hutten's respect for great personalities and for the religious appears in that he did not try to hold Luther to this program but stood aside, not piqued but admiring, when Luther declared before all the world that the religious element was decisive.

But what was to be done now in a political way, since the emperor and the princes had proved broken reeds? A direct alliance between Luther and Hutten was out of the question, for by this time it must have been abundantly apparent that Luther contemplated a much more comprehensive reform and would achieve it only through the inner power of the Word and the transformation of souls. We have already seen how deeply Hutten was smitten by

Luther's personality, as he saw him battle at Worms for his faith. In Luther, too, the anti-papal tendency was anything but extinguished. In his famous speech before the emperor and the estates he had made this almost an independent matter and had defended it in resounding national notes.[1] In this address his books were divided into three parts: those dealing with evangelical teaching, those against the Papacy, and those against individuals. He was not prepared to recant any one of these groups, although he conceded that the personal controversies had been conducted with a virulence unbecoming a Christian. As for his writings against the Papacy, said he, everybody knows how the conscience of the faithful has been scandalized, "and the goods of this famous German nation have been devoured and exploited." Were he now to retract his books against the Papacy and its abuses, he would thereby not only strengthen the tyranny and open the window, but also even the door to the abomination, and the advocates of the Papacy would then boast of the adherence of the emperor and the estates. He would not assume responsibility for furthering such evil and such tyranny.

Hutten would read this declaration with approbation because it could easily be interpreted as favorable to his own war program. Moreover, though an enthusiast, he was not a mere pupil of Luther. His war on Rome had been commenced before Luther's and besides Luther belonged to another order. Hutten retained a feeling for the cleavage between clergy and laity, religion and reason, between Christian and civil virtue—the more so in the moment when he thought to see in Luther the ideal of the earnest prophet and man of prayer. Here Hutten was throughout an Erasmian. In the *Enchiridion* Erasmus had said that he who is not equal to the genuine Christian warfare, who is not equipped with the qualities of heroism, can content himself with the preservation of the simpler civil virtues.[2]

1. M. Luther, *Werke,* VII, 814 ff.

2. Desiderius Erasmus Roterodamus, *Opera* (Leiden), V, 51; or *Opera Selecta,* edited by A. and H. Holborn (Munich, 1933), p. 111.

One might almost suppose that Hutten had these words in mind when in the first *Monitor* he made Luther say: "What I proclaimed applies only to the perfect. But one can be saved also in that middle rank. Christ has not made the Kingdom of Heaven so narrow, but he is most plenteous in mercy and after the highest and the heavenly he has ordained a second grade of more lenient and attainable precepts. If you cannot attain the perfect for which you strive with all your might, the other way will suffice for salvation."[3] The scholastic distinction between the "precepts" and the "counsels of perfection" was retained by Hutten as by Erasmus. Although Hutten made the casual remark in the second *Monitor* that the priests would have to give an answer for making two kinds of Christians, nevertheless the letters to and about Luther in the Worms period clearly reveal the ancient distinction between a higher and lower Christian perfection. Luther was for him the perfect priest, whereas he thought of himself as a knight. And as he began his campaign independently of Luther, so now he would carry it on, realizing that Luther was in a position to create something different and higher in the religious realm. This realization enabled Hutten to reconcile himself to the fact that during the days at Worms Luther had made no closer approaches to him. Hutten's program was still essentially on the old lines.

But what was the external situation now? Previous to the diet all of the spiritual cleavages had not come clearly to the fore, and in these days it looked as if the different groups might be able to get together. That was the greatest era of Hutten's literary activity. The objectives had not been clarified in the larger arena and men listened with eagerness to the prophets of a new ideal. But after the diet the political parties and groups split apart and Hutten's field of operations, which for the moment had been the whole world, was now greatly shrunk. From the breadth of the universal sphere he was suddenly thrown back upon the narrowness of his own personal existence

3. Hutten, *Opera,* IV, 345. See also II, 142.

and immediate environment. When the emperor and princes failed and Luther had further receded from politics, Hutten fell back on Sickingen and his circle of knights. These were the only ones who could be bolstered in their will to achieve a general alteration. Under such conditions Hutten's literary output was necessarily directed to influencing the local and class area in which he stood. It is no accident that he, who had more national feeling and less particularism than most of his contemporaries, should now in the midst of studies on the history and character of the Franks, expressly declare that his German ideal must be predominantly represented and conserved by the knights.

What we have here is not so much a conscious program worked out with reference to the restricted sphere now remaining, as rather an almost irrelevant and arbitrary relapse into conceptions which had always influenced his life and activity. The humanist knight had gained a wide audience in recent years as a pamphleteer. He had kindled enthusiasms and had thrown a heavy weight into the scales against Rome. Class consciousness and humanist feeling were here intimately combined. Now when literary activity by itself could achieve little further, he sought a substitute in the strong sword of the knight.

In the letter to Pirckheimer of the first of May, which was circulated in a German version, Hutten had given a concise survey of the events at Worms. "The priests are greatly elated for the moment. At once they will triumph, for they think a full stop has been set to the story, not realizing, poor fools, how far off the end is still and the last act is yet to be played." Closely connected with this passage is the description of Sickingen's adherence to the Lutheran cause. Hutten tells how Lutheran tracts were read at table and "Sickingen has imbibed them."[4]

That this account is accurate we may not doubt.[5] Actu-

4. Hutten, *Opera,* II, 59 ff.

5. Compare the reports by Aleander in T. Brieger, *Aleander und Luther,* pp. 132 ff., 206. Also *Gesprechbiechlin neüw Karsthans,* edited by E. Lehmann (Halle, 1930), p. 15.

ally in the circle of Sickingen a Lutheran congregation arose at a time when the like was not to be found save in Wittenberg and Nuremberg.[6] Martin Bucer, the future organizer of the church of Strassburg, itself a model for Geneva and England, was in Sickingen's service. So, too, was the Erasmian Oecolampadius, who later made life at Basel uncomfortable for Erasmus. The castles of Sickingen were, for a time, some of the most important centers of growing Protestantism. Luther stayed away from the Ebernburg, but did not forget it. On the first of June his tract *On Confession* was dedicated to the lord of these domains as an expression of "heartfelt thanks for much comfort and readiness to help."[7] And again in March, 1522, he sent greetings to "our friends in the faith, Franz and Ulrich von Hutten and as many more as may be."[8] No wonder that he was moved by Sickingen's death in 1523.

The opposite camp likewise was aware of Sickingen's pro-Lutheran tendencies. Aleander had early written from Worms to Rome that Sickingen studied Luther's works and absorbed them. Toward the end of the diet, that is in the month after Luther's appearance at Worms, the news was most alarming. The legate had heard of menaces of Sickingen against the clergy and the nuntios, yes even that Sickingen had plans against Trier.[9] As a matter of fact the idea of achieving a thorough reform of Church and Empire by a seizure of the Electorate of Trier seems to have been fully matured in these weeks. Sickingen was on the point of beginning in earnest.[10] Was Hutten's plot against the nuntios, which boded unpredictable consequences, connected with these plans? We do not know, but it is symptomatic that in Bucer's tract of these days, the

6. Compare H. Ulmann, *Franz von Sickingen,* pp. 164 ff., 261 ff. J. W. Baum, *Capito und Butzer* (Elberfeld, 1860). G. Anrich, *Martin Butzer* (Strassburg, 1914). H. Eells, *Martin Bucer* (New Haven, 1931).

7. M. Luther, *Werke,* VIII, 139.

8. *Ibid.,* X, Part 2, 53 ff. *Werke, Briefwechsel,* II, 484 ff.

9. T. Brieger, *Aleander und Luther,* p. 216.

10. F. Walser, *Die Politische Entwicklung Ulrichs von Hutten während der Entscheidungsjahre der Reformation,* p. 108.

"Neu-Karsthans," Sickingen again appears as the German Ziska.[11]

In any case Hutten did not succeed in bringing Sickingen to the point of action. On the contrary his patron decided definitely to accept the post of a general in the imperial war against France. The crucial audience with Charles V took place in Mainz on June 3. A month later he received his commission. Hutten was shaken by this turn of events which threw him upon his own resources. He left the Ebernburg and began his war against the Romanists independently. Whether their friendship, however, was thereby seriously affected is open to question, for Sickingen had accepted only military duties and had postponed his own projects for domestic and ecclesiastical politics to a more propitious time. Probably he wished to wait for the departure of the emperor from the Netherlands. Moreover as an imperial general he might assemble a larger army. We do not know whether he hoped to utilize the prestige of victory for the success of his plans. But this is plain that the final acceptance of service with the emperor did not mean the renunciation of his theological and humanist friends. If Hutten at all thought so when he forsook Sickingen's fortresses at the end of May or the beginning of June and undertook his own campaign, he was soon to find out that Sickingen had reserved a place for him in the army about to be assembled for the emperor. Authority was given to commission twenty-five nobles, among them Ulrich von Hutten.[12]

This, too, explains why Hutten's own undertakings failed of any real success. He began his campaign—apart from the assault on Aleander, which miscarried—with the commission to people on all hands (we do not know of what sort) to conduct a feud in his name against all the

11. Hutten, *Opera,* IV, 676 ff. *Neüw Karsthans,* edited by E. Lehmann (Halle, 1930), p. 15. Compare H. Ulmann, *Franz von Sickingen,* p. 268.

12. C. von Höfler, *Papst Adrian VI* (Wien, 1880), p. 58 n. 1. *Die Reichsregisterbücher Kaiser Karls V.,* edited by the K. und k. Haus-, Hof-, und Staatsarchiv, Part I (Vienna, 1913), p. 25.

priests dependent on Rome. He hoped avowedly to cast a torch far over the land, kindling onslaught against Roman dominance. "Conflagrations often arise from a spark," he says in a poem of that period.[13] His personal feud should become a war of wider proportions. The greater part of the knights should be enlisted. But in such hopes he was to be thoroughly disappointed as to the political situation. His sickness contributed to prevent a consistent prosecution of his plan. Before anything was actually done, a new attack drove him for recuperation to Sickingen's castle. He seems to have had the intention of joining Sickingen's army as soon as possible,[14] but in the meantime his protector's destiny began to run its course. The campaign was a failure. The French army under the celebrated knight, Bayard, drove the imperial forces from their first recoil to the Maas to a speedy retreat. Apparently this was not Sickingen's fault alone. The imperial government did not provide the necessary sinews. But Sickingen, in fact, had had no previous opportunity to develop strategetic ability and the court lost all enthusiasm for his further employ. To repay his loans was out of the question. The English ambassador wrote from the imperial court: "Money is so dear which seemeth to be a universal sickness. God amend it." The emperor was in truth in the greatest difficulties. The 20,000 gulden borrowed from Sickingen for the coronation were not once repaid with punctuality and the more recent loan of 76,000 gulden fared no better. Sickingen was forced to send home most of his soldiers with empty promises.

With his military star on the wane and his reputation as a provider for his men seriously impaired, his situation was highly precarious. At the court of the Netherlands there was fear that he might seize one of the Hapsburg territories in pledge. Instead he reverted to the deferred campaign against Trier.[15] Personal enmity of long stand-

13. Hutten, *Opera,* II, 93. 14. *Ibid.,* pp. 81 ff.

15. See H. Ulmann, *Franz von Sickingen,* pp. 261–399. K. H. Rendenbach, *Die Fehde Franz von Sickingens gegen Trier* (*Historische Studien,* Vol. 224, Berlin, 1933).

ing existed between him and the Elector of Trier, Archbishop Richard von Greiffenklau. During the imperial election the archbishop had been rightly suspected as a supporter of Francis I and at the Diet of Worms as an active opponent of Luther. What a fine opportunity to promote the Gospel by seizure of this spiritual electorate! Might not the emperor be forced by an accomplished fact to make Sickingen a prince of the *Reich?* And would not such a *coup d'état*, in the case of one of the pillars of the imperial constitution and arches between the Empire and the Roman Church, of necessity set in motion a general reform?

The circumstances seemed not unfavorable. The Council of the Empire, wrung from Charles V at Worms, was now sitting at Nuremberg and there the princes and the cities were in sharp conflict.[16] The princes were badly in the debt of the cities. If the cities made further concessions their political independence would be imperilled and likewise if they refused new grants until the old were repaid the appetite of the princes would be whetted for their political suppression. Here seemed to be a chance for Sickingen to make the cities his allies and Hutten's pen was not the only one at his service.[17]

But above all, now was the time to rally the free knights themselves for this great reform of the Empire. The name and the connections of Hutten in Mainz and Franconia would be highly serviceable at this juncture. To be sure the actual military help of the independent small lords did not prove later so significant as the indirect assistance of the imperial knights in the service of the princes. Here one recalls the policy of the court prefect of Mainz, Frowin von Hutten, for when Sickingen struck at Trier, Mainz not only refrained from rescue as obligated by im-

16. H. von Schubert, *Lazarus Spengler und die Einführung der Reformation in Nürnberg* (Leipsic, 1934), pp. 313 ff.

17. See in the first place Hartmuth von Cronberg, *Schriften,* edited by E. Kück (Halle, 1899). K. Schottenloher, *Flugschriften zur Ritterschaftsbewegung des Jahres 1523* (*Reformationsgeschichtliche Studien und Texte,* Vol. 53, Münster, 1929).

perial law, but even denied passage to the army of Philip of Hesse.[18] For this unauthorized blocking of the Rhine bridges Frowin von Hutten was penalized by the loss of his post and the Elector Albert by a heavy fine. But Richard von Trier might have lost his position had he not been one of the fighting German bishops. Tragic irony that Sickingen should find his David in a knight in vestments!

The campaign against Trier, commenced on August 29, 1522, had to be abandoned as hopeless after four weeks and now the united princes determined to deal with all the recalcitrant nobles. In the next months dozens of knights' bastions were smashed. Sickingen's castles, too, fell before the artillery of the princes. He himself died sore wounded before the eyes of his conquerors. An epoch of German chivalry sank with him. An independent political rôle was never played by the knights again. Their insignia and social position survived only because the levelling of the Peasants' War inclined the princes to the preservation of the stabilizing elements of the old order. As in the campaign against Sickingen they had given a new lease of life to the spiritual principalities, so they respected henceforth the old tradition of the independent knights.

Hutten had taken no part in the campaign against Trier because of his sickness. When the great blow "against tyranny" collapsed[19] and Sickingen was compelled to prepare his castles for the defense of naked existence, Hutten, sick and no good as a soldier, was compelled to flee.

During this period, that is, from the fall of 1521 to the fall of 1522, he had undertaken only two raids.[20] The first, in the year 1521, was against the Carthusians of Strassburg, who were despoiled of two thousand gulden. The city of Strassburg, which plainly suspected that Sickingen was back of Hutten's declaration of feud, brought

18. H. Ulmann, *Franz von Sickingen,* pp. 309 ff. P. Kalkoff, *Huttens Vagantenzeit und Untergang* (Weimar, 1925), p. 374.

19. Hutten, *Operum Supplementum,* II, 808. Compare *Jahrbuch der Luthergesellschaft,* 1923, p. 84.

20. See P. Kalkoff, *Hutten und die Reformation,* pp. 426 ff.

pressure on the order to pay the money, but when in the spring of 1522 Hutten sent a challenge to the "courtesans" of Frankfurt and Strassburg, the two imperial cities defended the ecclesiastics within their walls. The last act of this somewhat obscure war on the Romanists took place while Sickingen was attacking Trier. Hutten sent a mounted retainer into the Palatinate to enforce apostolic poverty upon two abbeys, but the Elector of the Palatinate caught the man and executed him for highway robbery.[21]

Nothing more came of Hutten's "war on the Romanists." The gauntlets thrown down disdainfully in the hope of a world reformation eventuated only in the reactionary license of the knightly class. One must not forget, however, that Hutten regarded these feuds as thoroughly warranted. It speaks for him that his trial before the *Reich* had not been conducted as he had a right to demand. Such personal experiences naturally confirmed his prejudices against the new legal reforms and confirmed his hate against the internal administration of the *Reich* by the princely class. The Diet of 1495 had forbidden feuds once and for all, and the Diet of Worms had declared a more extensive internal peace. But from the political point of view the people who profited from this peace were the princes. Their right to make war was not touched like that of the knights; and further, the princes had insured their control over the Cameral Tribunal. The knights were not prepared to accept this arrangement as final and in the following years members of their class in Franconia broke into a revolt against the law on internal peace of 1521, in place of which they sought to revive the courts of arbitration of the knights.[22] The key to Hutten's feud lies in the fluctuating struggle between the new and old legal forms.

21. S. Szamatolski, *Ulrichs von Hutten deutsche Schriften* (Strassburg, 1891), pp. 165 ff. J. Schlecht in *Briefmappe II* (*Reformationsgeschichtliche Studien und Texte,* Vol. 40, Munich, 1922), p. 96. Compare P. Joachimsen in *Historische Zeitschrift,* CXXXVI (1927), 344 ff.

22. R. Fellner, *Die fränkische Ritterschaft* (Berlin, 1905), pp. 212 ff.

When the new law denied him justice he reverted for the vindication of his honor to the old, which he always liked better.

Modern law is not the standard by which to judge Hutten's recourse to a feud or even the plundering which accompanied his forays. The old German law, like the English of the present day, allowed compensation for offenses to honor. But taking the law into one's own hands was a constant menace to peaceful commerce and the cities continually and properly complained that the knights took advantage of the law of feudal compensation to appropriate other people's property, since an offense against honor could easily be manufactured when some favored opponent was selected for spoliation. That Hutten's last campaigns, especially the plundering of the abbeys, should have differed so little from these forays of the knights is the more remarkable because he was ostensibly concerned for more than personal affairs. They were national questions. The declaration of feud was aimed at all Romanists and "courtesans." But shortly afterwards those alone were selected who had something to confiscate. The man who was deeply moved because Luther at Worms relied solely on his conscience now pacified his own conscience all too quickly, forgetting that if his person was to be identified with the general cause he must not fall back into the mere turbulence of his class. Previously he had given his picture of primitive German manliness a deep tinge of chivalry, but now this class tendency was extremely dangerous in the practical sphere. The fight for German freedom from foreign influences and pretensions was debased into class provincialism, into the anarchistic struggle of one knight for himself, whose deeds in 1522 could satisfy only his own ambition and not further the common weal. Hutten wanted to show that he was not slack, not unmanned by circumstances. He failed to realize how he exposed the cause not only by this turbulence but also by the unsavory conduct which rumor now bruited abroad. We cannot tell how much may be true in view of the paucity of the evidence, but one comes away with the impression that in the heat of the conflict he lacked the strength to live up to his own moral ideals. He contented himself with an external, forensic justification of the procedure which was to have inaugurated new historical developments. It looks as if he was not unaware of what contemporaries thought about the knights, but when once he had conceived of his affair and of the cause of ecclesiastical reform as a knightly enterprise such considerations influenced him no more. He would prove himself a good knight in combatting the dominant powers. The inconsistency which he discovered only confirmed his conviction that his cause was just. In struggling for new ends he was more obstinate than the ordinary knight in clinging to contested and outmoded legal forms.

Something of this sort drove him to dubious courses and rendered him futile in politics. One might say that neither in the moral nor in the political sphere was he enough of a realist to see the threatening snares. In both he refused to recognize that new spiritual forms are required for the mastery of a changed reality. The resistance of the princes to the Reformation enkindled to a high heat his old hate against "the tyranny." The tracts of the year 1522—the *Warning to Free and Imperial Cities of the German Nation* and the *Humble Exhortation to the Entire City of Worms*,[23] as well as the *Message to the Elector of the Palatinate*[24] called for a limitation of princely power. The nobles and the city should combine to bring this to pass. But such plans had small chance of success,[25] even granted that Hutten was not entirely mistaken when he saw in the princes a menace not only as formerly to the *Reich* but also to the Reformation. Lutheranism lost much in universal influence by the alliance with the territorial princes. Nevertheless it is highly questionable whether the knights and the cities could have provided an adequate basis for

23. Hutten, *Opera,* III, 527 ff.; II, 124 ff.
24. See note 21, above.
25. H. von Schubert, *Lazarus Spengler und die Einführung der Reformation in Nürnberg,* pp. 362 ff.

the Reformation and whether they would have been strong enough to carry through a reform both of the *Reich* and of the Church. For the cities and the knights too were already widely dependent on the princes. Things had come to such a pass in Germany that the peace of the land depended on the princes, and no longer, as previously, on the *Reich*. Their courts took care of the legal protection which the industry of the cities demanded. And, after all, the nobles profited too. However galling the restrictions of the free knighthood by the princely powers, the noble was glad to turn to the princes to provide the younger sons with civil posts or protect them in the enjoyment of ecclesiastical benefices. Some members of the noble chapter of Mainz—Hutten's relatives among them—might indeed take a hand with Sickingen to the prejudice of Mainz, but where the noble was to be found in a decisive case Sickingen was to discover to his cost in the campaign against the Archbishop of Trier. Most of the knights of Franconia were not willing to help, despite their restiveness under the renewal at Worms of the prohibition of feuds.[26]

For the combination which Hutten sought now to effect between the cities and the knights in the interests of the Reformation and Sickingen's undertakings the spiritual presuppositions were lacking. One scarcely needs to recall how the city dwellers felt toward the knights who imperilled their lines of communication, and it was highly dubious whether the cities would forget these ancient grievances. The noble on his side was far from being in a position to appreciate the contribution of the cities. Hutten himself, in his writings, did not emerge from the prejudices of the nobles. While admitting faults among the knights, he portrayed the cities as even further degenerated from the primitive German ideal of manliness and simplicity. The cities would have to cast off a long list of shortcomings before they would be fit comrades for the knights. These are the old complaints which Hutten now urgently

26. P. Kalkoff, *Huttens Vagantenzeit und Untergang*, pp. 376 ff.

renewed—complaints over the arrogant extravagance of urban life, over the corrosive influence of large scale commerce, over the menace of capitalism and monopolies. These objections were common in contemporary literature. That luxury exceeded all reason may be inferred from the many sumptuary regulations of the cities, for we are not to suppose that these laws were actuated by Calvinist asceticism so much as by civic moderation. It is odd, nevertheless, that Hutten should seek to excuse the feud of the knights against the cities on the ground that the knights would curb German luxury.[27]

27. Hutten, *Opera,* IV, 369 ff.

XII

HUTTEN'S CONTROVERSY WITH ERASMUS. LAST DAYS

HUTTEN'S efforts to win the cities, however unsuccessful otherwise, profited him at least personally in that they were ready to receive him when he was compelled to leave Sickingen's fortress. In November, 1522, Ulrich went by way of Schlettstadt to Basel. The City Council honored him on his arrival as a distinguished guest, but would not incur any inconvenience on his account. A polemical tract against a doctor who had plainly mistreated him, an attack on the Palatine Count Ludwig, and the continued propaganda for the war against the "courtesans" occasioned his dismissal a few months later. Hutten turned to Mühlhausen in Alsace, where he was harbored by the monks of Luther's order, the Augustinians.

Here in Mühlhausen was composed the *Expostulation*, the tract in which Hutten turned the weapons of his polemic against Erasmus, the ideal of his formative period.[1] Two years before, when he met Erasmus at Louvain, he might have sensed that the great humanist was not prepared for a decisive and warlike attack on the problem of church reform. But only when it became apparent that Erasmus would not only stand aside in pacific neutrality from the tumult, but would also try to mediate between the parties, did venomous contempt arise in Hutten against the man whom he had regarded as the spiritual director and stimulator of progress. In a letter of the fifteenth of August, 1520, to Erasmus,[2] the flames of mistrust leaped up around the ideal picture which Hutten had carried in

1. Hutten, *Opera*, II, 180 ff.
2. *Ibid.*, I, 367 ff. Allen, *Opus epistularum Erasmi*, Ep. 1135, IV, 328 ff.

his heart. Erasmus was warned not to conceal his reformatory tendencies from the potentates of the Church. He was mistaken if he thought he could persuade the opponents that he was not the precursor of Luther. But such concern for his own person would alienate his followers. Yet Hutten avoided pulling the cord of separation as he had done with Reuchlin. He sought rather to lure and persuade than to threaten and repel. Now he besought Erasmus at least to preserve silence and not to come out openly against his war. He still honored him and a letter written a little later from Ebernburg seems to regard the former idol as still a symbol of the future peace beyond the struggle for the restoration of German freedom. Now Hutten exhorted Erasmus to stay in Basel, far from the scene of conflict, and devote himself to scholarship.[3]

But the engulfing political turmoil caused such hopes to recede, and Luther as the moving personality in the struggle overshadowed Erasmus. The way in which men lined up with reference to Luther became for Hutten more and more the touchstone by which to measure them. Erasmus' deficiency in this regard weighed heavily, and had they met in Basel the debate would have been more acrimonious than in the letter of August, 1520. Already, in Schlettstadt, Hutten had complained to their friend Beatus Rhenanus over the attitude of Erasmus and desired to go to Basel to "bolster his courage." But there was no meeting. Erasmus advised Hutten not to visit him.

After the last meeting of the two, in the summer of 1520, the position of Erasmus had become more difficult. Hutten was right that the warring factions could not be appeased with half-explanations. Though at first Erasmus could justify his aloofness with the hope of casting the weight of his judgment for the settlement of the controversy, the sensitive man was soon driven to the defense of nothing more than his own personal existence against the mistrust and reproaches cast upon him from all sides. The

3. Hutten, *Opera,* I, 423. Allen, *Opus epistularum Erasmi,* Ep. 1161, IV, 380.

days were gone when he could greet the coming century with joyful enthusiasm in almost the words of Hutten. A century of peace it should have been for Erasmus, not an epoch of sectarianism. The horizon was dark for him, with the lowering clouds of dissension, and the storm ravished from his nostrils the air which he was accustomed to breathe. "He who likes this century is welcome to it. I consider it most calamitous."[4] He lived from now on in an inner disquietude occasioned by a concern for something deeper than his own personal defenselessness against the powers of darkness. It has been held against him that he had formerly preached the necessity of martyrdom for every Christian, but now, when the test drew near, he declared: "Not all have the strength for martyrdom. I am afraid, should tumult break out, I would imitate Peter."[5] But who will measure how much more inconsolable the old age of Erasmus was rendered precisely by the hesitant participation which he chose for himself?

At the beginning of the Reformation Erasmus was considered in general as one of the fathers of the new movement, and his criticism of the Church was publicly regarded as a prelude to Luther. This view of the matter was at bottom as little justified as its opposite. The wishes and the objectives of Erasmus moved in a direction of his own. The Erasmian standpoint taken to its logical conclusion was as revolutionary as the Lutheran. But when it came to a definite answer for or against Luther—and excited contemporaries would have nothing but yes or no—he was forced to line up with the conservative party. The teaching and ceremonies of the Catholic Church might seem to him in many respects alien and cramping. Nevertheless in the main he felt that he belonged within the unity of her life and historic continuity, because he could attribute to her institutions a moral and pedagogical justification. He believed in the natural development of history, which he desired to see interrupted neither by the

4. Hutten, *Opera,* II, 322.
5. Allen, *Opus epistularum Erasmi,* Ep. 1218, IV, 541.

political nor spiritual revolutions of individuals. This note is very characteristic in a long unrecovered letter to Luther of August 1, 1520, where his revulsion from the Lutheran cause is clearly foreshadowed: "A serious matter it is to provoke those who cannot be overcome save by great disturbance. Such disturbances I greatly fear because they often get out of hand. If the sea is undyked its waters cannot again be controlled. If the situation demands disturbance I would rather that someone else start it."[6] At that moment he went no farther indeed than to admonish Luther to abstain from an attack on the system of the Church and promised him assistance in that case. But when Luther in the *Babylonian Captivity* laid the axe directly at the root of the Church, the inner rupture was complete. Erasmus looked to the approved power of the Church and rejected a party which believed itself in league with God to shatter her unity. Hence he was driven to rely on traditional viewpoints and political currents alien to his spirit. For a while he hoped to mediate between the parties, but the time demanded from him a confession for or against Luther. Hutten gave to the question which was on so many lips the sharpest possible answer, when on quitting Basel he addressed his *Expostulation* to Erasmus.

The great humanist, in spite of the interview in Louvain and the letter of August, 1520, did not realize how wide the gulf had become. His fondness for Ulrich had received recent expression. To be sure, he regretted that Hutten was "withdrawn by this tumult from the Muses," and, in a letter to Pirckheimer, recognized Hutten's lack of political realism: "He who writes such invectives as those of Hutten against the nuntios must have an army ready for action behind him." Nevertheless he could praise Hutten's courage of conviction. The rejection of the visit, then, did not mean the rejection of the man, but merely a desire to avoid political complications. Just as he had requested

6. Not in Allen, *Opus epistularum Erasmi.* The letter was first published by O. Clemen in *Zeitschrift für Kirchengeschichte,* XLIX (1930), pp. 159 ff. and again in M. Luther, *Werke, Briefwechsel,* II, 155 ff.

Luther in August, 1520, not to cite him by name in his books in order not to increase his difficulties in orthodox Louvain, so now he begged Hutten to accept his critical circumstances as an excuse. Everything indicates that the wish of Erasmus was transmitted to Hutten in friendly and discreet fashion.[7] He may have been disappointed, but he was not immediately incensed. But when a few weeks later a letter of Erasmus to Marcus Laurinus appeared in print,[8] in which the writer repudiated before his friends in the Netherlands any connection with Lutheranism, Hutten allowed himself to be persuaded by the Protestant opponents of Erasmus in Basel to bring him to task. Now the rejection of the visit, which Erasmus in this letter incorrectly attributed to a divergence of opinion, came to be associated with the varied betrayals of the cause of the Reformation. The Basel episode having become a personal slight, the tract took on the embittered tone of an outlaw.

And yet in his own persecution Hutten did not become a mere persecutor of Erasmus. The gifts and services of his former patron counted for more than the pain of discourtesy. "The natural talents, the spiritual gifts and persuasiveness" of the great opponent were not discounted. The stimulus received from Erasmus was expressly acknowledged.[9] One would suppose that the independence of the Erasmian conceptions would have made more of an impression on Hutten and that he would have been the last to try to make Erasmus feel an obligation to the Lutheran cause. Hutten himself had not emerged from the theological point of view of Erasmus, and he was himself aware that he could not be called a Lutheran in the full sense of the term. "I admire Luther's spirit and his incomparable power in interpreting the secrets of scripture, but Luther has been neither my teacher nor my comrade."[10] But on the other hand Hutten had only in a measure appropri-

7. Compare the admirable study of W. Kaegi "Hutten und Erasmus," in *Historische Vierteljahrsschrift,* XXII (1924), 200 and 461 ff.

8. Hutten, *Opera,* II, 158 ff. Allen, *Opus epistularum Erasmi,* Ep. 1342.

9. Hutten, *Opera,* II, 195.

10. *Ibid.,* p. 223.

ated the ideas of Erasmus, and in so doing had given them a new turn by combining them with his romantic Germanic conceptions. For that reason he arrived at a very different judgment of the ecclesiastical hierarchy, and in the struggle with the Roman institutions for German freedom he could rejoice in the Lutheran religious renewal. So in the *Expostulation* he urged: "Although I am myself an independent and hate passionately to be reckoned to a party, nevertheless I will always belong to those who are opposed to the tyranny of the Roman Pope, who defend the truth and reject man-made precepts for the teaching of the Gospel. Because such people are commonly called Lutherans, I will suffer with equanimity the injustice of the name lest I seem in the end to deny the justice of the cause. . . . Here you have the explanation why I suffer myself to be nicknamed a 'Lutheran.' And in this sense it is easy to persuade every one that you are a Lutheran, too,—the more so because you are a better writer and a more persuasive speaker."

Hutten conceived of his own thoughts and intentions as the fruit of the Erasmian ideas, and Erasmus himself, even though beginning to write against Luther, was nevertheless in part on his side. "You are not so much against us as against your own spirit and books. You have to persuade against your own persuasiveness. Your books withstand each other."[11] Hutten was unable to explain the attitude of Erasmus on the basis of the objective situation. Even though he might renounce political leadership for the outward carrying out of the reform, nevertheless the reform was the reform, the necessity of which Erasmus himself had proclaimed among the loudest. If now, in the decisive hour, he vaunted his connection with the old Church, thereby he declined to champion the new ideas against opposition, and to do this was in Hutten's eyes the essential fruit of humanist training. The attitude of the watchful observer he could not tolerate even tempo-

11. Hutten, *Opera,* II, 247. Compare also II, 234.

rarily. "You say we should dissimulate for the moment. Such words scarcely beseem any Christian let alone a scholar and a theologian, when a pagan author condemns dissimulation in friendship as corrupting judgment of the true. How much less are simulation and dissimulation appropriate to one in your station. To do and to suffer all things arduous and adverse on behalf of liberty is our concern. But every one sees that your thought is to avoid offense and to labor without suspicion. If victory crowned such efforts no one would strive."[12]

The significance of the controversy between Hutten and Erasmus is to be discovered not merely in the conflict of romantic Germanism in Lutheran dress over against cosmopolitan rationalistic humanism, but in the friction between an activistic and quietistic humanist. Both failed to grasp the point. They saw their difference not as a contrast of spiritual conceptions and individual opinions, but as a difference in moral capacity.

Everything which Hutten formerly had falsely attributed to Erasmus or exaggerated in him now served as a moral reproach, as cowardice, egoism, ambition. "What you yourself sowed and planted, what you instituted and prompted, that you now discard with your violent eloquence as something to be expiated with a bloody sin offering. Could one conceive of a greater change?" The following indignant words are the sequel to the former praise of the German Erasmus: "The Germans are not like this, but rather the fickle and inconsistent foreigners, who turn like a weathercock. One finds this sort in Italy, among your confidants, the Roman cardinals, where each follows his own inclinations and pleasures. Or take those French Germans [the Netherlanders] who abound in all your characteristic faults. Unless you moderate these faults, to us intolerable, all Germans will have to ask you to go elsewhere, I think, and no longer imbue our youth by your example with a levity and inconsistency alien to our nation."[13]

12. Hutten, *Opera,* II, 196. 13. *Ibid.,* p. 239.

Erasmus did not find it difficult to rebut Hutten's reproaches. With regard to his relation to Reuchlin, Hutten had written: "I so championed his cause that his enemies always suffered, and far worse from me than from him. That was how he could swear a sacred oath that he assumed no responsibility for the complaints against me."[14] Erasmus could use this involuntary concession of Hutten as applied to their own relations. Hutten's political activities had always been foreign to him, and even his ties to the young knight had not been so intimate or binding as Hutten pretended. But Erasmus was not content to clarify these misunderstandings and thus to cut the ground from under the moral reproaches heaped upon him. He too was not quite willing to pull the cord which should separate him definitively from Hutten. "My writings show how cordially I have treasured Hutten's spirit and talents." And for that reason his reply would merely refute the accusations with brevity and not pile up "reproaches and revilings." But in spite of this preface, *The Sponge to Wipe Out the Aspersions of Hutten*,[15] is prolix, twice as long as the *Expostulation*. The temptation was consistently gratified to set Hutten's person in an unfavorable light. Hutten wrote thunderously and not without embittered and violent passion. Erasmus was prompted by a hate born of repressed fear.

Erasmus was especially nettled that Hutten's screed had appeared in a German version of unparalleled virulence for which the author was not responsible. This circumstance explains only in part, however, why Erasmus forgot himself in the choice of weapons. His inability to maintain an unimpassioned judgment arose not merely from the difficulty of his situation after the emergence of Luther, but also from a veiled human weakness. Only a careful comparison of these polemical tracts makes it quite apparent that the literary feud was not only the inevitable conflict of irreconcilable ideas beyond the region of acci-

14. *Ibid.*, p. 183.

15. *Ibid.*, pp. 265 ff.

dental outward irritations, but was also the product of far deeper forces. When one reads the tract of Erasmus one wonders why he was continually resorting to the weapons of defamation and contempt which he had promised to spurn, for on the whole he was able to show that Hutten's caricature rested only on details drawn from their context, and that amid all the changes of circumstances he himself had remained true to his initial persuasions, at any rate in the sense that "Consistent does not mean that one should always use the same language, but that one should always have the same objectives."[16] But that he should have forgotten all the cordial hopes he had entertained for humanism a few years before, that he should not be aware how easily his varied statements were capable of misunderstandings like those of Hutten, leaves a bad taste in the mouth. His tract against Hutten shows a curious exaggeration of the uniformity and success of his activity and suggests that he had need of such an ideal picture of himself in order to master an inner disquiet over his own being and position. In Hutten he met the same mood which rendered Luther unfathomable. To discover the like in Hutten was the more irritating because the affinity was otherwise greater in spite of the knight's armor. In both Luther and Hutten, Erasmus found the resolve to treat some one thing as the highest good and to confess it even though open revolution should result. Luther's position did not get under his skin so sharply because it could be rejected as "paradox." Luther sought to express in his formulations a new experience of God: that God is above and over against all learning, all philosophy, that He produces a new spirit and will, and in consequence here is the true sign of genuine believers, that they always constitute a minority. Erasmus simply could not comprehend this. He could not separate faith and reason, religious and philosophical truth, and it seemed to him impossible on the basis of the one to make war on the other, as he warned

16. Hutten, *Opera,* II, 295.

Luther: "If you utterly damn all philosophy you will have to reckon not only with all the universities, but also with all the ancients, and even with your own Augustine."[17] One should seek rather by comparison and criticism of varied opinions to recover the irreducible kernel, to mature human reason that it may be able to grasp the divine profundity. Hence one should not repudiate the storehouse of tradition. Only by making it available and sifting it can cultural progress be attained. In contrast to Luther, for whom the world and the powers of man belonged to Satan, and for whom history acquired definite meaning only in a break with tradition, Erasmus saw the divine plan unfolded in the continuity of history. Here for him lay the real appeal of the Catholic Church, and the division into laity and clergy seemed to him necessary, for only the learned can attain the highest degrees of truth. Authority consequently had a place. Luther's doctrine of the priesthood of all believers, and that the religious truth of Scripture is intelligible to the simple believer, was to Erasmus an abomination.

The ideas which Erasmus worked out and published have had an immense historical influence, and from their elaboration many a revolution and world convulsion have arisen. But in the form in which Erasmus expressed them, of the immanent holiness of history and the power of human reason, they were calculated rather to conserve the inherited and traditional—not in their entirety, of course, but in the main. Erasmus appealed to the perfectability of mankind, but his contemplative thought, and his theory of the germ of good already present in all things could not cow the demonic in man. It was a hardy Utopia to expect that the authorities and powers, even if they became his disciples, would heed his appeal, a Utopia which some day undoubtedly must kindle men, yet which arose from the impulse of one who by contemplation wished at once to rule and withdraw. We could understand how this illegiti-

17. M. Luther, *Werke, Briefwechsel,* II, 155 ff.

mate son of a priest, at home in no class of society and early compelled to be the guest of all nations, should have given a revolutionary tinge to his ideas. But he tried to fortify himself against his origin and his homelessness by winning a grasp on totality, through unremitting and unsparing toil. It is no accident that he rejected all offices, refused to take root in any particular locality, and made good his ambition to be a literary man. His lack of social class is responsible for the fact that he could feel at home in the university of the spirit but that he never came to grips with concrete life. This is the human basis of his approval of the authorities: he had suffered too much from the pitiableness of little potentates not to wish that for the future the great officials would keep them under their thumbs. Nevertheless he regarded the mixed character of his inner life, compounded of weakness and courage, as "fated." He could not rise above this fate. All hope for posthumous influence could not eradicate the feeling that he was but fulfilling his destiny, instead of being free to accept or reject. That is why, in his reply to Hutten, he could not remain cool and confine himself to the clarification of principles. That is why vengeance and hate flowed from his pen as he attacked the evil life and the political futility of his opponent in order to reinstate himself in the eyes of the world and in his own and to vindicate his antipathy to "revolution" and his love of *civilitas*.[18] The most clear-cut example perhaps is the passage where he tried to laugh off Hutten's philosophy of conflict, even against the odds of Fortune, by suggesting that he might go to Rome or Franco-Germany to seek the martyr's crown.[19] A sort of perverted envy comes to expression in the refutation of the apostate disciple Hutten, who was resolved to transfer the humanist ideals to the sphere of activity and to embrace "the party of paradoxes." Erasmus writes: "Hutten has fortresses and walls, troops and guns, firearms and swords,

18. See his "De libero arbitrio contra M. Lutherum," *Opera* (Leiden), X, 1283.

19. Hutten, *Opera,* II, 310.

declarations of feud—in short, all the munitions of war with which to defend himself. I exist only through the favor of the good and of a few powerful lords."

This contempt for a defenseless and despised fugitive shows, nevertheless, the unusual understanding of Erasmus for his fellow men. Hutten had not been actuated like Luther by a sense of religious compulsion, but by ancestry and blood. He was not a knight pure and simple; he was too much of a literary man for that. But the devotion of his writings to deeds, and finally the half-jocular, half-fanatical way in which he toyed with his own existence, bear the stamp of chivalry. Now, in the moment when the sun of knighthood sank forever, history permitted one from its ranks to share in the labor, care, and anguish of decisions, and thereby some of the ideal weapons with which chivalry so long had wrought became the plowshares of the future. German humanism, fostered from now on in the cities, brought forth for the first time in Lessing a personality who with similar passion sought to project spiritual achievements from the schoolroom into the world, mould realities in accord with their pattern. It cannot be regarded as accidental that the heirs of Lessing began to look back to his predecessors among the knights. Since patriotic feeling in the waning of the Holy Roman Empire did not go essentially beyond the national ideas of Hutten, his language for that reason remained thus far intelligible. Goethe, in speaking of the enthusiasm of the youth of his generation for the combination of national and cosmopolitan culture, remarked that these interests had their roots in the epoch between the fifteenth and sixteenth centuries. "The works of Ulrich von Hutten came into my hands and it seemed to me truly remarkable that what took place then should recur in our own days."

The pamphlet of Erasmus never reached Hutten's eyes. When the news came of the rout of Sickingen's knights and the death of their leader, Hutten had to flee from Mühlhausen to escape menacing fists. Security was possible now only outside of the limits of the *Reich.* Not only the princes but even the imperial authorities were active against him. Pope Hadrian had besought Archduke Ferdinand, in a brief composed by Cajetan, to take action as the emperor's representative against "the Mohammedan onslaughts" of Hutten, more dangerous than the incursions of the Turks.[20] There was, in consequence, no longer any place for him in the Empire and he turned again to Switzerland, where Zwingli was just in the process of carrying through a reform of the Church along humanist lines. He gave Hutten an asylum. To do so was an act of courage. The attitude of the people was still dubious and favor to Hutten meant disfavor with Erasmus, to whom Zwingli owed so much of his spiritual life. On the tenth of August, 1523, Erasmus wrote to the Council of Zurich warning them against sheltering Hutten.[21] Nevertheless Zwingli stood his ground. This was the most significant direct effect of the controversy between Hutten and Erasmus, that the Swiss reformer began to dissociate himself from Erasmus and to move in the direction of active reform.

During the winter of 1520–1521 Crotus had opened the eyes of his friend to what would be involved in a war against the Romanists. In the dialogue *Huttenus illustris* the goddess of truth addresses her champion, Hutten, in the rôle of the *miles Christianus:* "You will not think of wife, nor child, nor gold. All these you will esteem as trifles. You will love your country. For her liberty you will forsake the paternal roof and live in some cave or deserted tower. You will obtain as many books as you can and the best, especially those dealing with the Gospel of Christ and if any one bans or condemns further you will take it without bitterness."[22] Save for slight discrepancies this is exactly what did happen. In exile he was practically without resources, for he did not dare lay claim to his mother's in-

20. P. Balan, *Monumenta reformationis Lutheranae* (Ratisbonae, 1884), p. 298.

21. Hutten, *Opera,* II, 256. Allen, *Opus epistularum Erasmi,* Ep. 1379, IV, 311.

22. Hutten, *Opera,* IV, 598.

heritance lest his family be involved in the interdict. Also the greater part of his books and the large collection of his humanist correspondence were part of the spoils after Sickingen's debacle.

The shades of death began to close about the man who was only just turned thirty-five. In swift and almost continuous succession the disease attacked him. But nothing could separate him from his ideals and his nature. Once more in the last letter which he sent to Germany we hear all the old tones responding to his master touch: "Is there any measure and any end to dire fortune pursuing us so bitterly? I doubt it. Nevertheless we have enough spirit to endure her insults. She who subjects us to all other injuries leaves us this one solace and refuge. My flight brings me to Switzerland. And it may be I must go even further. Germany, in her present state, cannot suffer me, though I hope soon to see a glorious transformation when the tyrants are expelled. A respite from carnage has given me leisure for literary pursuits. I will set myself hard to writing. Fortune has conferred this one boon upon us that after great and hateful strife she has brought us back to the tranquil quietude of studies."[23] And yet in these very last studies he was making war on Fortune. A pamphlet which he sent to a friend with an urgent plea for publication is not extant. He called it a tract "Against Tyrants," and said it was written that "posterity might know who they were who set themselves with base audacity against honesty, laws, justice, faith, and religion." One might suppose for a moment that this was the letter despatched the year before to the Elector of the Palatinate in defense of the campaigns, were it not that "tyrants" is here in the plural. Was he gathering up his life-long polemic against the barbarian theologians, the absolutist princes, the robbing "courtesans," the inquisitorial churchmen, and the craven humanists?

We do not know, for the tract was not printed. Ger-

23. *Ibid.*, II, 252 ff.

many was nervous and individual personalities were overshadowed by social groups and classes and political institutions. The day of single combat was over. The colors of life became more drab. Hutten was not only banished, but also abandoned by his German contemporaries. He himself had reached the last station of his life. Death overtook him on the twenty-ninth of August, 1523, on the island of Ufnau on Lake Zurich, where he had sought the medical attention of John Klarer, both pastor and doctor.[24] When the inhabitants learned through the death announcement the identity of the stranger entertained in their midst, Hutten's last host was compelled to flee in haste. Thus even in death he who all his life had incited men to action and decision was to cast fire on the earth.

His achievements and his frustration bear the marks of human greatness. Still a kindling force in modern German history is he who first wrestled with her deepest problem: that of a genuine synthesis of spiritual freedom with the external needs of the nation. Throughout the centuries with all their variations the appeal to Ulrich von Hutten belongs only to those for whom the nation is a way of ascent to *Humanitas*.

24. See D. Fretz, "Johannes Klarer, genannt Schnegg, der letzte Gastgeber Huttens," in *Festgabe für H. Escher* (Zurich, 1927), pp. 127 ff.

BIBLIOGRAPHICAL NOTE

No historical period has received so much attention of late from bibliographers as that of the German Reformation. An exhaustive treatment at this point is, therefore, superfluous. Gustav Wolf made a beginning toward a comprehensive bibliography in his *Quellenkunde der deutschen Reformationsgeschichte* (Gotha, 1915–23). The survey in the ninth edition of Dahlmann-Waitz, *Quellenkunde zur deutschen Geschichte* (Leipsic, 1931), likewise from the pen of G. Wolf, was extensive though by no means so comprehensive as the massive collection assembled with astonishing industry by Karl Schottenloher in his *Bibliographie zur deutschen Geschichte im Zeitalter der Glaubensspaltung, 1517–1585* (edited by the *Kommission zur Erforschung der Geschichte der Reformation und Gegenreformation,* Leipsic, 1933 ff.). In addition to these works the reader may profitably consult Franz Schnabel, *Deutschlands geschichtliche Quellen und Darstellungen in der Neuzeit,* Vol. I: *Das Zeitalter der Reformation, 1500–1550* (Leipsic, 1931). I wrote the section on the Reformation in the American Historical Association's *Guide to Historical Literature* edited by George Frederick Howe and others (New York, 1961), pp. 551 ff.

The magnificent edition of Hutten's works by Eduard Böcking remains to this day the initial source for all investigation of the man. There is nothing comparable to it in the area of humanist research except the edition of the letters of Erasmus by P. S. Allen. Eduard Böcking was a distinguished legal historian from the school of Savigny, professor of law at Bonn, a man of wide training and fine artistic taste, a friend of August Wilhelm Schlegel, himself one of the leaders of the romantic school in Germany. Böcking fulfilled the wish of Herder, who in 1776 complained that Germany had not discharged her debt to Hutten by erecting a monument in the publication of his works. As a matter of fact the *Opera Ulrichi Hutteni equitis Germani* (five volumes, Leipsic, 1859–62, and two supplementary volumes, Leipsic, 1864–70) is more than a monument. It is a quarry of the first rank for the history of German humanism in the period from 1510 to 1523, because we have here not only the writings of Hutten, but also the letters to him, as well as documents about him and writings commonly attributed to him, which are useful for comparison with his own.

After 1870 a whole series of additions to Hutten's biography came to light, but nothing which detracted seriously from Böcking's work. All of these contributions are utilized in the notes to the present work. Among these discoveries only one needs to be mentioned here, namely that of S. Szamatólski, *Ulrich von Huttens deutsche Schriften* (Strassburg, 1891), because these letters constitute an important enlargement of our sources for the decisive years of Hutten's life from 1520 to 1523. They show, too, that the epistolary material available to Böcking, though relatively extensive, was nevertheless only a small portion of Hutten's correspondence. He referred himself at the end of his life to a collection of 2,000 letters which he had collected. To this day they remain unrecovered and among the resulting gaps in our sources are the great losses in the exchange with Luther and Erasmus. All researches in the archives of the Hutten family have thus far proved vain. Only Szamatólski was lucky enough to discover a bundle of authentic documents.

On the other hand, the sources for the general history of the time have been very greatly augmented since Böcking, especially in the case of literary history. In this area only a few examples may be cited. The first place is accorded to the magnificent work of P. S. Allen, *Opus epistularum Erasmi Roterodami* (Oxford, 1906 ff.). Editions of the German humanists have been undertaken in recent years by the *Kommission zur Erforschung der Geschichte der Reformation und Gegenreformation,* to which reference has already been made. A beginning was made by E. König in the publication of Konrad Peutinger's correspondence (Munich, 1926). Then after a long interval followed the letters of Johann Cuspinian edited by H. Ankwicz von Kleehoven, and of Conrad Celtis by H. Rupprich (Munich, 1933 and 1934).

Besides the humanists, Luther and a host of popular pamphleteers of the Reformation must be consulted in any treatment of Hutten. One turns first to the great critical edition of Luther's works *Kritische Gesamtausgabe der Werke Martin Luthers* commonly referred to as the *Weimarer Ausgabe*. Particular attention should be called to the most recent section, the correspondence edited by O. Clemen (seven volums so far, 1930 ff.), which is in process of superseding the older edition of Enders and Kawerau.

For the popular literature the following sources are the more important:

"Flugschriften aus der Reformationszeit," in *Neudrucke deutscher Literaturwerke des XVI. und XVII. Jahrhunderts,* edited by W. Braune (Halle, 1877 ff.).

Flugschriften aus den ersten Jahren der Reformation, edited by O. Clemen (Halle and Leipsic, 1906 ff.).

Flugschriften aus der Reformationszeit in Facsimiledrucken, edited by O. Clemen (Leipsic, 1921 ff.).

SECONDARY WORKS

Modern concern for Hutten goes back to Herder, who between 1776 and 1793 renewed interest in the man as a great German and thereby evoked a strong echo. Goethe it was who especially followed him in this enthusiasm. The "Goetz von Berlichingen" and "Faust" demonstrate that he was powerfully drawn to this great century of German history and the autobiography *Poetry and Truth* testifies to the impetus derived from Hutten's writings. For this early renaissance of Hutten studies one will find the sources in Herder's *Werke,* edited by Suphan, IX, 476 ff.; XVI, 273 ff. and in Goethe, *Dichtung und Wahrheit* (III, 12 and 13). An English author, Anthony Aufrere, observed these early beginnings and happening to find an anonymous article by Herder in the *Deutsche Merkur,* mistook it for the work of Goethe whose star was just swinging into the European heaven, and translated it with the title, "A Tribute to the memory of Ulric of Hutten, contemporary with Erasmus and Luther; one of the most zealous antagonists, as well of the papal powers as of all despotic government, and one of the most elegant Latin authors of his time; translated from the German of Goethe, the celebrated author of the Sorrows of Werther, London, 1789."

The development of Hutten's portrait since Goethe cannot be pursued here in detail, but we must call attention to the richest and soundest appraisal of the man, which stands the fire of contemporary criticism, namely the treatment from the pen of Leopold Ranke in his *History of Germany in the Period of the Reformation.* Yet the few lines which he was able to devote to the subject did not take the place of a biography. The impetus came from the Böcking edition of the works, but was not from the pen of the learned editor, but rather from an influential author of the time, David Friedrich Strauss, at whose disposal Böcking generously placed his entire collection. Strauss, who had exiled himself from academic life through the storm occasioned by his *Life of Jesus* (1835), devoted himself thereafter frequently to biographies of figures exclusively drawn from the leaders of the European Enlightenment, fighters against clerical or political dominance. Hutten was portrayed in the same vein as a precursor of the movement for German unification.

The biography, which appeared in the first edition in 1858 and then in a new form directly after the unification of Germany, was naturally a great success, because in accord with the national enthusiasm and the anticlericalism of the liberals. For the first time the writings of Hutten in extensive citations were made accessible to a wider public. The literary merits of the work were great and have made the book one of the most widely read biographies in Germany. The *Life of Jesus* was speedily forgotten, but the *Hutten* enjoyed frequent reprinting. The last edition was that of O. Clemen (Leipsic, 1927). An abbreviated English edition was translated by Mrs. G. Sturge (London, 1874).

Really, however, the biography is not the work of an historian in command of the general history of the sixteenth century. Strauss was acquainted only in a superficial way with the political and social relations of the age, and likewise in the history of ideas he was not at home. Luther's theology was a closed book to him. As a liberal rationalist he had an eye only for the negative contribution of Luther, the demolition of the medieval church, and not for the positive content of his piety.

For fifty years Strauss' picture was dominant and found further dissemination through the Swiss poet Conrad Ferdinand Meyer in his cycle *Huttens letzte Tage*. On Meyer consult the edition of R. B. Roulston, *Huttens letzte Tage* (Baltimore, 1933). The historical specialists were well aware of the weaknesses of Strauss' book. Nevertheless the biographies of the next years introduced but slight modifications of Strauss. They are: G. Wolf, *Ulrich von Hutten* (Berlin, 1906); K. Jordan, *Ulrich von Hutten* (Berlin, 1908); O. Harnack, "Ulrich von Hutten," in *Im Morgenrot der Reformation*, edited by J. von Pflugk-Hartung (Hersfeld, 1912, 4th ed., Basel, 1922).

Criticism made itself heard in the general treatments, for example in F. von Bezold's *Geschichte der deutschen Reformation* (Berlin, 1890), or in F. Paulsen's *Geschichte des gelehrten Unterrichts auf den deutschen Schulen und Universitäten* (Leipsic, 1885; 2nd ed. 1896). The last book treated humanism as a disturbing factor in the history of German education. Consequently an important part of Hutten's national contribution was eliminated. The Catholic scholars were not ready to accord Hutten a positive rôle in history. On the contrary, F. W. Kampschulte in his book *Die Universität Erfurt in ihrem Verhältnis zu dem Humanismus und der Reformation* (Trier, 1858 ff.) and Johannes Janssen in his *Geschichte des deutschen Volkes seit dem Ausgang des Mittelalters* (1876–1888) utilized the revolutionary aspects of Hutten's career in order to call in question Luther's religious motives for his break with Rome. By stressing the ephemeral "alliance" between Luther and Hutten in the conflict with Rome the religious reformer could be transformed into a secular politician.

If my judgment is correct, such treatments lead Kalkoff (d. 1928) to deny to Hutten any rôle of importance in the history of the German Reformation. This conservative Protestant scholar undertook in his last years to treat Hutten as an anarchistic spirit, of no significance for the Reformation and of only the third rank as a humanist. Kalkoff did make a contribution in relating Hutten's career to the social and political conditions of the period in which the historian was well versed. Nevertheless the picture of Hutten is fundamentally unsound. Presuppositions again and again result in grotesque caricature and even the appraisal of particular episodes can seldom be accepted without reservation. Kalkoff's studies are published in two works: *Ulrich von Hutten und die Entscheidungsjahre der Reformation* (Leipsic, 1920) and *Ulrich von Huttens Vagantenzeit und Untergang* (Weimar, 1925); and in a whole series of articles among which only the most important can be noticed: "Erasmus und Hutten in ihrem Verhältnis zu Luther," in *Historische Zeitschrift,* CXXII (1920), 260 ff.; "Der geschichtliche Ulrich von Hutten in seinem Verhältnis zu Luther," *Jahrbuch der Luther-Gesellschaft* (1923), pp. 22 ff.; "Die Stellung der deutschen Humanisten zur Reformation," *Zeitschrift für Kirchengeschichte,* XLVI (1927), 162 ff.; "Hutten als Humanist," *Zeitschrift für Geschichte des Oberrheins,* XLII (1928), 3 ff.

Important as are these books and studies of Kalkoff, the way to a deeper understanding than that of the liberal and Catholic historiographers of the nineteenth century had to come from other quarters. One thinks in the first instance, of that outstanding specialist in the history of German humanism, the late Paul Joachimsen (d. 1930). His first extensive study, *Geschichtsauffassung und Geschichtsschreibung in Deutschland unter dem Einfluss des Humanismus* (Leipsic, 1910), already contained valuable contributions toward a new judgment of Hutten and the like was true of his later works, which are cited in the course of the present book. We may mention further only the testament of this great scholar of German humanism, the posthumous *Die Reformation als Epoche der deutschen Geschichte,* O. Schottenloher (editor), (Munich, 1951). His lengthy reviews of Kalkoff in the *Historische Zeitschrift,* CXXV 1921), 487 ff., and CXXXVI (1927), 336 f., are especially valuable and have helped me greatly. I myself have presented a survey of German history in the age of the Reformation in my *A History of Modern Germany: The Reformation* (New York, 1959).

Of similar importance is Kuno Francke's occupation with Hutten. Before the appearance of Kalkoff's books he sensed that the figure of Hutten had been improperly neglected in German historical writing. In his *Personality in German Literature before Luther* (Cambridge, 1916) he attempted very successfully to find a new way to Hutten from the background of the literary history of the Middle Ages. The little book is a very independent and interesting contribution to Hutten studies and has in my judgment permanent worth. Among German literary historians since Kalkoff, F. Gundolf has concerned himself with Hutten's poetry in his *Hutten, Klopstock, Arndt* (Heidelberg, 1924).

I have myself broken a lance with Kalkoff, shortly before the completion of the first draft of this book, in the *Deutsche Literaturzeitung,* XLVII (1926), 1598 ff., and then again, at the time of the German publication of the present work, in the *Zeitschrift für Geschichte des Oberrheins,* XLII (1929), 617 ff.

My own treatment (Leipsic, 1929) has been favored with a whole series of reviews. P. Joachimsen bestowed his approval in the *Deutsche Vierteljahrschrift für Literaturwissenschaft und Geistesgeschichte,* VIII (1930), 461 ff., and so did W. Köhler in the *Historische Zeitschrift,* CXLII, 348. For English opinion see the *English Historical Review,* XLV (1930), 681 ff.

In the present edition I have subjected my own standpoint to critical scrutiny but without approaching any closer to Kalkoff's position. Here and there suggestions have come through the book of Otto Flake, *Ulrich von Hutten* (Berlin, 1929), which came out a few weeks after my own. The attempt was made to harmonize Strauss and Kalkoff. Except on literary points the author was almost lacking in judgments of his own. The most recent treatment of Hutten is the superficial sketch by Otto Graf zu Stolberg-Wernigerode, *Ulrich von Hutten* (Lübeck, 1934, Colemans kleine Biographien, Heft 40). From recent studies in the general field I was able to derive useful addenda.

INDEX OF NAMES

Revised February 1966

harper torchbooks

HUMANITIES AND SOCIAL SCIENCES

American Studies: General

THOMAS C. COCHRAN: The Inner Revolution: *Essays on the Social Sciences in History* TB/1140

EDWARD S. CORWIN: American Constitutional History. *Essays edited by Alpheus T. Mason and Gerald Garvey* TB/1136

CARL N. DEGLER, Ed.: Pivotal Interpretations of American History TB/1240, TB/1241

A. HUNTER DUPREE: Science in the Federal Government: *A History of Policies and Activities to 1940* TB/573

OSCAR HANDLIN, Ed.: This Was America: *As Recorded by European Travelers in the Eighteenth, Nineteenth and Twentieth Centuries. Illus.* TB/1119

MARCUS LEE HANSEN: The Atlantic Migration: 1607-1860. *Edited by Arthur M. Schlesinger. Introduction by Oscar Handlin* TB/1052

MARCUS LEE HANSEN: The Immigrant in American History. *Edited with a Foreword by Arthur M. Schlesinger* TB/1120

JOHN HIGHAM, Ed.: The Reconstruction of American History TB/1068

ROBERT H. JACKSON: The Supreme Court in the American System of Government TB/1106

JOHN F. KENNEDY: A Nation of Immigrants. *Illus. Revised and Enlarged. Introduction by Robert F. Kennedy* TB/1118

RALPH BARTON PERRY: Puritanism and Democracy TB/1138

ARNOLD ROSE: The Negro in America: *The Condensed Version of Gunnar Myrdal's* An American Dilemma TB/3048

MAURICE R. STEIN: The Eclipse of Community: *An Interpretation of American Studies* TB/1128

W. LLOYD WARNER and Associates: Democracy in Jonesville: *A Study in Quality and Inequality* || TB/1129

W. LLOYD WARNER: Social Class in America: *The Evaluation of Status* TB/1013

American Studies: Colonial

BERNARD BAILYN, Ed.: The Apologia of Robert Keayne: *Self-Portrait of a Puritan Merchant* TB/1201

BERNARD BAILYN: The New England Merchants in the Seventeenth Century TB/1149

JOSEPH CHARLES: The Origins of the American Party System TB/1049

LAWRENCE HENRY GIPSON: The Coming of the Revolution: 1763-1775. † *Illus.* TB/3007

LEONARD W. LEVY: Freedom of Speech and Press in Early American History: *Legacy of Suppression* TB/1109

PERRY MILLER: Errand Into the Wilderness TB/1139

PERRY MILLER & T. H. JOHNSON, Eds.: The Puritans: *A Sourcebook of Their Writings* Vol. I TB/1093; Vol. II TB/1094

EDMUND S. MORGAN, Ed.: The Diary of Michael Wigglesworth, 1653-1657: *The Conscience of a Puritan*

EDMUND S. MORGAN: The Puritan Family: *Religion and Domestic Relations in Seventeenth-Century New England* TB/1227

RICHARD B. MORRIS: Government and Labor in Early America TB/1244

KENNETH B. MURDOCK: Literature and Theology in Colonial New England TB/99

WALLACE NOTESTEIN: The English People on the Eve of Colonization: 1603-1630. † *Illus.* TB/3006

LOUIS B. WRIGHT: The Cultural Life of the American Colonies: 1607-1763. † *Illus.* TB/3005

American Studies: From the Revolution to 1860

JOHN R. ALDEN: The American Revolution: 1775-1783. † *Illus.* TB/3011

MAX BELOFF, Ed.: The Debate on the American Revolution, 1761-1783: *A Sourcebook* TB/1225

RAY A. BILLINGTON: The Far Western Frontier: 1830-1860. † *Illus.* TB/3012

EDMUND BURKE: On the American Revolution: *Selected Speeches and Letters.* ‡ *Edited by Elliott Robert Barkan* TB/3068

WHITNEY R. CROSS: The Burned-Over District: *The Social and Intellectual History of Enthusiastic Religion in Western New York, 1800-1850* TB/1242

GEORGE DANGERFIELD: The Awakening of American Nationalism: 1815-1828. † *Illus.* TB/3061

CLEMENT EATON: The Freedom-of-Thought Struggle in the Old South. *Revised and Enlarged. Illus.* TB/1150

CLEMENT EATON: The Growth of Southern Civilization: 1790-1860. † *Illus.* TB/3040

LOUIS FILLER: The Crusade Against Slavery: 1830-1860. † *Illus.* TB/3029

DIXON RYAN FOX: The Decline of Aristocracy in the Politics of New York: 1801-1840. ‡ *Edited by Robert V. Remini* TB/3064

FELIX GILBERT: The Beginnings of American Foreign Policy: *To the Farewell Address* TB/1200

FRANCIS J. GRUND: Aristocracy in America: *Social Class in the Formative Years of the New Nation* TB/1001

ALEXANDER HAMILTON: The Reports of Alexander Hamilton. ‡ *Edited by Jacob E. Cooke* TB/3060

THOMAS JEFFERSON: Notes on the State of Virginia. ‡ *Edited by Thomas P. Abernethy* TB/3052

JAMES MADISON: The Forging of American Federalism: *Selected Writings of James Madison. Edited by Saul K. Padover* TB/1226

† The New American Nation Series, edited by Henry Steele Commager and Richard B. Morris.

‡ American Perspectives series, edited by Bernard Wishy and William E. Leuchtenburg.

* The Rise of Modern Europe series, edited by William L. Langer.

|| Researches in the Social, Cultural, and Behavioral Sciences, edited by Benjamin Nelson.

§ The Library of Religion and Culture, edited by Benjamin Nelson.

Σ Harper Modern Science Series, edited by James R. Newman.

° Not for sale in Canada.

BERNARD MAYO: Myths and Men: *Patrick Henry, George Washington, Thomas Jefferson* TB/1108
JOHN C. MILLER: Alexander Hamilton and the Growth of the New Nation TB/3057
RICHARD B. MORRIS, Ed.: The Era of the American Revolution TB/1180
R. B. NYE: The Cultural Life of the New Nation: 1776-1801. † *Illus.* TB/3026
FRANCIS S. PHILBRICK: The Rise of the West, 1754-1830. † *Illus.* TB/3067
TIMOTHY L. SMITH: Revivalism and Social Reform: *Protestantism on the Eve of the Civil War* TB/1229
FRANK THISTLETHWAITE: America and the Atlantic Community: *Anglo-American Aspects, 1790-1850* TB/1107
A. F. TYLER: Freedom's Ferment: *Phases of American Social History from the Revolution to the Outbreak of the Civil War. 31 illus.* TB/1074
GLYNDON G. VAN DEUSEN: The Jacksonian Era: 1828-1848. † *Illus.* TB/3028
LOUIS B. WRIGHT: Culture on the Moving Frontier TB/1053

American Studies: The Civil War to 1900

THOMAS C. COCHRAN & WILLIAM MILLER: The Age of Enterprise: *A Social History of Industrial America* TB/1054
W. A. DUNNING: Essays on the Civil War and Reconstruction. *Introduction by David Donald* TB/1181
W. A. DUNNING: Reconstruction, Political and Economic: 1865-1877 TB/1073
HAROLD U. FAULKNER: Politics, Reform and Expansion: 1890-1900. † *Illus.* TB/3020
HELEN HUNT JACKSON: A Century of Dishonor: *The Early Crusade for Indian Reform. ‡ Edited by Andrew F. Rolle* TB/3063
ALBERT D. KIRWAN: Revolt of the Rednecks: *Mississippi Politics, 1876-1925* TB/1199
ROBERT GREEN MCCLOSKEY: American Conservatism in the Age of Enterprise: 1865-1910 TB/1137
WHITELAW REID: After the War: *A Tour of the Southern States, 1865-1866. ‡ Edited by C. Vann Woodward* TB/3066
CHARLES H. SHINN: Mining Camps: *A Study in American Frontier Government. ‡ Edited by Rodman W. Paul* TB/3062
VERNON LANE WHARTON: The Negro in Mississippi: 1865-1890 TB/1178

American Studies: 1900 to the Present

RAY STANNARD BAKER: Following the Color Line: *American Negro Citizenship in Progressive Era. ‡ Illus. Edited by Dewey W. Grantham, Jr.* TB/3053
RANDOLPH S. BOURNE: War and the Intellectuals: *Collected Essays, 1915-1919. ‡ Ed. by Carl Resek* TB/3043
A. RUSSELL BUCHANAN: The United States and World War II. † *Illus.* Vol. I TB/3044; Vol. II TB/3045
ABRAHAM CAHAN: The Rise of David Levinsky: *a documentary novel of social mobility in early twentieth century America. Intro. by John Higham* TB/1028
THOMAS C. COCHRAN: The American Business System: *A Historical Perspective, 1900-1955* TB/1080
FOSTER RHEA DULLES: America's Rise to World Power: 1898-1954. † *Illus.* TB/3021
JOHN D. HICKS: Republican Ascendancy: 1921-1933. † *Illus.* TB/3041
SIDNEY HOOK: Reason, Social Myths, and Democracy TB/1237
ROBERT HUNTER: Poverty: *Social Conscience in the Progressive Era. ‡ Edited by Peter d'A. Jones* TB/3065
WILLIAM L. LANGER & S. EVERETT GLEASON: The Challenge to Isolation: *The World Crisis of 1937-1940 and American Foreign Policy* Vol. I TB/3054; Vol. II TB/3055
WILLIAM E. LEUCHTENBURG: Franklin D. Roosevelt and the New Deal: 1932-1940. † *Illus.* TB/3025
ARTHUR S. LINK: Woodrow Wilson and the Progressive Era: 1910-1917. † *Illus.* TB/3023
GEORGE E. MOWRY: The Era of Theodore Roosevelt and the Birth of Modern America: 1900-1912. † *Illus.* TB/3022
RUSSEL B. NYE: Midwestern Progressive Politics: *A Historical Study of its Origins and Development, 1870-1958* TB/1202
WALTER RAUSCHENBUSCH: Christianity and the Social Crisis. ‡ *Edited by Robert D. Cross* TB/3059
PHILIP SELZNICK: TVA and the Grass Roots: *A Study in the Sociology of Formal Organization* TB/1230
GEORGE B. TINDALL, Ed.: A Populist Reader ‡ TB/3069
TWELVE SOUTHERNERS: I'll Take My Stand: *The South and the Agrarian Tradition. Intro. by Louis D. Rubin, Jr. Biographical Essays by Virginia Rock* TB/1072
WALTER E. WEYL: The New Democracy: *An Essay on Certain Political Tendencies in the United States. ‡ Edited by Charles B. Forcey* TB/3042

Anthropology

JACQUES BARZUN: Race: *A Study in Superstition. Revised Edition* TB/1172
JOSEPH B. CASAGRANDE, Ed.: In the Company of Man: *Twenty Portraits of Anthropological Informants. Illus.* TB/3047
W. E. LE GROS CLARK: The Antecedents of Man: *Intro. to Evolution of the Primates.* ° *Illus.* TB/559
CORA DU BOIS: The People of Alor. *New Preface by the author. Illus.* Vol. I TB/1042; Vol. II TB/1043
RAYMOND FIRTH, Ed.: Man and Culture: *An Evaluation of the Work of Bronislaw Malinowski* || ° TB/1133
DAVID LANDY: Tropical Childhood: *Cultural Transmission and Learning in a Rural Puerto Rican Village* || TB/1235
L. S. B. LEAKEY: Adam's Ancestors: *The Evolution of Man and His Culture. Illus.* TB/1019
ROBERT H. LOWIE: Primitive Society. *Introduction by Fred Eggan* TB/1056
EDWARD BURNETT TYLOR: The Origins of Culture. *Part I of "Primitive Culture." § Intro. by Paul Radin* TB/33
EDWARD BURNETT TYLOR: Religion in Primitive Culture. *Part II of "Primitive Culture." § Intro. by Paul Radin* TB/34
W. LLOYD WARNER: A Black Civilization: *A Study of an Australian Tribe.* || *Illus.* TB/3056

Art and Art History

WALTER LOWRIE: Art in the Early Church. *Revised Edition. 452 illus.* TB/124
EMILE MÂLE: The Gothic Image: *Religious Art in France of the Thirteenth Century. § 190 illus.* TB/44
MILLARD MEISS: Painting in Florence and Siena after the Black Death: *The Arts, Religion and Society in the Mid-Fourteenth Century. 169 illus.* TB/1148
ERICH NEUMANN: The Archetypal World of Henry Moore. *107 illus.* TB/2020
DORA & ERWIN PANOFSKY: Pandora's Box: *The Changing Aspects of a Mythical Symbol. Revised Edition. Illus.* TB/2021
ERWIN PANOFSKY: Studies in Iconology: *Humanistic Themes in the Art of the Renaissance. 180 illustrations* TB/1077
ALEXANDRE PIANKOFF: The Shrines of Tut-Ankh-Amon. *Edited by N. Rambova. 117 illus.* TB/2011
JEAN SEZNEC: The Survival of the Pagan Gods: *The Mythological Tradition and Its Place in Renaissance Humanism and Art. 108 illustrations* TB/2004
OTTO VON SIMSON: The Gothic Cathedral: *Origins of Gothic Architecture and the Medieval Concept of Order. 58 illus.* TB/2018
HEINRICH ZIMMER: Myths and Symbols in Indian Art and Civilization. *70 illustrations* TB/2005

Business, Economics & Economic History

REINHARD BENDIX: Work and Authority in Industry: *Ideologies of Management in the Course of Industrialization* TB/3035
GILBERT BURCK & EDITORS OF FORTUNE: The Computer Age: *And Its Potential for Management* TB/1179
THOMAS C. COCHRAN: The American Business System: *A Historical Perspective, 1900-1955* TB/1080
THOMAS C. COCHRAN: The Inner Revolution: *Essays on the Social Sciences in History* TB/1140
THOMAS C. COCHRAN & WILLIAM MILLER: The Age of Enterprise: *A Social History of Industrial America* TB/1054
ROBERT DAHL & CHARLES E. LINDBLOM: Politics, Economics, and Welfare: *Planning & Politico-Economic Systems Resolved into Basic Social Processes* TB/3037
PETER F. DRUCKER: The New Society: *The Anatomy of Industrial Order* TB/1082
EDITORS OF FORTUNE: America in the Sixties: *The Economy and the Society* TB/1015
ROBERT L. HEILBRONER: The Great Ascent: *The Struggle for Economic Development in Our Time* TB/3030
FRANK H. KNIGHT: The Economic Organization TB/1214
FRANK H. KNIGHT: Risk, Uncertainty and Profit TB/1215
ABBA P. LERNER: Everybody's Business: *Current Assumptions in Economics and Public Policy* TB/3051
ROBERT GREEN MCCLOSKEY: American Conservatism in the Age of Enterprise, 1865-1910 TB/1137
PAUL MANTOUX: The Industrial Revolution in the Eighteenth Century: *The Beginnings of the Modern Factory System in England* ° TB/1079
WILLIAM MILLER, Ed.: Men in Business: *Essays on the Historical Role of the Entrepreneur* TB/1081
RICHARD B. MORRIS: Government and Labor in Early America TB/1244
HERBERT SIMON: The Shape of Automation: *For Men and Management* TB/1245
PERRIN STRYKER: The Character of the Executive: *Eleven Studies in Managerial Qualities* TB/1041
PIERRE URI: Partnership for Progress: *A Program for Transatlantic Action* TB/3036

Contemporary Culture

JACQUES BARZUN: The House of Intellect TB/1051
JOHN U. NEF: Cultural Foundations of Industrial Civilization TB/1024
NATHAN M. PUSEY: The Age of the Scholar: *Observations on Education in a Troubled Decade* TB/1157
PAUL VALÉRY: The Outlook for Intelligence TB/2016

Historiography & Philosophy of History

JACOB BURCKHARDT: On History and Historians. *Intro. by H. R. Trevor-Roper* TB/1216
WILHELM DILTHEY: Pattern and Meaning in History: *Thoughts on History and Society.* ° *Edited with an Introduction by H. P. Rickman* TB/1075
J. H. HEXTER: Reappraisals in History: *New Views on History & Society in Early Modern Europe* TB/1100
H. STUART HUGHES: History as Art and as Science: *Twin Vistas on the Past* TB/1207
RAYMOND KLIBANSKY & H. J. PATON, Eds.: Philosophy and History: *The Ernst Cassirer Festschrift. Illus.* TB/1115
GEORGE H. NADEL, Ed.: Studies in the Philosophy of History: *Selected Essays from* History and Theory TB/1208
JOSE ORTEGA Y GASSET: The Modern Theme. *Introduction by Jose Ferrater Mora* TB/1038
KARL R. POPPER: The Open Society and Its Enemies
Vol. I: The Spell of Plato TB/1101
Vol. II: The High Tide of Prophecy: Hegel, Marx and the Aftermath TB/1102
KARL R. POPPER: The Poverty of Historicism ° TB/1126
G. J. RENIER: History: Its Purpose and Method TB/1209
W. H. WALSH: Philosophy of History: *An Introduction* TB/1020

History: General

L. CARRINGTON GOODRICH: A Short History of the Chinese People. *Illus.* TB/3015
DAN N. JACOBS & HANS H. BAERWALD: Chinese Communism: *Selected Documents* TB/3031
BERNARD LEWIS: The Arabs in History TB/1029

History: Ancient

A. ANDREWES: The Greek Tyrants TB/1103
ADOLF ERMAN, Ed.: The Ancient Egyptians: *A Sourcebook of Their Writings. New material and Introduction by William Kelly Simpson* TB/1233
MICHAEL GRANT: Ancient History ° TB/1190
SAMUEL NOAH KRAMER: Sumerian Mythology TB/1055
NAPHTALI LEWIS & MEYER REINHOLD, Eds.: Roman Civilization. *Sourcebook I: The Republic* TB/1231
NAPHTALI LEWIS & MEYER REINHOLD, Eds.: Roman Civilization. *Sourcebook II: The Empire* TB/1232

History: Medieval

P. BOISSONNADE: Life and Work in Medieval Europe: *The Evolution of the Medieval Economy, the 5th to the 15th Century.* ° *Preface by Lynn White, Jr.* TB/1141
HELEN CAM: England before Elizabeth TB/1026
NORMAN COHN: The Pursuit of the Millennium: *Revolutionary Messianism in Medieval and Reformation Europe* TB/1037
G. G. COULTON: Medieval Village, Manor, and Monastery TB/1022
HEINRICH FICHTENAU: The Carolingian Empire: *The Age of Charlemagne* TB/1142
F. L. GANSHOF: Feudalism TB/1058
EDWARD GIBBON: The Triumph of Christendom in the Roman Empire *(Chaps. XV-XX of "Decline and Fall," J. B. Bury edition). § Illus.* TB/46
W. O. HASSALL, Ed.: Medieval England: *As Viewed by Contemporaries* TB/1205
DENYS HAY: The Medieval Centuries ° TB/1192
J. M. HUSSEY: The Byzantine World TB/1057
FERDINAND LOT: The End of the Ancient World and the Beginnings of the Middle Ages. *Introduction by Glanville Downey* TB/1044
G. MOLLAT: The Popes at Avignon: 1305-1378 TB/308
CHARLES PETIT-DUTAILLIS: The Feudal Monarchy in France and England: *From the Tenth to the Thirteenth Century* ° TB/1165
HENRI PIERENNE: Early Democracies in the Low Countries: *Urban Society and Political Conflict in the Middle Ages and the Renaissance. Introduction by John H. Mundy* TB/1110
STEVEN RUNCIMAN: A History of the Crusades.
Volume I: *The First Crusade and the Foundation of the Kingdom of Jerusalem. Illus.* TB/1143
Volume II: *The Kingdom of Jerusalem and the Frankish East, 1100-1187. Illus.* TB/1243
FERDINAND SCHEVILL: Siena: *The History of a Medieval Commune. Intro. by William M. Bowsky* TB/1164
SULPICIUS SEVERUS et al.: The Western Fathers: *Being the Lives of Martin of Tours, Ambrose, Augustine of Hippo, Honoratus of Arles and Germanus of Auxerre. Edited and translated by F. R. Hoare* TB/309
HENRY OSBORN TAYLOR: The Classical Heritage of the Middle Ages. *Foreword and Biblio. by Kenneth M. Setton* TB/1117
F. VAN DER MEER: Augustine the Bishop: *Church and Society at the Dawn of the Middle Ages* TB/304
J. M. WALLACE-HADRILL: The Barbarian West: *The Early Middle Ages, A.D. 400-1000* TB/1061

History: Renaissance & Reformation

JACOB BURCKHARDT: The Civilization of the Renaissance in Italy. *Intro. by Benjamin Nelson & Charles Trinkaus. Illus.* Vol. I TB/40; Vol. II TB/41
JOHN CALVIN & JACOPO SADOLETO: A Reformation Debate. *Edited by John C. Olin* TB/1239
ERNST CASSIRER: The Individual and the Cosmos in Renaissance Philosophy. *Translated with an Introduction by Mario Domandi* TB/1097
FEDERICO CHABOD: Machiavelli and the Renaissance TB/1193
EDWARD P. CHEYNEY: The Dawn of a New Era, 1250-1453. * *Illus.* TB/3002
R. TREVOR DAVIES: The Golden Century of Spain, 1501-1621 ° TB/1194
DESIDERIUS ERASMUS: Christian Humanism and the Reformation: *Selected Writings. Edited and translated by John C. Olin* TB/1166
WALLACE K. FERGUSON et al.: Facets of the Renaissance TB/1098
WALLACE K. FERGUSON et al.: The Renaissance: *Six Essays. Illus.* TB/1084
JOHN NEVILLE FIGGIS: The Divine Right of Kings. *Introduction by G. R. Elton* TB/1191
JOHN NEVILLE FIGGIS: Political Thought from Gerson to Grotius: 1414-1625: *Seven Studies. Introduction by Garrett Mattingly* TB/1032
MYRON P. GILMORE: The World of Humanism, 1453-1517.* *Illus.* TB/3003
FRANCESCO GUICCIARDINI: Maxims and Reflections of a Renaissance Statesman *(Ricordi). Trans. by Mario Domandi. Intro. by Nicolai Rubinstein* TB/1160
J. H. HEXTER: More's Utopia: *The Biography of an Idea. New Epilogue by the Author* TB/1195
HAJO HOLBORN: Ulrich von Hutten and the German Reformation TB/1238
JOHAN HUIZINGA: Erasmus and the Age of Reformation. *Illus.* TB/19
ULRICH VON HUTTEN et al.: On the Eve of the Reformation: *"Letters of Obscure Men." Introduction by Hajo Holborn* TB/1124
PAUL O. KRISTELLER: Renaissance Thought: *The Classic, Scholastic, and Humanist Strains* TB/1048
PAUL O. KRISTELLER: Renaissance Thought II: *Papers on Humanism and the Arts* TB/1163
NICCOLÒ MACHIAVELLI: History of Florence and of the Affairs of Italy: *from the earliest times to the death of Lorenzo the Magnificent. Introduction by Felix Gilbert* TB/1027
ALFRED VON MARTIN: Sociology of the Renaissance. *Introduction by Wallace K. Ferguson* TB/1099
GARRETT MATTINGLY et al.: Renaissance Profiles. *Edited by J. H. Plumb* TB/1162
MILLARD MEISS: Painting in Florence and Siena after the Black Death: *The Arts, Religion and Society in the Mid-Fourteenth Century. 169 illus.* TB/1148
J. E. NEALE: The Age of Catherine de Medici ° TB/1085
ERWIN PANOFSKY: Studies in Iconology: *Humanistic Themes in the Art of the Renaissance. 180 illustrations* TB/1077
J. H. PARRY: The Establishment of the European Hegemony: 1415-1715: *Trade and Exploration in the Age of the Renaissance* TB/1045
J. H. PLUMB: The Italian Renaissance: *A Concise Survey of Its History and Culture* TB/1161
CECIL ROTH: The Jews in the Renaissance. *Illus.* TB/834
A. L. ROWSE: The Expansion of Elizabethan England. ° *Illus.* TB/1220
GORDON RUPP: Luther's Progress to the Diet of Worms ° TB/120
FERDINAND SCHEVILL: The Medici. *Illus.* TB/1010
FERDINAND SCHEVILL: Medieval and Renaissance Florence. *Illus.* Volume I: *Medieval Florence* TB/1090
Volume II: *The Coming of Humanism and the Age of the Medici* TB/1091
G. M. TREVELYAN: England in the Age of Wycliffe, 1368-1520 ° TB/1112
VESPASIANO: Renaissance Princes, Popes, and Prelates: *The Vespasiano Memoirs: Lives of Illustrious Men of the XVth Century. Intro. by Myron P. Gilmore* TB/1111

History: Modern European

FREDERICK B. ARTZ: Reaction and Revolution, 1815-1832. * *Illus.* TB/3034
MAX BELOFF: The Age of Absolutism, 1660-1815 TB/1062
ROBERT C. BINKLEY: Realism and Nationalism, 1852-1871. * *Illus.* TB/3038
ASA BRIGGS: The Making of Modern England, 1784-1867: *The Age of Improvement* ° TB/1203
CRANE BRINTON: A Decade of Revolution, 1789-1799. * *Illus.* TB/3018
D. W. BROGAN: The Development of Modern France. ° Volume I: *From the Fall of the Empire to the Dreyfus Affair* TB/1184
Volume II: *The Shadow of War, World War I, Between the Two Wars. New Introduction by the Author* TB/1185
J. BRONOWSKI & BRUCE MAZLISH: The Western Intellectual Tradition: *From Leonardo to Hegel* TB/3001
GEOFFREY BRUUN: Europe and the French Imperium, 1799-1814. * *Illus.* TB/3033
ALAN BULLOCK: Hitler, A Study in Tyranny. ° *Illus.* TB/1123
E. H. CARR: The Twenty Years' Crisis, 1919-1939: *An Introduction to the Study of International Relations* ° TB/1122
GORDON A. CRAIG: From Bismarck to Adenauer: *Aspects of German Statecraft. Revised Edition* TB/1171
WALTER L. DORN: Competition for Empire, 1740-1763. * *Illus.* TB/3032
FRANKLIN L. FORD: Robe and Sword: *The Regrouping of the French Aristocracy after Louis XIV* TB/1217
CARL J. FRIEDRICH: The Age of the Baroque, 1610-1660. * *Illus.* TB/3004
RENÉ FUELOEP-MILLER: The Mind and Face of Bolshevism: *An Examination of Cultural Life in Soviet Russia. New Epilogue by the Author* TB/1188
M. DOROTHY GEORGE: London Life in the Eighteenth Century TB/1182
LEO GERSHOY: From Despotism to Revolution, 1763-1789. * *Illus.* TB/3017
C. C. GILLISPIE: Genesis and Geology: *The Decades before Darwin* § TB/51
ALBERT GOODWIN: The French Revolution TB/1064
ALBERT GUERARD: France in the Classical Age: *The Life and Death of an Ideal* TB/1183
CARLTON J. H. HAYES: A Generation of Materialism, 1871-1900. * *Illus.* TB/3039
J. H. HEXTER: Reappraisals in History: *New Views on History & Society in Early Modern Europe* TB/1100
STANLEY HOFFMANN et al.: In Search of France: *The Economy, Society and Political System in the Twentieth Century* TB/1219
A. R. HUMPHREYS: The Augustan World: *Society, Thought, and Letters in 18th Century England* ° TB/1105
DAN N. JACOBS, Ed.: The New Communist Manifesto *& Related Documents. Third edition, Revised* TB/1078
HANS KOHN: The Mind of Germany: *The Education of a Nation* TB/1204
HANS KOHN, Ed.: The Mind of Modern Russia: *Historical and Political Thought of Russia's Great Age* TB/1065
FRANK E. MANUEL: The Prophets of Paris: *Turgot, Condorcet, Saint-Simon, Fourier, and Comte* TB/1218
KINGSLEY MARTIN: French Liberal Thought in the Eighteenth Century: *A Study of Political Ideas from Bayle to Condorcet* TB/1114
L. B. NAMIER: Personalities and Powers: *Selected Essays* TB/1186

L. B. NAMIER: Vanished Supremacies: *Essays on European History, 1812-1918* ° TB/1088
JOHN U. NEF: Western Civilization Since the Renaissance: *Peace, War, Industry, and the Arts* TB/1113
FREDERICK L. NUSSBAUM: The Triumph of Science and Reason, 1660-1685. * *Illus.* TB/3009
JOHN PLAMENATZ: German Marxism and Russian Communism. ° *New Preface by the Author* TB/1189
RAYMOND W. POSTGATE, Ed.: Revolution from 1789 to 1906: *Selected Documents* TB/1063
PENFIELD ROBERTS: The Quest for Security, 1715-1740. * *Illus.* TB/3016
PRISCILLA ROBERTSON: Revolutions of 1848: *A Social History* TB/1025
ALBERT SOREL: Europe Under the Old Regime. *Translated by Francis H. Herrick* TB/1121
N. N. SUKHANOV: The Russian Revolution, 1917: *Eyewitness Account. Edited by Joel Carmichael* Vol. I TB/1066; Vol. II TB/1067
A. J. P. TAYLOR: The Habsburg Monarch, 1809-1918: *A History of the Austrian Empire and Austria-Hungary* ° TB/1187
JOHN B. WOLF: The Emergence of the Great Powers, 1685-1715. * *Illus.* TB/3010
JOHN B. WOLF: France: 1814-1919: *The Rise of a Liberal-Democratic Society* TB/3019

Intellectual History & History of Ideas

HERSCHEL BAKER: The Image of Man: *A Study of the Idea of Human Dignity in Classical Antiquity, the Middle Ages, and the Renaissance* TB/1047
R. R. BOLGAR: The Classical Heritage and Its Beneficiaries: *From the Carolingian Age to the End of the Renaissance* TB/1125
RANDOLPH S. BOURNE: War and the Intellectuals: *Collected Essays, 1915-1919.* ‡ *Edited by Carl Resek* TB/3043
J. BRONOWSKI & BRUCE MAZLISH: The Western Intellectual Tradition: *From Leonardo to Hegel* TB/3001
ERNST CASSIRER: The Individual and the Cosmos in Renaissance Philosophy. *Translated with an Introduction by Mario Domandi* TB/1097
NORMAN COHN: The Pursuit of the Millennium: *Revolutionary Messianism in Medieval and Reformation Europe* TB/1037
C. C. GILLISPIE: Genesis and Geology: *The Decades before Darwin* § TB/51
G. RACHEL LEVY: Religious Conceptions of the Stone Age *and Their Influence upon European Thought. Illus. Introduction by Henri Frankfort* TB/106
ARTHUR O. LOVEJOY: The Great Chain of Being: *A Study of the History of an Idea* TB/1009
FRANK E. MANUEL: The Prophets of Paris: *Turgot, Condorcet, Saint-Simon, Fourier, and Comte* TB/1218
PERRY MILLER & T. H. JOHNSON, Editors: The Puritans: *A Sourcebook of Their Writings* Vol. I TB/1093; Vol. II TB/1094
MILTON C. NAHM: Genius and Creativity: *An Essay in the History of Ideas* TB/1196
ROBERT PAYNE: Hubris: *A Study of Pride. Foreword by Sir Herbert Read* TB/1031
RALPH BARTON PERRY: The Thought and Character of William James: *Briefer Version* TB/1156
GEORG SIMMEL et al.: Essays on Sociology, Philosophy, and Aesthetics. || *Edited by Kurt H. Wolff* TB/1234
BRUNO SNELL: The Discovery of the Mind: *The Greek Origins of European Thought* TB/1018
PAGET TOYNBEE: Dante Alighieri: *His Life and Works. Edited with Intro. by Charles S. Singleton* TB/1206
ERNEST LEE TUVESON: Millennium and Utopia: *A Study in the Background of the Idea of Progress.* || *New Preface by the Author* TB/1134
PAUL VALÉRY: The Outlook for Intelligence TB/2016
PHILIP P. WIENER: Evolution and the Founders of Pragmatism. *Foreword by John Dewey* TB/1212

Literature, Poetry, The Novel & Criticism

JAMES BAIRD: Ishmael: *The Art of Melville in the Contexts of International Primitivism* TB/1023
JACQUES BARZUN: The House of Intellect TB/1051
W. J. BATE: From Classic to Romantic: *Premises of Taste in Eighteenth Century England* TB/1036
RACHEL BESPALOFF: On the Iliad TB/2006
R. P. BLACKMUR et al.: Lectures in Criticism. *Introduction by Huntington Cairns* TB/2003
ABRAHAM CAHAN: The Rise of David Levinsky: *a documentary novel of social mobility in early twentieth century America. Intro. by John Higham* TB/1028
ERNST R. CURTIUS: European Literature and the Latin Middle Ages TB/2015
GEORGE ELIOT: Daniel Deronda: *a novel. Introduction by F. R. Leavis* TB/1039
ADOLF ERMAN, Ed.: The Ancient Egyptians: *A Sourcebook of Their Writings. New Material and Introduction by William Kelly Simpson* TB/1233
ÉTIENNE GILSON: Dante and Philosophy TB/1089
ALFRED HARBAGE: As They Liked It: *A Study of Shakespeare's Moral Artistry* TB/1035
STANLEY R. HOPPER, Ed.: Spiritual Problems in Contemporary Literature § TB/21
A. R. HUMPHREYS: The Augustan World: *Society, Thought and Letters in 18th Century England* ° TB/1105
ALDOUS HUXLEY: Antic Hay & The Giaconda Smile. ° *Introduction by Martin Green* TB/3503
ALDOUS HUXLEY: Brave New World & Brave New World Revisited. ° *Introduction by Martin Green* TB/3501
HENRY JAMES: Roderick Hudson: *a novel. Introduction by Leon Edel* TB/1016
HENRY JAMES: The Tragic Muse: *a novel. Introduction by Leon Edel* TB/1017
ARNOLD KETTLE: An Introduction to the English Novel. Volume I: *Defoe to George Eliot* TB/1011
Volume II: *Henry James to the Present* TB/1012
ROGER SHERMAN LOOMIS: The Development of Arthurian Romance TB/1167
JOHN STUART MILL: On Bentham and Coleridge. *Introduction by F. R. Leavis* TB/1070
KENNETH B. MURDOCK: Literature and Theology in Colonial New England TB/99
SAMUEL PEPYS: The Diary of Samuel Pepys. ° *Edited by O. F. Morshead. Illus. by Ernest Shepard* TB/1007
ST.-JOHN PERSE: Seamarks TB/2002
GEORGE SANTAYANA: Interpretations of Poetry and Religion § TB/9
HEINRICH STRAUMANN: American Literature in the Twentieth Century. *Third Edition, Revised* TB/1168
PAGET TOYNBEE: Dante Alighieri: *His Life and Works. Edited with Intro. by Charles S. Singleton* TB/1206
DOROTHY VAN GHENT: The English Novel: *Form and Function* TB/1050
E. B. WHITE: One Man's Meat. *Introduction by Walter Blair* TB/3505
MORTON DAUWEN ZABEL, Editor: Literary Opinion in America Vol. I TB/3013; Vol. II TB/3014

Myth, Symbol & Folklore

JOSEPH CAMPBELL, Editor: Pagan and Christian Mysteries. *Illus.* TB/2013
MIRCEA ELIADE: Cosmos and History: *The Myth of the Eternal Return* § TB/2050
MERCEA ELIADE: Rites and Symbols of Initiation: *The Mysteries of Birth and Rebirth* § TB/1236
C. G. JUNG & C. KERÉNYI: Essays on a Science of Mythology: *The Myths of the Divine Child and the Divine Maiden* TB/2014
DORA & ERWIN PANOFSKY: Pandora's Box: *The Changing Aspects of a Mythical Symbol. Revised Edition. Illus.* TB/2021

ERWIN PANOFSKY: Studies in Iconology: *Humanistic Themes in the Art of the Renaissance. 180 illustrations* TB/1077
JEAN SEZNEC: The Survival of the Pagan Gods: *The Mythological Tradition and its Place in Renaissance Humanism and Art. 108 illustrations* TB/2004
HELLMUT WILHELM: Change: *Eight Lectures on the I Ching* TB/2019
HEINRICH ZIMMER: Myths and Symbols in Indian Art and Civilization. *70 illustrations* TB/2005

Philosophy

G. E. M. ANSCOMBE: An Introduction to Wittgenstein's Tractatus. *Second edition, Revised.* ° TB/1210
HENRI BERGSON: Time and Free Will: *An Essay on the Immediate Data of Consciousness* ° TB/1021
H. J. BLACKHAM: Six Existentialist Thinkers: *Kierkegaard, Nietzsche, Jaspers, Marcel, Heidegger, Sartre* ° TB/1002
CRANE BRINTON: Nietzsche. *New Preface, Bibliography and Epilogue by the Author* TB/1197
ERNST CASSIRER: The Individual and the Cosmos in Renaissance Philosophy. *Translated with an Introduction by Mario Domandi* TB/1097
ERNST CASSIRER: Rousseau, Kant and Goethe. *Introduction by Peter Gay* TB/1092
FREDERICK COPLESTON: Medieval Philosophy ° TB/376
F. M. CORNFORD: Principium Sapientiae: *A Study of the Origins of Greek Philosophical Thought. Edited by W. K. C. Guthrie* TB/1213
F. M. CORNFORD: From Religion to Philosophy: *A Study in the Origins of Western Speculation* § TB/20
WILFRID DESAN: The Tragic Finale: *An Essay on the Philosophy of Jean-Paul Sartre* TB/1030
A. P. D'ENTRÈVES: Natural Law: *An Historical Survey* TB/1223
HERBERT FINGARETTE: The Self in Transformation: *Psychoanalysis, Philosophy and the Life of the Spirit* || TB/1177
PAUL FRIEDLÄNDER: Plato: *An Introduction* TB/2017
ÉTIENNE GILSON: Dante and Philosophy TB/1089
WILLIAM CHASE GREENE: Moira: *Fate, Good, and Evil in Greek Thought* TB/1104
W. K. C. GUTHRIE: The Greek Philosophers: *From Thales to Aristotle* ° TB/1008
F. H. HEINEMANN: Existentialism and the Modern Predicament TB/28
ISAAC HUSIK: A History of Medieval Jewish Philosophy JP/3
EDMUND HUSSERL: Phenomenology and the Crisis of Philosophy. *Translated with an Introduction by Quentin Lauer* TB/1170
IMMANUEL KANT: The Doctrine of Virtue, *being Part II of* The Metaphysic of Morals. *Trans. with Notes & Intro. by Mary J. Gregor. Foreword by H. J. Paton* TB/110
IMMANUEL KANT: Groundwork of the Metaphysic of Morals. *Trans. & analyzed by H. J. Paton* TB/1159
IMMANUEL KANT: Lectures on Ethics. § *Introduction by Lewis W. Beck* TB/105
IMMANUEL KANT: Religion Within the Limits of Reason Alone. § *Intro. by T. M. Greene & J. Silber* TB/67
QUENTIN LAUER: Phenomenology: *Its Genesis and Prospect* TB/1169
GABRIEL MARCEL: Being and Having: *An Existential Diary. Intro. by James Collins* TB/310
GEORGE A. MORGAN: What Nietzsche Means TB/1198
PHILO, SAADYA GAON, & JEHUDA HALEVI: Three Jewish Philosophers. *Ed. by Hans Lewy, Alexander Altmann, & Isaak Heinemann* TB/813
MICHAEL POLANYI: Personal Knowledge: *Towards a Post-Critical Philosophy* TB/1158
WILLARD VAN ORMAN QUINE: Elementary Logic: *Revised Edition* TB/577
WILLARD VAN ORMAN QUINE: From a Logical Point of View: *Logico-Philosophical Essays* TB/566
BERTRAND RUSSELL et al.: The Philosophy of Bertrand Russell. *Edited by Paul Arthur Schilpp*
Vol. I TB/1095; Vol. II TB/1096
L. S. STEBBING: A Modern Introduction to Logic TB/538
ALFRED NORTH WHITEHEAD: Process and Reality: *An Essay in Cosmology* TB/1033
PHILIP P. WIENER: Evolution and the Founders of Pragmatism. *Foreword by John Dewey* TB/1212
WILHELM WINDELBAND: A History of Philosophy
Vol. I: *Greek, Roman, Medieval* TB/38
Vol. II: *Renaissance, Enlightenment, Modern* TB/39
LUDWIG WITTGENSTEIN: The Blue and Brown Books ° TB/1211

Political Science & Government

JEREMY BENTHAM: The Handbook of Political Fallacies. *Introduction by Crane Brinton* TB/1069
KENNETH E. BOULDING: Conflict and Defense: *A General Theory* TB/3024
CRANE BRINTON: English Political Thought in the Nineteenth Century TB/1071
EDWARD S. CORWIN: American Constitutional History: *Essays edited by Alpheus T. Mason and Gerald Garvey* TB/1136
ROBERT DAHL & CHARLES E. LINDBLOM: Politics, Economics, and Welfare: *Planning and Politico-Economic Systems Resolved into Basic Social Processes* TB/3037
JOHN NEVILLE FIGGIS: The Divine Right of Kings. *Introduction by G. R. Elton* TB/1191
JOHN NEVILLE FIGGIS: Political Thought from Gerson to Grotius: 1414-1625: *Seven Studies. Introduction by Garrett Mattingly* TB/1032
F. L. GANSHOF: Feudalism TB/1058
G. P. GOOCH: English Democratic Ideas in Seventeenth Century TB/1006
J. H. HEXTER: More's Utopia: *The Biography of an Idea. New Epilogue by the Author* TB/1195
SIDNEY HOOK: Reason, Social Myths and Democracy TB/1237
ROBERT H. JACKSON: The Supreme Court in the American System of Government TB/1106
DAN N. JACOBS, Ed.: The New Communist Manifesto & *Related Documents. Third edition, Revised* TB/1078
DAN N. JACOBS & HANS BAERWALD, Eds.: Chinese Communism: *Selected Documents* TB/3031
ROBERT GREEN MCCLOSKEY: American Conservatism in the Age of Enterprise, 1865-1910 TB/1137
KINGSLEY MARTIN: French Liberal Thought in the Eighteenth Century: *Political Ideas from Bayle to Condorcet* TB/1114
ROBERTO MICHELS: First Lectures in Political Sociology. *Edited by Alfred De Grazia* || ° TB/1224
JOHN STUART MILL: On Bentham and Coleridge. *Introduction by F. R. Leavis* TB/1070
BARRINGTON MOORE, JR.: Political Power and Social Theory: *Seven Studies* || TB/1221
BARRINGTON MOORE, JR.: Soviet Politics—The Dilemma of Power: *The Role of Ideas in Social Change* || TB/1222
JOHN B. MORRALL: Political Thought in Medieval Times TB/1076
JOHN PLAMENATZ: German Marxism and Russian Communism. ° *New Preface by the Author* TB/1189
KARL R. POPPER: The Open Society and Its Enemies
Vol. I: *The Spell of Plato* TB/1101
Vol. II: *The High Tide of Prophecy: Hegel, Marx, and the Aftermath* TB/1102
HENRI DE SAINT-SIMON: Social Organization, The Science of Man, and Other Writings. *Edited and Translated by Felix Markham* TB/1152
JOSEPH A. SCHUMPETER: Capitalism, Socialism and Democracy TB/3008

CHARLES H. SHINN: Mining Camps: *A Study in American Frontier Government.* ‡ *Edited by Rodman W. Paul* TB/3062

Psychology

ALFRED ADLER: The Individual Psychology of Alfred Adler. *Edited by Heinz L. and Rowena R. Ansbacher* TB/1154

ALFRED ADLER: Problems of Neurosis. *Introduction by Heinz L. Ansbacher* TB/1145

ANTON T. BOISEN: The Exploration of the Inner World: *A Study of Mental Disorder and Religious Experience* TB/87

HERBERT FINGARETTE: The Self in Transformation: *Psychoanalysis, Philosophy and the Life of the Spirit* ‖ TB/1177

SIGMUND FREUD: On Creativity and the Unconscious: *Papers on the Psychology of Art, Literature, Love, Religion.* § *Intro. by Benjamin Nelson* TB/45

C. JUDSON HERRICK: The Evolution of Human Nature TB/545

WILLIAM JAMES: Psychology: *The Briefer Course. Edited with an Intro. by Gordon Allport* TB/1034

C. G. JUNG: Psychological Reflections TB/2001

C. G. JUNG: Symbols of Transformation: *An Analysis of the Prelude to a Case of Schizophrenia. Illus.* Vol. I: TB/2009; Vol. II TB/2010

C. G. JUNG & C. KERÉNYI: Essays on a Science of Mythology: *The Myths of the Divine Child and the Divine Maiden* TB/2014

JOHN T. MC NEILL: A History of the Cure of Souls TB/126

KARL MENNINGER: Theory of Psychoanalytic Technique TB/1144

ERICH NEUMANN: Amor and Psyche: *The Psychic Development of the Feminine* TB/2012

ERICH NEUMANN: The Archetypal World of Henry Moore. *107 illus.* TB/2020

ERICH NEUMANN: The Origins and History of Consciousness Vol. I *Illus.* TB/2007; Vol. II TB/2008

C. P. OBERNDORF: A History of Psychoanalysis in America TB/1147

RALPH BARTON PERRY: The Thought and Character of William James: *Briefer Version* TB/1156

JEAN PIAGET, BÄRBEL INHELDER, & ALINA SZEMINSKA: The Child's Conception of Geometry ° TB/1146

JOHN H. SCHAAR: Escape from Authority: *The Perspectives of Erich Fromm* TB/1155

Sociology

JACQUES BARZUN: Race: *A Study in Superstition. Revised Edition* TB/1172

BERNARD BERELSON, Ed.: The Behavioral Sciences Today TB/1127

ABRAHAM CAHAN: The Rise of David Levinsky: *A documentary novel of social mobility in early twentieth century America. Intro. by John Higham* TB/1028

THOMAS C. COCHRAN: The Inner Revolution: *Essays on the Social Sciences in History* TB/1140

ALLISON DAVIS & JOHN DOLLARD: Children of Bondage: *The Personality Development of Negro Youth in the Urban South* ‖ TB/3049

ST. CLAIR DRAKE & HORACE R. CAYTON: Black Metropolis: *A Study of Negro Life in a Northern City. Revised and Enlarged. Intro. by Everett C. Hughes* Vol. I TB/1086; Vol. II TB/1087

EMILE DURKHEIM et al.: Essays on Sociology and Philosophy: *With Analyses of Durkheim's Life and Work.* ‖ *Edited by Kurt H. Wolff* TB/1151

LEON FESTINGER, HENRY W. RIECKEN & STANLEY SCHACHTER: When Prophecy Fails: *A Social and Psychological Account of a Modern Group that Predicted the Destruction of the World* ‖ TB/1132

ALVIN W. GOULDNER: Wildcat Strike: *A Study in Worker-Management Relationships* ‖ TB/1176

FRANCIS J. GRUND: Aristocracy in America: *Social Class in the Formative Years of the New Nation* TB/1001

KURT LEWIN: Field Theory in Social Science: *Selected Theoretical Papers.* ‖ *Edited with a Foreword by* Dorwin Cartwright TB/1135

R. M. MACIVER: Social Causation TB/1153

ROBERT K. MERTON, LEONARD BROOM, LEONARD S. COTTRELL, JR., Editors: Sociology Today: *Problems and Prospects* ‖ Vol. I TB/1173; Vol. II TB/1174

ROBERTO MICHELS: First Lectures in Political Sociology. *Edited by Alfred De Grazia* ‖ ° TB/1224

BARRINGTON MOORE, JR.: Political Power and Social Theory: *Seven Studies* ‖ TB/1221

BARRINGTON MOORE, JR.: Soviet Politics—The Dilemma of Power: *The Role of Ideas in Social Change* ‖ TB/1222

TALCOTT PARSONS & EDWARD A. SHILS, Editors: Toward a General Theory of Action: *Theoretical Foundations for the Social Sciences* TB/1083

JOHN H. ROHRER & MUNRO S. EDMONSON, Eds.: The Eighth Generation Grows Up: *Cultures and Personalities of New Orleans Negroes* ‖ TB/3050

ARNOLD ROSE: The Negro in America: *The Condensed Version of Gunnar Myrdal's* An American Dilemma TB/3048

KURT SAMUELSSON: Religion and Economic Action: *A Critique of Max Weber's* The Protestant Ethic and the Spirit of Capitalism. ‖ ° *Trans. by E. G. French. Ed. with Intro. by D. C. Coleman* TB/1131

PHILIP SELZNICK: TVA and the Grass Roots: *A Study in the Sociology of Formal Organization* TB/1230

GEORG SIMMEL et al.: Essays on Sociology, Philosophy, and Aesthetics. ‖ *Edited by Kurt H. Wolff* TB/1234

HERBERT SIMON: The Shape of Automation: *For Men and Management* TB/1245

PITIRIM A. SOROKIN: Contemporary Sociological Theories. *Through the First Quarter of the 20th Century* TB/3046

MAURICE R. STEIN: The Eclipse of Community: *An Interpretation of American Studies* TB/1128

FERDINAND TÖNNIES: Community and Society: *Gemeinschaft und Gesellschaft. Translated and edited by Charles P. Loomis* TB/1116

W. LLOYD WARNER & Associates: Democracy in Jonesville: *A Study in Quality and Inequality* TB/1129

W. LLOYD WARNER: Social Class in America: *The Evaluation of Status* TB/1013

RELIGION

Ancient & Classical

J. H. BREASTED: Development of Religion and Thought in Ancient Egypt. *Introduction by John A. Wilson* TB/57

HENRI FRANKFORT: Ancient Egyptian Religion: *An Interpretation* TB/77

G. RACHEL LEVY: Religious Conceptions of the Stone Age *and their Influence upon European Thought. Illus. Introduction by Henri Frankfort* TB/106

MARTIN P. NILSSON: Greek Folk Religion. *Foreword by Arthur Darby Nock* TB/78

ALEXANDRE PIANKOFF: The Shrines of Tut-Ankh-Amon. *Edited by N. Rambova. 117 illus.* TB/2011

H. J. ROSE: Religion in Greece and Rome TB/55

Biblical Thought & Literature

W. F. ALBRIGHT: The Biblical Period from Abraham to Ezra TB/102

C. K. BARRETT, Ed.: The New Testament Background: *Selected Documents* TB/86

C. H. DODD: The Authority of the Bible TB/43

M. S. ENSLIN: Christian Beginnings TB/5

M. S. ENSLIN: The Literature of the Christian Movement TB/6

JOHN GRAY: Archaeology and the Old Testament World. *Illus.* TB/127
JAMES MUILENBURG: The Way of Israel: *Biblical Faith and Ethics* TB/133
H. H. ROWLEY: The Growth of the Old Testament TB/107
D. WINTON THOMAS, Ed.: Documents from Old Testament Times TB/85

The Judaic Tradition

LEO BAECK: Judaism and Christianity. *Trans. with Intro. by Walter Kaufmann* JP/23
SALO W. BARON: Modern Nationalism and Religion JP/18
MARTIN BUBER: Eclipse of God: *Studies in the Relation Between Religion and Philosophy* TB/12
MARTIN BUBER: The Knowledge of Man: *Selected Essays. Edited with an Introduction by Maurice Friedman. Translated by Maurice Friedman and Ronald Gregor Smith* TB/135
MARTIN BUBER: Moses: *The Revelation and the Covenant* TB/27
MARTIN BUBER: Pointing the Way. *Introduction by Maurice S. Friedman* TB/103
MARTIN BUBER: The Prophetic Faith TB/73
MARTIN BUBER: Two Types of Faith: *the interpenetration of Judaism and Christianity* ° TB/75
ERNST LUDWIG EHRLICH: A Concise History of Israel: *From the Earliest Times to the Destruction of the Temple in A.D. 70* ° TB/128
MAURICE S. FRIEDMAN: Martin Buber: *The Life of Dialogue* TB/64
LOUIS GINZBERG: Students, Scholars and Saints JP/2
SOLOMON GRAYZEL: A History of the Contemporary Jews TB/816
WILL HERBERG: Judaism and Modern Man TB/810
ABRAHAM J. HESCHEL: God in Search of Man: *A Philosophy of Judaism* JP/7
ISAAC HUSIK: A History of Medieval Jewish Philosophy JP/3
FLAVIUS JOSEPHUS: The Great Roman-Jewish War, *with* The Life of Josephus. *Introduction by William R. Farmer* TB/74
JACOB R. MARCUS The Jew in the Medieval World TB/814
MAX L. MARGOLIS & ALEXANDER MARX: A History of the Jewish People TB/806
T. J. MEEK: Hebrew Origins TB/69
C. G. MONTEFIORE & H. LOEWE, Eds.: A Rabbinic Anthology. JP/32
JAMES PARKES: The Conflict of the Church and the Synagogue: *The Jews and Early Christianity* JP/21
PHILO, SAADYA GAON, & JEHUDA HALEVI: Three Jewish Philosophers. *Ed. by Hans Lewey, Alexander Altmann, & Isaak Heinemann* TB/813
HERMAN L. STRACK: Introduction to the Talmud and Midrash TB/808
JOSHUA TRACHTENBERG: The Devil and the Jews: *The Medieval Conception of the Jew and its Relation to Modern Anti-Semitism* JP/22

Christianity: General

ROLAND H. BAINTON: Christendom: *A Short History of Christianity and its Impact on Western Civilization. Illus.* Vol. I TB/131; Vol. II TB/132

Christianity: Origins & Early Development

AUGUSTINE: An Augustine Synthesis. *Edited by Erich Przywara* TB/335
ADOLF DEISSMANN: Paul: *A Study in Social and Religious History* TB/15
EDWARD GIBBON: The Triumph of Christendom in the Roman Empire *(Chaps. XV-XX of "Decline and Fall," J. B. Bury edition).* § *Illus.* TB/46
MAURICE GOGUEL: Jesus and the Origins of Christianity. ° *Introduction by C. Leslie Mitton*
Volume I: *Prolegomena to the Life of Jesus* TB/65
Volume II: *The Life of Jesus* TB/66
EDGAR J. GOODSPEED: A Life of Jesus TB/1
ADOLF HARNACK: The Mission and Expansion of Christianity *in the First Three Centuries. Introduction by Jaroslav Pelikan* TB/92
R. K. HARRISON: The Dead Sea Scrolls: *An Introduction* ° TB/84
EDWIN HATCH: The Influence of Greek Ideas on Christianity. § *Introduction and Bibliography by Frederick C. Grant* TB/18
ARTHUR DARBY NOCK: Early Gentile Christianity and Its Hellenistic Background TB/111
ARTHUR DARBY NOCK: St. Paul ° TB/104
ORIGEN: On First Principles. *Edited by G. W. Butterworth. Introduction by Henri de Lubac* TB/310
JAMES PARKES: The Conflict of the Church and the Synagogue: *The Jews and Early Christianity* JP/21
SULPICIUS SEVERUS et al.: The Western Fathers: *Being the Lives of Martin of Tours, Ambrose, Augustine of Hippo, Honoratus of Arles and Germanus of Auxerre. Edited and translated by F. R. Hoare* TB/309
F. VAN DER MEER: Augustine the Bishop: *Church and Society at the Dawn of the Middle Ages* TB/304
JOHANNES WEISS: Earliest Christianity: *A History of the Period A.D. 30-150. Introduction and Bibliography by Frederick C. Grant* Volume I TB/53
Volume II TB/54

Christianity: The Middle Ages and The Reformation

JOHN CALVIN & JACOPO SADOLETO: A Reformation Debate. *Edited by John C. Olin* TB/1239
JOHANNES ECKHART: Meister Eckhart: *A Modern Translation by R. B. Blakney* TB/8
DESIDERIUS ERASMUS: Christian Humanism and the Reformation: *Selected Writings. Edited and translated by John C. Olin* TB/1166
ÉTIENNE GILSON: Dante and Philosophy TB/1089
WILLIAM HALLER: The Rise of Puritanism TB/22
HAJO HOLBORN: Ulrich von Hutten and the German Reformation TB/1238
JOHAN HUIZINGA: Erasmus and the Age of Reformation. *Illus.* TB/19
A. C. MCGIFFERT: Protestant Thought Before Kant. *Preface by Jaroslav Pelikan* TB/93
JOHN T. MCNEILL: Makers of the Christian Tradition: *From Alfred the Great to Schleiermacher* TB/121
G. MOLLAT: The Popes at Avignon, 1305-1378 TB/308
GORDON RUPP: Luther's Progress to the Diet of Worms ° TB/120

Christianity: The Protestant Tradition

KARL BARTH: Church Dogmatics: *A Selection* TB/95
KARL BARTH: Dogmatics in Outline TB/56
KARL BARTH: The Word of God and the Word of Man TB/13
RUDOLF BULTMANN et al.: Translating Theology into the Modern Age: *Historical, Systematic and Pastoral Reflections on Theology and the Church in the Contemporary Situation. Volume 2 of* Journal for Theology and the Church, *edited by Robert W. Funk in association with Gerhard Ebeling* TB/252
WINTHROP HUDSON: The Great Tradition of the American Churches TB/98
SOREN KIERKEGAARD: Edifying Discourses. *Edited with an Introduction by Paul Holmer* TB/32
SOREN KIERKEGAARD: The Journals of Kierkegaard. ° *Edited with an Introduction by Alexander Dru* TB/52
SOREN KIERKEGAARD: The Point of View for My Work as an Author: *A Report to History.* § *Preface by Benjamin Nelson* TB/88

SOREN KIERKEGAARD: The Present Age. § *Translated and edited by Alexander Dru. Introduction by Walter Kaufmann* TB/94
SOREN KIERKEGAARD: Purity of Heart TB/4
SOREN KIERKEGAARD: Repetition: *An Essay in Experimental Psychology. Translated with Introduction & Notes by Walter Lowrie* TB/117
SOREN KIERKEGAARD: Works of Love: *Some Christian Reflections in the Form of Discourses* TB/122
WALTER LOWRIE: Kierkegaard: *A Life* Vol. I TB/89; Vol. II TB/90
JOHN MACQUARRIE: The Scope of Demythologizing: *Bultmann and his Critics* TB/134
PERRY MILLER & T. H. JOHNSON, Editors: The Puritans: *A Sourcebook of Their Writings* Vol. I TB/1093; Vol. II TB/1094
JAMES M. ROBINSON et al.: The Bultmann School of Biblical Interpretation: New Directions? *Volume 1 of* Journal of Theology and the Church, *edited by Robert W. Funk in association with Gerhard Ebeling* TB/251
F. SCHLEIERMACHER: The Christian Faith. *Introduction by Richard R. Niebuhr* Vol. I TB/108; Vol. II TB/109
F. SCHLEIERMACHER: On Religion: *Speeches to Its Cultured Despisers. Intro. by Rudolf Otto* TB/36
PAUL TILLICH: Dynamics of Faith TB/42
EVELYN UNDERHILL: Worship TB/10
G. VAN DER LEEUW: Religion in Essence and Manifestation: *A Study in Phenomenology. Appendices by Hans H. Penner* Vol. I TB/100; Vol. II TB/101

Christianity: The Roman and Eastern Traditions

DOM CUTHBERT BUTLER: Western Mysticism: *The Teaching of Augustine, Gregory and Bernard on Contemplation and the Contemplative Life* § ° TB/312
A. ROBERT CAPONIGRI, Ed.: Modern Catholic Thinkers I: *God and Man* TB/306
A. ROBERT CAPONIGRI, Ed.: Modern Catholic Thinkers II: *The Church and the Political Order* TB/307
THOMAS CORBISHLEY, S. J.: Roman Catholicism TB/112
CHRISTOPHER DAWSON: The Historic Reality of Christian Culture TB/305
G. P. FEDOTOV: The Russian Religious Mind: *Kievan Christianity, the 10th to the 13th Centuries* TB/70
G. P. FEDOTOV, Ed.: A Treasury of Russian Spirituality TB/303
DAVID KNOWLES: The English Mystical Tradition TB/302
GABRIEL MARCEL: Being and Having: *An Existential Diary. Introduction by James Collins* TB/310
GABRIEL MARCEL: Homo Viator: *Introduction to a Metaphysic of Hope* TB/397
GUSTAVE WEIGEL, S. J.: Catholic Theology in Dialogue TB/301

Oriental Religions: Far Eastern, Near Eastern

TOR ANDRAE: Mohammed: *The Man and His Faith* TB/62
EDWARD CONZE: Buddhism: *Its Essence and Development. ° Foreword by Arthur Waley* TB/58
EDWARD CONZE et al., Editors: Buddhist Texts Through the Ages TB/113
ANANDA COOMARASWAMY: Buddha and the Gospel of Buddhism. *Illus.* TB/119
H. G. CREEL: Confucius and the Chinese Way TB/63
FRANKLIN EDGERTON, Trans. & Ed.: The Bhagavad Gita TB/115
SWAMI NIKHILANANDA, Trans. & Ed.: The Upanishads: *A One-Volume Abridgment* TB/114
HELLMUT WILHELM: Change: *Eight Lectures on the I Ching* TB/2019

Philosophy of Religion

NICOLAS BERDYAEV: The Beginning and the End § TB/14
NICOLAS BERDYAEV: Christian Existentialism: *A Berdyaev Synthesis. Ed. by Donald A. Lowrie* TB/130
NICOLAS BERDYAEV: The Destiny of Man TB/61
RUDOLF BULTMANN: History and Eschatology: *The Presence of Eternity* ° TB/91
RUDOLF BULTMANN AND FIVE CRITICS: Kerygma and Myth: *A Theological Debate* TB/80
RUDOLF BULTMANN and KARL KUNDSIN: Form Criticism: *Two Essays on New Testament Research. Translated by Frederick C. Grant* TB/96
MIRCEA ELIADE: The Sacred and the Profane TB/81
LUDWIG FEUERBACH: The Essence of Christianity. § *Introduction by Karl Barth. Foreword by H. Richard Niebuhr* TB/11
ADOLF HARNACK: What is Christianity? § *Introduction by Rudolf Bultmann* TB/17
FRIEDRICH HEGEL: On Christianity: *Early Theological Writings. Ed. by R. Kroner & T. M. Knox* TB/79
KARL HEIM: Christian Faith and Natural Science TB/16
IMMANUEL KANT: Religion Within the Limits of Reason Alone. § *Intro. by T. M. Greene & J. Silber* TB/67
JOHN MACQUARRIE: An Existentialist Theology: *A Comparison of Heidegger and Bultmann. ° Preface by Rudolf Bultmann* TB/125
PAUL RAMSEY, Ed.: Faith and Ethics: *The Theology of H. Richard Niebuhr* TB/129
PIERRE TEILHARD DE CHARDIN: The Divine Milieu ° TB/384
PIERRE TEILHARD DE CHARDIN: The Phenomenon of Man ° TB/83

Religion, Culture & Society

JOSEPH L. BLAU, Ed.: Cornerstones of Religious Freedom in America: *Selected Basic Documents, Court Decisions and Public Statements. Revised and Enlarged Edition* TB/118
C. C. GILLISPIE: Genesis and Geology: *The Decades before Darwin* § TB/51
KYLE HASELDEN: The Racial Problem in Christian Perspective TB/116
WALTER KAUFMANN, Ed.: Religion from Tolstoy to Camus: *Basic Writings on Religious Truth and Morals. Enlarged Edition* TB/123
JOHN T. MCNEILL: A History of the Cure of Souls TB/126
KENNETH B. MURDOCK: Literature and Theology in Colonial New England TB/99
H. RICHARD NIEBUHR: Christ and Culture TB/3
H. RICHARD NIEBUHR: The Kingdom of God in America TB/49
RALPH BARTON PERRY: Puritanism and Democracy TB/1138
PAUL PFUETZE: Self, Society, Existence: *Human Nature and Dialogue in the Thought of George Herbert Mead and Martin Buber* TB/1059
WALTER RAUSCHENBUSCH: Christianity and the Social Crisis. ‡ *Edited by Robert D. Cross* TB/3059
KURT SAMUELSSON: Religion and Economic Action: *A Critique of Max Weber's* The ˘rotestant Ethic and the Spirit of Capitalism. ‖ ° *Trans. by E. G. French. Ed. with Intro. by D. C. Coleman* TB/1131
TIMOTHY L. SMITH: Revivalism and Social Reform: *Protestantism on the Eve of the Civil War* TB/1229
ERNST TROELTSCH: The Social Teaching of the Christian Churches ° Vol. I TB/71; Vol. II TB/72

NATURAL SCIENCES AND MATHEMATICS

Biological Sciences

CHARLOTTE AUERBACH: The Science of Genetics Σ TB/568
MARSTON BATES: The Natural History of Mosquitoes. *Illus.* TB/578
A. BELLAIRS: Reptiles: *Life History, Evolution, and Structure. Illus.* TB/520

LUDWIG VON BERTALANFFY: Modern Theories of Development: *An Introduction to Theoretical Biology* TB/554
LUDWIG VON BERTALANFFY: Problems of Life: *An Evaluation of Modern Biological and Scientific Thought* TB/521
HAROLD F. BLUM: Time's Arrow and Evolution TB/555
JOHN TYLER BONNER: The Ideas of Biology. Σ *Illus.* TB/570
A. J. CAIN: Animal Species and their Evolution. *Illus.* TB/519
WALTER B. CANNON: Bodily Changes in Pain, Hunger, Fear and Rage. *Illus.* TB/562
W. E. LE GROS CLARK: The Antecedents of Man: *Intro. to Evolution of the Primates.* ° *Illus.* TB/559
W. H. DOWDESWELL: Animal Ecology. *Illus.* TB/543
W. H. DOWDESWELL: The Mechanism of Evolution. *Illus.* TB/527
R. W. GERARD: Unresting Cells. *Illus.* TB/541
DAVID LACK: Darwin's Finches. *Illus.* TB/544
J. E. MORTON: Molluscs: *An Introduction to their Form and Functions. Illus.* TB/529
ADOLF PORTMANN: Animals as Social Beings. ° *Illus.* TB/572
O. W. RICHARDS: The Social Insects. *Illus.* TB/542
P. M. SHEPPARD: Natural Selection and Heredity. *Illus.* TB/528
EDMUND W. SINNOTT: Cell and Psyche: *The Biology of Purpose* TB/546
C. H. WADDINGTON: How Animals Develop. *Illus.* TB/553
C. H. WADDINGTON: The Nature of Life: *The Main Problems and Trends in Modern Biology* TB/580

Chemistry

J. R. PARTINGTON: A Short History of Chemistry. *Illus.* TB/522
J. READ: A Direct Entry to Organic Chemistry. *Illus.* TB/523
J. READ: Through Alchemy to Chemistry. *Illus.* TB/561

Communication Theory

J. R. PIERCE: Symbols, Signals and Noise: *The Nature and Process of Communication* TB/574

Geography

R. E. COKER: This Great and Wide Sea: *An Introduction to Oceanography and Marine Biology. Illus.* TB/551
F. K. HARE: The Restless Atmosphere TB/560

History of Science

W. DAMPIER, Ed.: Readings in the Literature of Science. *Illus.* TB/512
A. HUNTER DUPREE: Science in the Federal Government: *A History of Policies and Activities to 1940* TB/573
ALEXANDRE KOYRÉ: From the Closed World to the Infinite Universe: *Copernicus, Kepler, Galileo, Newton, etc.* TB/31
A. G. VAN MELSEN: From Atomos to Atom: *A History of the Concept* Atom TB/517
O. NEUGEBAUER: The Exact Sciences in Antiquity TB/552
H. T. PLEDGE: Science Since 1500: *A Short History of Mathematics, Physics, Chemistry and Biology. Illus.* TB/506
HANS THIRRING: Energy for Man: *From Windmills to Nuclear Power* TB/556
LANCELOT LAW WHYTE: Essay on Atomism: *From Democritus to 1960* TB/565
A. WOLF: A History of Science, Technology and Philosophy in the 16th and 17th Centuries. ° *Illus.* Vol. I TB/508; Vol. II TB/509
A. WOLF: A History of Science, Technology, and Philosophy in the Eighteenth Century. ° *Illus.* Vol. I TB/539; Vol. II TB/540

Mathematics

E. W. BETH: The Foundations of Mathematics: *A Study in the Philosophy of Science* TB/581
H. DAVENPORT: The Higher Arithmetic: *An Introduction to the Theory of Numbers* TB/526
H. G. FORDER: Geometry: *An Introduction* TB/548
GOTTLOB FREGE: The Foundations of Arithmetic: *A Logico-Mathematical Enquiry* TB/534
S. KÖRNER: The Philosophy of Mathematics: *An Introduction* TB/547
D. E. LITTLEWOOD: Skeleton Key of Mathematics: *A Simple Account of Complex Algebraic Problems* TB/525
GEORGE E. OWEN: Fundamentals of Scientific Mathematics TB/569
WILLARD VAN ORMAN QUINE: Mathematical Logic TB/558
O. G. SUTTON: Mathematics in Action. ° *Foreword by James R. Newman. Illus.* TB/518
FREDERICK WAISMANN: Introduction to Mathematical Thinking. *Foreword by Karl Menger* TB/511

Philosophy of Science

R. B. BRAITHWAITE: Scientific Explanation TB/515
J. BRONOWSKI: Science and Human Values. *Revised and Enlarged Edition* TB/505
ALBERT EINSTEIN et al.: Albert Einstein: Philosopher-Scientist. *Edited by Paul A. Schilpp* Vol. I TB/502 Vol. II TB/503
WERNER HEISENBERG: Physics and Philosophy: *The Revolution in Modern Science* TB/549
JOHN MAYNARD KEYNES: A Treatise on Probability. ° *Introduction by N. R. Hanson* TB/557
KARL R. POPPER: The Logic of Scientific Discovery TB/576
STEPHEN TOULMIN: Foresight and Understanding: *An Enquiry into the Aims of Science. Foreword by Jacques Barzun* TB/564
STEPHEN TOULMIN: The Philosophy of Science: *An Introduction* TB/513
G. J. WHITROW: The Natural Philosophy of Time ° TB/563

Physics and Cosmology

STEPHEN TOULMIN & JUNE GOODFIELD: The Fabric of the Heavens: *The Development of Astronomy and Dynamics. Illus.* TB/579
DAVID BOHM: Causality and Chance in Modern Physics. *Foreword by Louis de Broglie* TB/536
P. W. BRIDGMAN: The Nature of Thermodynamics TB/537
P. W. BRIDGMAN: A Sophisticate's Primer of Relativity TB/575
A. C. CROMBIE, Ed.: Turning Point in Physics TB/535
C. V. DURELL: Readable Relativity. *Foreword by Freeman J. Dyson* TB/530
ARTHUR EDDINGTON: Space, Time and Gravitation: *An Outline of the General Relativity Theory* TB/510
GEORGE GAMOW: Biography of Physics Σ TB/567
MAX JAMMER: Concepts of Force: *A Study in the Foundation of Dynamics* TB/550
MAX JAMMER: Concepts of Mass *in Classical and Modern Physics* TB/571
MAX JAMMER: Concepts of Space: *The History of Theories of Space in Physics. Foreword by Albert Einstein* TB/533
EDMUND WHITTAKER: History of the Theories of Aether and Electricity
Volume I: *The Classical Theories* TB/531
Volume II: *The Modern Theories* TB/532
G. J. WHITROW: The Structure and Evolution of the Universe: *An Introduction to Cosmology. Illus.* TB/504